Political Behavior of the American Electorate

Political Behavior of the American Electorate

Twelfth Edition

William H. Flanigan
University of Minnesota

and

Nancy H. Zingale
University of St. Thomas

CQ PRESS

A Division of SAGE
Washington, D.C.

CQ Press
2300 N Street, NW, Suite 800
Washington, DC 20037

Phone: 202-729-1900; toll-free, 1-866-4CQ-PRESS (1-866-427-7737)

Web: www.cqpress.com

Cover design: Jeffrey Everett/El Jefe Design
Composition: C&M Digitals (P) Ltd.

⊗ The paper used in this publication exceeds the requirements of the
American National Standard for Information Sciences—Permanence of
Paper for Printed Library Materials, ANSI Z39.48-1992.

Printed and bound in the United States of America

13   12   11   10   09   1   2   3   4   5

Library of Congress Cataloging-in-Publication Data

Flanigan, William H.
  Political behavior of the American electorate / William H. Flanigan and
Nancy H. Zingale. — Twelfth ed.
     p. cm.
  Includes bibliographical references and index.
  ISBN 978-1-60426-521-7 (pbk. : alk. paper) 1. Voting—United States.
I. Zingale, Nancy H. II. Title.

  JK1967.F38 2010
  324.973—dc22

                                                                2009044996

To the memory of
Ruth M. Flanigan
Edwin N. Flanigan
Amy K. Hill
James S. Hill

Contents

Tables and Figures   xi

Acknowledgments   xv

Introduction   1

c h a p t e r   o n e

Political Culture and American Democracy   11

Fair, Free, and Competitive Elections   12
Political Culture as a Foundation for Democracy   18
Maintaining a Democracy   33
Notes   36
Suggested Readings   37
Internet Resources   38

c h a p t e r   t w o

Suffrage and Turnout   39

Extensions of Suffrage   39
Restrictions on Suffrage   42
Turnout in American Elections Historically   44
High- and Low-Stimulus Elections   48
Voters and Nonvoters   52
Registration as a Barrier to Voting   56
Is the Level of Turnout in the United States a Cause for Concern?   60
Notes   64
Suggested Readings   65
Internet Resources   66

c h a p t e r   t h r e e

Partisanship   67

Party Loyalty   67
Party Identification   69
Types of Electoral Change   72
Party Systems and Realignments   75
Are Conditions Right for a Realignment?   83
Notes   86
Suggested Readings   86
Internet Resources   87

c h a p t e r   f o u r

Partisans and Partisan Change   89

Voting Behavior   89
Are Independents Apolitical?   95
Partisan Change   99
The Future of Parties and Partisanship   107
Notes   108
Suggested Readings   109
Internet Resources   110

c h a p t e r   f i v e

Social Characteristics of Partisans and Independents 111

The Social Composition of Partisan Groups   115
Social Group Analysis   116
Red and Blue States   126
Social Cross-Pressures   129
Notes   132
Suggested Readings   133
Internet Resources   134

c h a p t e r   s i x

Public Opinion and Ideology   135

The Measurement of Public Opinion   137
Domestic Economic Issues   138

Racial Issues   142
Social Issues   148
Homeland Security and Terrorism   153
International Affairs   154
Issues and Partisanship   159
Political Ideology   160
Public Opinion and Political Leadership   166
Notes   168
Suggested Readings   170
Internet Resources   170

c h a p t e r   s e v e n

Political Communication and the Mass Media   173

Functions of Opinions for Individuals   174
Opinion Consistency and Dissonance   175
Political Communication and Attitude Change   176
Attention to the Media   179
Did Iraq Have Weapons of Mass Destruction?   184
The Media and Presidential Approval Ratings   186
Campaigns   190
Presidential Primary Campaigns   199
Campaign Strategy   202
Notes   204
Suggested Readings   206
Internet Resources   207

c h a p t e r   e i g h t

Vote Choice and Electoral Decisions   209

Social Characteristics and Presidential Vote Choice 210
Partisanship and Ideology   212
Short-Term Forces   214
Determinants of Vote Choice   226
The Popular Vote and the Electoral College   230
Vote Choice in Other Types of Elections   233
The Meaning of an Election   235
Notes   238
Suggested Readings   239
Internet Resources   239

a p p e n d i x

Survey Research Methods   241

Survey Data Collection   242
Validity of Survey Questions   248
Validity versus Continuity   250
Notes   251
Suggested Readings   251
Internet Resources   252

Index   253

Tables and Figures

Tables

1-1 Political Influentials versus the Electorate, Responses
     to Items Expressing Belief in Democratic Values,
     1964 and 2004   23
1-2 Ninth Graders' Views on What Is Good and Bad for
     Democracy, 1999   32
2-1 Interest and Partisanship of Registered Voters and
     Nonvoters and Unregistered Citizens, 2008   58
3-1 Party Identification of the Electorate, 1952–2008   79
3-2 Party Identification of the Electorate for the Nation,
     the Non-South, and the South, 1952–2008   80
4-1 The Distribution of Votes for President by Independents,
     1948–2008   96
4-2 Party Identifiers, Self-Identified Independents, and
     People Claiming No Preference, 1968–2008   97
4-3 Stability and Change of Partisanship, 1965–1997   104
5-1 Party Identification, by Social Characteristics, 2008   112
5-2 Reported Vote Preferences of Primary Groups, by
     Respondent's Reported Vote for President, 2000   118
5-3 Political and Social Characteristics of Safe Red States,
     Safe Blue States, and Battleground States, 2008   128
6-1 Attitudes toward Cutting Spending versus Increasing
     Government Services, by Party Identification, 2008   142
6-2 Attitudes on Health Care, by Party Identification, 2008   143
6-3 Public Attitudes on School Integration and
     Employment Practices   145

6-4   Whites' Views on Abortion, by Religion and Frequency
      of Church Attendance, 2008   151
6-5   Attitudes on Abortion, by Party Identification, 2008   152
6-6   Attitudes toward Gay Marriage, by Party Identification, 2008   153
6-7   Attitudes toward the War in Iraq according to Party
      Identification, 2004 and 2008   158
6-8   Attitudes toward Possible Foreign Policy Goals according
      to Party Identification, 2008   159
6-9   Distribution of Ideological Identification, 1972–2008   161
6-10 Relationship between Ideological Self-Identification
      and Party Identification, 2008   162
6-11 Distribution of the Levels of Conceptualization, 1956–2000   164
6-12 Relationship between Ideological Identification and
      Liberal Positions on Issues, 1972–2008   167
7-1   Most Closely Followed News Stories and Other Selected
      News Items, 1986–2009   181
8-1   Presidential Vote, by Party Identification, 2008   213
8-2   Presidential Vote, by Ideological Identification, 2008   215
8-3   Presidential Vote and Attitude toward Government
      Services, 2008   223
8-4   Presidential Vote and Attitude toward Government
      Help for Blacks, 2008   223
8-5   Presidential Vote and Attitude toward Abortion, 2008   224
8-6   Presidential Vote and Attitude toward War in Iraq, 2008   224
8-7   Net Impact of Six Attitudinal Components in
      Determining Vote Choice, 1952–1984 and 2000–2004   228
8-8   Determinants of Presidential Vote Choice, Barack Obama
      versus John McCain, 2008   229
A-1   Recalled Vote for President in 1960, 1962, and 1964   250

Figures

1-1   Attitudes toward Politics and the Political System,
      1952–2009   26
1-2   Children's and Teachers' Understanding of the
      Concept of Democracy   31
2-1   Estimated Turnout of Eligible Voters in Presidential
      Elections in the Nation, the South, and the Non-South,
      1860–2008   45
2-2   Estimated Turnout of Eligible Voters in Presidential and
      Congressional Elections, 1868–2008   49
2-3   Relationship between Electoral Participation and Interest,
      Involvement, and Information   52

2-4 Percentage of the Electorate Reporting Having
Registered and Voted in the 2008 Election, by Age   54
2-5 Turnout in the 2008 Election, by Age and Education   55
2-6 Percentage of Adults Who Have Never Voted, by Race and
Gender, for the South and the Non-South, 1952–1980   57
3-1 Partisan Division of the Presidential Vote in the Nation,
1824–2008   68
3-2 Democratic Expected Vote in Presidential Elections,
1840–1968   71
3-3 Republican Expected Vote in Presidential Elections,
1872–1968   72
3-4 Democratic Normal Vote with Presidential Vote, 1968–2008   73
3-5 Republican Normal Vote with Presidential Vote, 1968–2008   74
3-6 Democratic Vote for Congress, North and South, 1936–2008   83
3-7 Democratic Identification among Southern and
Non-Southern Whites, 1952–2008   84
4-1 Defection Rates by Party Identifiers in Presidential Voting,
1952–2008   90
4-2 Defection Rates by Party Identifiers in Congressional
Voting, 1952–2008   92
4-3 Voting by Partisans and Independents in Presidential,
Congressional, and Presidential Primary Elections   94
4-4 Percentage of Turnout, High Interest, and Democratic
Vote for President by Partisanship, 2008   99
4-5 Distribution of Independents, by Age Cohorts, 1958,
1968, 1988, and 2008   101
4-6 Party Identification of High School Seniors and
Their Parents, 1965   105
4-7 Party Identification of High School Seniors and
Their Parents, 1997   106
5-1 Social Composition of Partisans and Independents,
by Race, Ethnicity, Religion, and Education, 2008   114
5-2 Net Partisan Advantage among White Married and
Unmarried Men and Women, 2008   119
5-3 Voting and Political Identification for White
Fundamentalists and Evangelicals according to
Church Attendance, 2008   123
5-4 The Relationship between Social Class Identification
and Party Identification, 1952–2008   125
6-1 Attitudes toward Domestic Spending, 1973–2008   140
6-2 Attitudes toward Cutting Spending versus Increasing
Government Services, by Race, Ethnicity, Religion,
and Education, 2008   141

6-3   Public Attitudes toward School Integration and Fair
       Employment Practices, 1942–2008   144
6-4   Attitudes toward Abortion among Catholics and
       Protestants, by Frequency of Church Attendance, 2008   150
6-5   Attitudes toward the War on Terrorism according to
       Party Identification, 2008   155
6-6   Ideological Identification, by Race, Ethnicity, Religion,
       and Education, 2008   163
7-1   Hypothetical Relationship between Mass Media Attention
       and Stability of Voting Behavior   184
7-2   Percentages Believing Iraq Has Weapons of Mass
       Destruction by Attention to the Campaign and Vote
       Intention, 2004   185
7-3   Approval Ratings of Presidents George H. W. Bush and
       George W. Bush before and after Middle Eastern Wars,
       August 1990–January 1992 and October 2002–March 2004   188
7-4   Approval Ratings of President George W. Bush in
       Handling His Job as President, the Economy, the
       War in Iraq, and Terrorism, 2001–2008   189
7-5   Trial Heat Results from the Democratic Presidential
       Primary and the General Election, 2008   193
8-1   Vote for President, by Race, Ethnicity, Religion,
       and Education, 2008   211
8-2   Social Composition of the Vote for President, by Race,
       Ethnicity, Religion, and Education, 2008   212
8-3   Democratic and Republican Presidential Candidate
       Evaluations, 1968–2008   216
8-4   Party Better Able to Handle the Nation's Economy and
       Keep the Country Out of War, 1988–2008   220
8-5   Vote for President according to Voters' Ideological
       Identification and Perceptions of the Candidates'
       Ideology, 2008   225

Acknowledgments

THIS BOOK, as well as research in the area of political behavior generally, has benefited tremendously from an innovative step taken by scholars at the University of Michigan fifty years ago. The late Angus Campbell, at the time director of the Institute for Social Research at the University of Michigan, first opened the data archives of the Survey Research Center to outside scholars. This generous act was the beginning of a tradition of data-sharing that has characterized this area of the social sciences ever since. The late Warren Miller, former director of the Center for Political Studies, expanded these archival activities through the creation of the Inter-university Consortium for Political and Social Research (ICPSR). The ICPSR, composed of more than five hundred academic and research institutions, has made available to an extensive clientele not only the archives of the Survey Research Center but also thousands of other major data collections. Scholars and students have benefited in incalculable ways from the ability to use these data for their own research. The study of political science has likewise benefited from the ability to verify, replicate, and build upon earlier work.

A second consequential development grew out of the first. The Survey Research Center at the University of Michigan had begun its state-of-the-art biennial election surveys in 1948, the fruit of which was being made widely available through the ICPSR by the mid-1960s. The critical importance of this for scholarship was recognized and institutionalized in 1977, when the National Science Foundation agreed to fund the surveys of the American National Election Studies (ANES) as a national research resource. Under this arrangement, intellectual control of the development of the surveys passed to an independent board, composed of scholars drawn from several universities, with input from the political science community more generally and with data freely available via download from its Web site.

This book relies heavily on these institutional innovations in two ways. First, we base our analyses primarily on the large quantities of survey data collected by the ANES and the aggregate data contained in the ICPSR Historical Archive. Second, several generations of scholars whose work we cite have similarly benefited from the availability of these resources. We are pleased to acknowledge our great debt to the individuals involved in both the ICPSR and the ANES who have contributed to the establishment of these resources and services. We must hasten to add that they bear no responsibility for the analysis and interpretation presented here. We can only hope that any weaknesses of this work will not reflect upon the worthiness and excellence of the open archives that the ICPSR and the ANES provide.

We also wish to thank our editors at CQ Press, past and present—Brenda Carter, Charisse Kiino, Allie McKay, Shana Wagger, Kerry Kern, Tracy Villano, Ann O'Malley, Debbie Hardin, Christopher Karlsten, Talia Greenberg, Colleen McGuiness, Jennifer Campi, and Belinda Josey—for their shepherding of the last six editions of this book to publication. It is a pleasure to work with such competent and pleasant people.

W. H. F.
N. H. Z.

Introduction

BY ANY MEASURE, THE ELECTION of 2008 was historic, bringing to office the first African American president, Barack Obama. On the way to the nomination, Obama defeated the first serious woman candidate for president, Hillary Rodham Clinton, whose strong showing in the primaries represented another first. Riding a wave of disenchantment with the administration of President George W. Bush, Obama's victory was the largest popular vote margin since 1984. The new president took office buoyed by an outpouring of euphoria and hope for a new beginning, hopes tempered by the realization that tremendous challenges awaited: an economy and financial system in crisis, wars in Iraq and Afghanistan, and a bundle of campaign promises in need of attention.

The 2008 presidential campaign season opened with widespread and growing unhappiness with the Bush administration. In the congressional elections in 2006, the Democrats had won a sweeping victory, taking back both the House and Senate from the Republicans without losing a single incumbent of their own.[1] Prospects for a Democratic victory in the 2008 presidential election looked good. Public opinion polls showed President Bush's job approval rating to be nearing all-time lows, and the percentage of people thinking the country was off on the wrong track was at an all-time high. The war in Iraq dragged on, and even though the violence had decreased, there was no apparent end in sight.

The 2008 election would be the first presidential contest since 1952 without a sitting president or vice president seeking election. This situation attracted a large field of candidates on both sides. Among the eight Democratic candidates, former first lady and current senator Hillary Clinton was the acknowledged front-runner, although former vice presidential candidate John Edwards and newcomer Barack Obama

1

(first elected to the Senate in 2004) had supporters among those who feared a Hillary Clinton candidacy carried too much baggage from her husband's years in the White House.

The Republican field appeared more wide open, so much so that in the fall of 2007 some political commentators wondered if the nomination would not be decided until the Republican National Convention in the late summer—something that had not happened for several decades. Rudolph Giuliani, former mayor of New York City, had name recognition and homeland security credentials and typically led all other Republican candidates in public opinion polls, as well as in trial heats with possible Democratic candidates. Former governor Mitt Romney of Massachusetts also had a familiar name in Republican circles and a track record of success in a heavily Democratic state. Sen. John McCain was a war hero and a favorite of the press corps, with demonstrated appeal to moderates and independents. And the relatively unknown former governor of Arkansas, Mike Huckabee, was proving an engaging figure on the campaign trail who could appeal to the conservative southern and evangelical base of the Republican Party.

Despite early predictions that the Republican primary vote would be splintered in several directions, Senator McCain had all but locked up the nomination by February 5, while the Democratic contest continued on for months. Two factors allowed McCain to sew up the nomination early. First and probably most important is the "winner-take-all" nature of most Republican primaries. Unlike the Democrats, who adopted a proportional representation system in the 1970s, the Republican Party has for the most part kept the traditional system in which the winner of the primary wins all (or almost all) of the delegate votes from that state, regardless of how small a plurality he or she has won. In a fractured field of candidates, a candidate can win virtually all of the delegates from a state with a relatively small percentage of the vote, provided that the share is more than any other candidate. Thus on February 5, in California, McCain won 42 percent of the vote in the Republican primary to 35 percent for Romney, but walked away with 158 of California's 173 delegates. This pattern was repeated in state after state. In Florida's January 29 primary, McCain won all 57 delegates, having defeated Romney by the relatively narrow margin of 36 percent to 31 percent.[2]

The second factor contributing to McCain's early win was the self-destruction of Giuliani's candidacy. Perhaps it was never realistic to think that a moderate, pro-choice, twice-divorced New Yorker could win the Republican nomination, but he sealed his fate by forgoing the Iowa caucuses and several early primaries to concentrate on Florida, with its abundance of transplanted New Yorkers. By the time the Florida primary arrived on January 29, McCain's bandwagon was rolling and Giuliani was no longer a factor. (Giuliani ran behind

McCain and Romney in Florida, garnering only 15 percent of the vote.) Governor Huckabee stayed in the race for another two months, and Rep. Ron Paul, a libertarian-style Republican from Texas, remained a declared candidate until the Republican convention, but the Republican race was essentially over in early February.

Meanwhile, the Democrats settled in for a long primary battle. Clinton's initial advantage disappeared after she placed third in the Iowa caucuses in early January, the first event of the primary season. Although she came back with a surprise win in New Hampshire, her aura of inevitability was gone, as well as a lot of her financial war chest. After she and Obama split the Super Tuesday I primaries in early February, Obama reeled off a string of lopsided victories in caucus states and small-state primaries. His strategists were claiming that the delegate math was in his favor and Clinton could not make up the difference, an assertion that proved to be correct—although it took until early June to prove it.

Unlike the Republicans, the Democratic Party uses a system of proportion representation in allocating the delegate votes won in a primary. The idea, born after the riot-marred Democratic National Convention of 1968, is to assure that the candidates' strength at the national nominating convention reflects their strength in the popular vote in the primaries. A narrow win in a primary nets a candidate more delegates than an opponent, but often by very little. (Indeed, depending on how delegates are divided among congressional districts, the winner may get fewer delegates than other candidates. Clinton won the statewide popular vote in New Hampshire—and a lot of favorable publicity as a comeback candidate—but Obama actually won more delegates in that primary.)

Obama's campaign strategy was to contest every caucus and primary nationwide—and he had the Internet fund-raising and organizing skill to implement this strategy successfully. Caucuses are neighborhood meetings to select convention delegates. They typically attract highly committed party activists willing to spend an evening at such a function. In 2008 party caucuses were flooded with people enthusiastic for Obama, and in many caucus states this led to overwhelming margins for him, allowing him to claim a lopsided share of the delegates in those states while Clinton was winning by narrow margins in primary states.

The Clinton strategy was a serious miscalculation. Her team had planned for quick victories early in the process, after which all her rivals would bow out. When this did not happen, she had no plan in place to compete effectively in the caucus states, and not enough money to outgun Obama elsewhere. Clinton was left claiming that the Michigan and Florida delegations should be seated despite their holding of nonconforming primaries, and making the apples-and-oranges argument that caucus-goers and primary voters should be added together to give her more votes nationwide than Obama had.

Obama's final edge among the "pledged" delegates (those who had been won in the primaries and caucuses where party rules specified that they were bound to their candidate on the first convention ballot unless released by the candidate) was very narrow and could have been overcome by the so-called "super-delegates." Super-delegates are party officials and elected officeholders of the party in each of the states who become convention delegates by virtue of their positions. The Democratic Party added super-delegates to the roster of convention delegates in 1984, in hopes that these party "pros" would counterbalance the primary electorates' tendency to vote for candidates who turned out to be unelectable in the general election because they were too liberal, too inexperienced, or too unknown. Given this intent, the super-delegates might have been expected to back Hillary Clinton over the newcomer, Barack Obama. Ironically, however, most were unwilling to be seen as "going against the choice of the voters" in their home states or nationwide, perhaps because party and elected officials themselves depend on support from constituents and party activists for their positions.

Although at the time Democrats worried that the long primary fight would doom the party's chances in the fall, it probably made Obama a better candidate. Certainly, he evolved as a better debater, becoming more conversant with the issues over that time. A spate of bad news, most notably the fiery sermons and unfortunate views of his pastor, the Reverend Jeremiah Wright, and Obama's alleged friendship with 1960s domestic terrorist William Ayers, were fully aired, explained, debunked, or rationalized in ways that would not have been possible if they had appeared in the shortened time frame of the fall general election campaign. Obama's personal strengths also became more evident during the primary campaign. Without any executive experience on his résumé, his ability to run a successful campaign with a savvy, efficient, leak-proof, drama-free organization helped to answer some critics.

By modern standards, both political conventions were attention-grabbing. The Democratic convention featured Bill Clinton one night and Hillary Clinton the next, and uncertainty about their level of enthusiasm for the soon-to-be nominee provided an element of suspense. Obama's acceptance speech in a football stadium filled with eighty thousand supporters played to his celebrity status as well as grassroots excitement over his candidacy. On the Republican side, the traditionally celebratory first night of the convention was downplayed and deliberately low-key as a hurricane approached New Orleans and threatened to be a reminder of the Republican disaster that was Katrina three years before. The high point of the Republican convention, however, was the surprise selection of Gov. Sarah Palin of Alaska as the vice presidential candidate.

McCain's choice of Palin as his running mate was a huge gamble. She was an attractive and charismatic candidate, with appeal to the Republican conservative base and a hope of winning over women who were disappointed that Clinton was not on the Democratic ticket. She was also unknown and inexperienced and, it turned out, not a quick or willing learner. Palin made a tremendous initial splash at the Republican convention before a national audience with her well-received acceptance speech, reportedly written several weeks before her selection in a way that it could serve, with minor additions, no matter whom McCain chose.

The following weeks, however, saw a disastrous interview with *CBS News* anchor Katie Couric and a long-running spoof on *Saturday Night Live* featuring Tina Fey's dead-on impersonation of Governor Palin. By the end of the campaign, most political commentators had concluded that the Palin choice had hurt McCain's campaign, taking away the issue of Obama's inexperience and calling attention to the seventy-two-year-old McCain's age, as voters worried about Palin's capabilities should she be called upon to assume the presidency. It also raised questions about the judgment of a man who would make such a high-risk choice. Nevertheless, Palin remained a star attraction throughout the campaign, drawing bigger and more enthusiastic crowds than McCain himself.

When the campaigns for the nominations began in 2007, it was widely assumed that Iraq would be the major issue in the ensuing election. Attitudes toward the war were particularly important in the Democratic primary race and generally benefited Obama, who had opposed the war from the outset, while most of his Democratic opponents, most notably Hillary Clinton, had voted for the legislation that enabled Bush to go to war. On the Republican side, McCain's credentials were acknowledged to be in foreign and military policy.

When the U.S. economy fell off a cliff in mid-September 2008, it seriously rearranged campaign strategies. A Democratic candidate has a natural advantage at such moments—the Democratic Party has long been viewed as the party of prosperity, and its support of greater government intervention to regulate business and provide economic security to the middle class seemed like the right prescription for the moment. For his part, McCain stumbled badly, with an ill-timed announcement that he was "suspending" his campaign to go back to Washington to deal with the crisis after acknowledging that economics was not his strong point.

With this sudden new emphasis on the economy, the presidential debates—originally intended to have one deal with foreign policy, one with domestic policy, and the third devoted to audience questions—all took on the domestic economy. The debates themselves contained no major gaffes by either candidate. But as the less-experienced newcomer, Obama benefited from the opportunity to demonstrate his ability to look suitably presidential.

Obama's prowess as a fund-raiser gave his campaign a serious advantage over McCain. In the spring of 2008, as his ability to outraise and outspend Clinton became obvious, Obama had reversed his pledge to accept public financing for the general election. Although both candidates benefited from expenditures by independent groups supporting them and attacking their opponent, Obama's campaign outspent McCain's on an order of four-to-one in the final days before the election.

The renewed focus on the economy sealed a Democratic victory. By election day, Obama was courting votes in usually reliably Republican states like North Carolina and Indiana, while McCain had suspended campaign operations in former battleground states like Michigan to defend normally Republican strongholds.

On election day, Obama was aided by high turnout and solid support from African Americans, higher than usual turnout among young people, and high support and good turnout among Hispanic voters, giving him wins in Florida, North Carolina, New Mexico, and Colorado. He was also aided by somewhat depressed turnout among some traditionally Republican areas.

The comfortable victory margin of 53 percent to 46 percent for Obama in the presidential race was accompanied by gains in the House of Representatives and, even more impressively, in the Senate, where Democrats added three votes to their existing fifty-five-vote majority on election day. (A fifty-ninth vote was added three months later when Sen. Arlen Specter of Pennsylvania switched from the Republican caucus to the Democratic, and a sixtieth arrived in July when a recount in Minnesota was finally settled.) The gains in both the House and Senate were a continuation of the Democratic tide that began in the midterm elections of 2006.

The Democratic victories in 2006 and 2008 need to be seen against a backdrop of the two preceding presidential elections in 2000 and 2004 that were, in contrast, very close and very polarizing. The presidential contest in 2000 between Vice President Al Gore and Texas governor George W. Bush was the closest in more than a hundred years. More remarkable, the election remained undecided for more than a month because of the uncertainty of the outcome in Florida. The voting was extremely close in Florida, and an alarming number of irregular procedures and events occurred both before and after the election that called into question the validity of many votes. An unprecedented series of political and legal steps eventually led to a 5-4 U.S. Supreme Court decision, *Bush v. Gore,* that ended the recount then in progress and effectively gave a narrow electoral college victory to Bush. The legal maneuvering and the actions of officials in Florida and Washington, D.C., made those on both sides worry about the sanctity of the American electoral process and caused many on the Democratic side to feel that an election had been stolen from them.

Other electoral oddities occurred in 2000. For the first time since 1888 the popular vote winner was not the electoral college winner. Gore was the popular vote winner by a margin of more than five hundred thousand votes, but he lost the electoral college by four votes. Ralph Nader, a minor-party candidate with a small percentage of the popular vote, denied the presidency to a candidate who otherwise would have won. This had not happened since 1912.

Dead heats were not limited to the presidential election. The results of the 2000 election left the U.S. Senate evenly divided between the Democrats and Republicans, with the Republican vice president holding the tie-breaking vote. Then in the late spring, Sen. James M. Jeffords of Vermont switched from Republican to independent and denied the Republicans control of the Senate. So in June following the election the Democrats reorganized the Senate. It was the first time that party control of the Senate had changed during a session.

Against this backdrop of close partisan division and lingering resentment over the election results, the horrific events of September 11, 2001, took place. In the immediate aftermath of the attacks, the nation and its political leadership united behind President Bush to face and fight the threat of terrorism. Bush's approval ratings in public opinion polls soared, at least temporarily. The war in Afghanistan, undertaken in the following months, and an array of homeland security measures were widely accepted by Congress and the public as necessary steps to take.

One might expect that the awfulness of the attacks and the outburst of patriotism that followed would have a lasting impact on the political divisions in the country, but they did not. Instead, partisan division in the nation returned to the level it had been in 2000. A crucial variable in solidifying these divisions was the Bush administration's decision to go to war in Iraq. Suspicions about the veracity of intelligence reports that Iraqi leader Saddam Hussein possessed weapons of mass destruction and concerns that Iraq was a distraction from the "real" war on terrorism in Afghanistan followed existing partisan divisions among the public.

In this highly charged political atmosphere entering the 2004 election cycle, the task of the Democratic Party was to choose a candidate to challenge President Bush. The intensity of the negative feelings toward

Bush was perhaps best illustrated by the unusually high level of commitment of rank-and-file Democrats, Democratic activists, and elected officials to choose someone as their nominee who could beat him. When Sen. John Kerry of Massachusetts won the Iowa caucuses, upsetting early front-runner Howard Dean, whose campaign imploded in the final days leading up to the caucuses, Democratic hunger for a winner was so great that other early states fell in line behind Kerry, and he had virtually wrapped up the nomination by early February—at the time, an unprecedented early date.

The campaign for the presidency in 2004 was fought primarily in the so-called "battleground states"—the dozen or so states where the outcome was close enough in 2000 to give the other side hope of victory. Republican themes focused on President Bush's leadership in the war on terrorism and pointed to Kerry's alleged "flip-flops" on issues. The Democrats, in turn, focused on criticism of the Bush administration's handling of the war in Iraq—dishonesty in making the case for going to war, continued poor planning in carrying it out, and responsibility for providing the impetus for a new wave of terrorism—along with traditional Democratic economic themes. The Massachusetts Supreme Court made gay marriage a campaign issue by declaring it a constitutional right in Kerry's home state. Although Kerry's position was that state legislatures, not the courts, should decide such matters, the issue energized and brought to the polls anti–gay marriage activists in many states where gay marriage bans were on the ballot.

The outcome in 2004 was close—but not as close as 2000. Bush won the popular vote by almost three million, versus a loss by over a half million votes in 2000. The electoral college was a close copy of 2000, with only Iowa, New Mexico, and New Hampshire changing columns.[3] In 2004 a slight change in voting in Ohio would have given the state to Kerry, making him the winner of the electoral college while losing the popular vote nationwide. Thus two elections in a row were extremely close in popular voting and in the electoral college, with the possibility or actuality of the popular vote and the electoral college vote diverging. Few elections in American history have been as close as 2000 and 2004.

Thus the Obama victory in 2008 came against a recent history of partisan polarization and close division. It remains to be seen whether the new president's calls for bipartisanship in meeting the serious challenges facing the country will fall on receptive ears. Early signs have not been promising.

The first edition of this book was published in 1967. The plan of the book then, as now, was to present basic analysis and generalizations about the political behavior of Americans. What was unknowable at the time was that a decade of political trauma was beginning for the American polity. Not only would some basic changes in political life take place in the late 1960s, but these changes would call into question some of the things political scientists thought they knew about the way Americans behave politically. The years since then have seen their quiet periods and their moments of political upheaval. Much has changed in the political landscape—the impeachment and forced resignation of presidents, the dismantling of the welfare state under Ronald Reagan, the Republican "revolution" in the House of Representatives in 1994, the focus on homeland security in the post–September 11 world, and the stunning election of the first African American president in U.S. history. Over the years since that first edition, however, we have been impressed with the overall continuity in the behavior of the electorate, even in the midst of significant changes in the political environment.

In this twelfth edition we continue to focus attention on the major concepts and characteristics that shape Americans' responses to politics: Are Americans committed to upholding basic democratic values? Who votes and why? How does partisanship affect political behavior? How and why does partisanship change? How do economic and social characteristics influence individuals' politics? How much influence do the mass media have on the electorate's attitudes and political choices? How do party loyalties, candidates' personalities, and issues influence voters' choices among candidates? Throughout the book we place the answers to these and other questions in the context of the changes that have occurred in American political behavior over the past sixty years. Specifically, we are concerned with trends in voter turnout, the loss of trust in government that many citizens have expressed, and the drop in voter attachment to political parties coupled with an increasing polarization of political activists and elites.

A second major focus of this book is to illustrate and document these trends in American political behavior with the best longitudinal data available. We rely heavily, although not exclusively, on data from surveys conducted by the American National Election Study (ANES). The ANES surveys, covering a broad range of political topics and offering the best time-series data available, have been conducted during the fall of every election year (except 2006) since 1952. Unless otherwise noted, the data come from this extraordinarily rich series of studies. We hope that the numerous tables and figures contained in this book will be used not only for documenting the points made in the book but also for learning to read and interpret data. Students can also explore a much wider range of data from the ANES on its Web site at www.elec tionstudies.org. The data from the ANES and other studies are available for classroom use through the Inter-university Consortium for Political and Social Research (ICPSR). (To see the full range of political studies available to the academic community, visit the ICPSR Web site at www .icpsr.umich.edu.) An especially good introduction to the analysis of

ANES data is a Web site at the University of California, Berkeley, that is open to all users: http://sda.berkeley.edu. One of our purposes is to provide an impetus for obtaining high-quality data to answer questions prompted, but not answered, by this book.

Notes

1. The exception was Sen. Joseph Lieberman of Connecticut, who left the party after being defeated in the Democratic primary and then went on to win reelection as an independent. He continues to caucus with the Democrats, however.
2. These figures are *New York Times* projections of the delegate count. See politics .nytimes.com/election-guide/2008/results/gopdelegates/index.html.
3. A reallocation of electoral votes following the 2000 census accounts for an additional switch of seven votes to the Republicans, as the population—and thus electoral votes—shifted from "blue" to "red" states.

Political Culture and American Democracy

SUCCESSFUL DEMOCRACIES rest on the consent of the governed and widespread public support. In representative democracies, regular, free, and fair elections are held to choose political leaders and, when necessary, to turn these leaders out of office. A democratic system of government, at a minimum, affords its citizens the opportunity to organize, to speak freely, and to select its leaders.

This simple view, which assumes a crucial role for the people in choosing their representatives and emphasizes the individual as an autonomous actor with inherent political rights, is widely agreed upon. Less consensus exists on what is required of citizens in a democracy. On the one hand is the vision of a well-informed electorate making decisions based on rational calculations of its own best interest or, possibly, a public good. On the other hand is the picture, drawn by some critics, of a deluded public, manipulated by political elites to hold views and support policies that are in the interests of the elites instead of the people. Somewhere in between is the view that the electorate responds to generalized policy promises and symbolic issues in selecting its leaders, setting broad and vague outer limits on decision makers. Specific policies, however, are negotiated between public officials and subsets of the attentive public who are unrepresentative of the general public, both in terms of their degree of interest in a particular policy and in the political resources available to them with which to exert influence. In the chapters that follow, you will have the opportunity to judge for yourself the level of information and capacity for rational decision making that the American public displays.

In this chapter we consider two topics. First, we examine an issue brought starkly into focus by the disputed outcome of the 2000 presidential election. What are the requirements for fair and free elections in a democracy, and how closely does the U.S. system come to meeting them? Second, we look at the cultural and attitudinal requirements for instituting and sustaining a democratic system and examine the extent to which they are met in the United States. How widespread is support for the political system in the United States and for the democratic values on which it is based? How confident are Americans that a democratic system is the best route to satisfactory policy outcomes? How confident are they that their government is playing by democratic rules? Looking at democracy from a different vantage point, what expectations do citizens have about their own roles in a democratic system? How are democratic values and appropriate citizen roles learned and transmitted from generation to generation?

Fair, Free, and Competitive Elections

Elections are a basic component of a democratic political system. They are the formal mechanism by which the people maintain or alter the existing political leadership. At regular intervals, competitive elections give ordinary citizens the power to choose their leaders and, just as important, to throw them out of office. Although the choices available to voters in a general election may not be numerous or even particularly dissimilar, democratic systems must provide for competition, usually by means of political parties, in presenting alternative candidates.

If elections are to be competitive, political leaders and organizations must be able to compete for the support of voters, and voters should have leaders competing for their support. (If some voters have no leaders competing for their support, the system must be open to the entry of new leaders who will seek the support of these unrepresented voters.)

Competitive elections require that all citizens must be free to participate fully in campaign activities before the election itself. Such campaign activities include the freedom to express one's views and the freedom to organize with others during the nominating phase and the campaign to make preferences known and to persuade others. Implicit in this is the freedom to receive information about the choices before the voters.

Citizens must be free to vote, and the right to vote should not be undermined by substantial economic or administrative barriers. No physical or social intimidation should take place. Citizens legally eligible to vote should have full and convenient access to polling places. The right to vote and the right to express one's choices freely require a secret ballot. In fair elections the ballots cast should reflect the intention of the

---

Requirements for Free and Fair Elections

A democratic system requires political leaders to compete for public support in fair and free elections. For elections to be fair and free, they must meet the following conditions.

- Freedom of citizens to form or join organizations in support of candidates
- Freedom to express preferences
- Alternative sources of information
- Ability of new leaders to enter the system and compete for support
- Right to vote without administrative barriers or intimidation
- Votes counted fairly
- Votes translated into representation fairly
- Due process and equal protection under the law

---

voters, and the votes should be counted accurately. Votes should be weighted equally in translating votes into representation.

Finally, the requirements of free and fair elections should be established in law and be enforceable through the judicial system. Both citizens and leaders must enjoy equal treatment under the law.

Recent presidential elections provide an opportunity to reassess the extent to which the requirements for being fair and free have been met in the American political system. Elections in the twenty-first century have been close and intensely contested. An impressive array of independent, nonparty groups formed in support of specific candidates. While some such groups were "letterhead organizations," and others not truly independent of the parties or candidates, the number and vigor of these groups, such as MoveOn.org, were noteworthy. The availability of the Internet as a place for groups to "meet" has facilitated the ability to join with like-minded people in support of one's preferred candidate. In 2008 Barack Obama's campaign took the use of the Internet to a new level, as a way to raise funds, turn out crowds, and organize at the grassroots level.

Freedom of political expression is guaranteed by the First Amendment to the U.S. Constitution, and few legal limits are placed on what can be said about a political opponent. Local and state ordinances and ethics commissions keep outright falsehoods from the candidates and their campaigns in check, but citizens, supporters, and talk-show hosts generally can and do get away with expressing all manner of opinions regarding current and potential officeholders. The most critical issue with freedom of expression in the television age is the imbalance in resources available to get one's views to a wide audience. Although the two major political parties are well funded, candidates seeking the presidential nomination through the primaries, minor-party candidates, and citizens with views not represented by the major parties may find themselves unable to get a hearing.

Given the vast amounts of money spent on political advertising in presidential election campaigns—much of it highly negative—the focus has often been on how to place limits on it. For years the U.S. Supreme Court has ruled that issue advocacy by individuals or independent groups is protected by First Amendment guarantees, and the Court and Congress have wrestled with the problem of placing limits on it. The bigger problem for a democracy such as the United States is reconciling freedom of expression with the disparity of resources that allows some groups to get a hearing for their views and others not.

Concerns have been raised in recent years about the concentration of ownership of mass media outlets in fewer hands. Although this has certainly happened, it is probably more than offset by the proliferation of new sources of information from the Internet and cable and satellite television. The problem likely is not whether alternative information sources exist, but whether consumers can sort through them to find credible sources and whether they will avail themselves of varied and competing views. The decline of newspapers, with their higher journalistic standards for fact-checking, nonbiased reporting, and civility, makes this situation potentially worse.

Despite the tight competition between the two major-party candidates and the fairly open competition among candidates within the parties' primaries, the barriers to entry into the competition by other parties' candidates are severe. Although other candidates—Pat Buchanan and Ralph Nader in 2000, Nader in 2004, and Nader and Robert Barr in 2008—were on the ballot in virtually every state, and Buchanan had access to public financing, the obstacles to competing effectively are serious. All these candidates were denied a place in the nationally televised debates, and the electoral college arrangements encourage voters to see a vote for such candidates as a wasted vote. Many of the rules governing elections in the United States are designed to weed out "nuisance" candidates and to limit attention to those with some degree of public support. Public financing, participation in the debates, and place on the ballot all require demonstration of some minimum level of support. On an informal level, coverage of a candidate's campaign by the mass media also requires such a demonstration. Unfortunately, minor candidates are faced with a chicken-and-egg dilemma: they cannot gain access to these important resources unless they are competitive, but they cannot become competitive unless they have access to these resources.

Registering to vote has become easier in most states in recent years; in consequence, registration has increased. (We will treat the topic of voter registration and turnout more fully in chapter 2.) Efforts also are evident in many states to make it easier for registered voters to vote by allowing vote by mail, easing restrictions on the use of absentee ballots, and setting up in-person, early voting opportunities. Administrative problems remain, however, and fall unevenly on the citizenry. For example, officials in some states have been slow to process new registrations, so that individuals who have correctly followed registration procedures find themselves not registered when they get to the polling place.

The Help American Vote Act (HAVA) of 2002 was fashioned to deal with some of these problems. One provision, in effect in time for the 2004 elections, was to allow voters who thought they were registered but did not appear on the registration lists to cast a provisional ballot that would be sealed and held, but not counted until the voter's eligibility to vote had been established. Another provision of HAVA was to mandate establishment of a statewide electronic database so problems of verifying registration can be resolved more quickly.

Nevertheless, as the competition between the two major parties has become closer and more intense, the willingness to use measures to restrict participation (or discourage fraud or both) has increased. These tendencies were at work in the presidential election in Florida in 2000 and in Ohio in 2004, both hotly contested states. (Whatever voting irregularities may have existed in 2008 were overshadowed by Obama's relatively comfortable winning margin in both the popular and electoral vote.)

An unusual registration problem in Florida in 2000 received a considerable amount of attention from the U.S. Commission on Civil Rights.[1] Because significant fraud came to light in some recent Florida elections, before the 2000 election the state legislature enacted legislation to purge the registration lists of ineligible voters (such as the dead or otherwise departed). The state contracted with a private firm to purge from the registration lists felons, who are not eligible to vote in Florida, but this process removed many nonfelons from the registration lists, due to inaccurate felon lists and computer mismatches of names. Some people were informed that they had been purged before the election, but the procedures for reinstatement were confusing. Others were not informed beforehand and arrived at their polling place only to be told that they were ineligible to vote. The Civil Rights Commission also heard testimony of black citizens in Florida who reported being stopped by state police on the way to the polls. If such obstruction was intentional and systematic, it would be a denial of fair access to a polling place.

Simple administrative bungling can have the same effect—for example, providing incorrect or conflicting information to would-be voters. In Ohio in 2004, voting equipment was reallocated to precincts on the basis of turnout in previous elections, not on the number of registered voters. This usually meant sending voting equipment from central city areas to suburban areas. When turnout increased substantially in 2004, voters in Cleveland and Columbus (areas with high Democratic concentrations) stood in line, reportedly for hours, waiting to vote. Doubtless, some voters did not stick it out. Also the Republican secretary of state, Kenneth Blackwell, ruled that provisional ballots, provided under HAVA, would be counted only if they were cast in the precinct in which the voter lived. This was a permissible ruling, according to the Federal Election Assistance Commission, but nonetheless was the kind of restrictive interpretation that serves to decrease participation in elections.

Because so much information is available on the vote-counting process in Florida in the aftermath of the 2000 election, it can be used as a test of the requirement that votes be counted accurately. The 2000 election in Florida demonstrated that voting procedures themselves can deny voters their vote. Voting devices can fail to record votes in various ways. On punch-hole ballots the paper chad might not be dislodged and, therefore, the ballot would not be counted; on scanned ballots the choices might not be detected; and on most voting devices the voter can inadvertently void the ballot by various kinds of inappropriate marking. (In party primary elections, in which voters are required to vote in only one party's races but the ballot form allows voting in more than one party primary, large percentages of the ballots are invalidated for this reason.[2]) Voting machines do exist that detect such errors and give the voter another chance to cast a ballot correctly, but they are relatively expensive. Another provision of HAVA required that states give voters an opportunity to check and correct their ballots before the ballot is cast. It also mandated standards for voter systems (eliminating punch cards with their hanging chads) and appropriated funds to states to assist in their purchase. Among the requirements for an approved voting system is a "paper trail" to enable a recount process when necessary.

The marked ballot should accurately reflect the voter's intention. In 2000 in Broward County, Florida, for example, the butterfly ballot, which was enlarged to help elderly voters read it better, resulted in a considerable number of voters mistakenly casting their votes for Buchanan when they intended to vote for Al Gore. Election officials in different counties used different rules for determining the voter's intent on flawed ballots during the various phases of the recount. Some officials allowed votes to be counted if the voter's intention could be reasonably inferred from the marks or punches on the ballot. In other counties, even ballots with a clear declaration of intent—such as that of the frustrated voter who wrote "I want to vote for Gore" on the ballot—were disallowed.

The counting of votes is overseen by representatives of the competing political parties, and they are expected to keep each other honest. Even so, standardizing procedures in different election districts is difficult.* For example, many months after the 2000 election, the Republican Party was revealed to have pursued a two-part strategy in Florida: in Republican counties, it insisted that all ballots be counted even if the ballots were flawed in various ways; in Democratic counties, Republican officials followed the strict letter of the law to disallow identically flawed ballots.

A fair election must allow for a thorough and accurate recount to ensure that the official results faithfully reflect the voters' choices. All vote-counting procedures are susceptible to error and fraud, so the occasional authentication of official returns is crucial to maintaining the legitimacy of elections in general. Typically in the United States recounts have uncovered a certain amount of clerical error and little fraud. The long-running recount in the 2008 Senate election in Minnesota revealed a net swing of only about five hundred votes out of three million cast (a small number, but enough to change the outcome from election night). It also revealed a surprising array of ways in which voters can spoil their ballots and substantial variation in the handling of ballots—especially absentee ballots—across different counties. Even after the HAVA provisions were in place, and in a state that was a pioneer in easing the burdens of voter registration, twelve thousand absentee voters did not have their ballots counted.

The election of 2000, in which the popular vote winner did not win in the electoral college and did not become president, puts in stark relief the problem of translating votes into representation. How can votes be considered equal if the state in which they are cast determines how much influence they have in determining the winner? The rationale lies in the nature of a federal system. States, as well as individual citizens, are actors in such a system, and their role was preserved in the electoral college as a part of the price of establishing the Union. It is one of many ways in which the American system departs from a purely representative democracy. Electoral outcomes such as 2000 are

---

*Following the Florida election controversy, a consortium of eight news organizations was formed to recount the presidential vote for the entire state. Using a number of different rules for counting disputed ballots, they found that systematically following the rules advocated by the Gore advisers would have led to a George W. Bush victory and following the rules preferred by the Bush organization would have produced a Gore victory.

rare, however. The only other presidential elections that resulted in a popular vote loser winning the electoral college were those of 1876 and 1888.[3] If one wants to consider a far more perverse case of bad translation of votes into representation, one should look at the U.S. Senate, where the votes of 16 percent of the population can elect a majority of that body.

Finally, in 2000 the partisan overtones to the involvement of the Florida Supreme Court (which ruled to benefit the Democrat) and the U.S. Supreme Court (which ruled to benefit the Republican) in deciding the election raise questions about the extent to which elections in the United States are subject to the rule of law. The election of 2000 tested the public's confidence in the fairness of the American electoral system. The tight competitiveness of the contest led both sides to campaign aggressively for every possible vote—and, in the confused aftermath of the election, to use every conceivable tactic to gain an advantage for their side. The challenge in a democratic electoral system is to be highly competitive without compromising the integrity of the election process. A few months after his inauguration in 2001, only half the public reported believing that George W. Bush "won fair and square."[4] By 2004, little had changed in these feelings. Fifty percent thought the 2000 election was "fair," whereas 49 percent thought it was not—and most on both sides felt strongly. In contrast, only about 15 percent thought the 2004 election was unfair.[5] In a postelection survey in 2008 by the Pew Research Center for the People and the Press, 81 percent of the public said they were very or fairly satisfied with the way U.S. democracy works. This was about the same percentage as in 1996 and 2004.[6]

Political Culture as a Foundation for Democracy

Political culture is the set of values and beliefs that support (or sometimes undermine) political processes and institutions. In democratic theory, much depends upon those beliefs and values. Citizens need to accept the idea of rule by the majority and, equally, to believe that the rights of the minority should be respected. They should have some sense of their rights and obligations to participate in the political process, at a minimum through exercising the right to vote. The political elite—those who hold elected or appointed office and those involved in putting them there—need to be willing to play by the democratic rules of the game and respect the will of the majority, even when it means the loss of their positions. In the remainder of this chapter we will examine the content of American political culture and assess it as a foundation for the maintenance of democracy. We will of necessity focus on the values of the dominant national culture, though you should keep in mind that political subcultures exist that may support contrary values and attitudes.

System Support

Governments, whether democratic or nondemocratic, require some level of support from the public to stay in power. Their holding of power must be seen, in some sense, as *legitimate*. The source of that legitimacy could be the divine right of kings (in hereditary monarchies of the past), religious authority (as with the imams of present-day Iran), or the consent of the people (in modern democracies). An important element in maintaining legitimacy is the belief that officeholders gained their position through appropriate means (through fair and free elections in the case of democracies) and exercise their power according to prescribed procedures and within prescribed limits. In a simplified scenario, if the public in a democratic system believes in democratic values, it will support leaders who come to office through democratic elections and govern according to democratic procedures. Furthermore, it would withdraw support from any leader or would-be leader who attempts to gain office or govern by undemocratic means.

A complicating factor in the consideration of system support is the impact of governmental *effectiveness* on public perceptions of legitimacy. A tyrannical government that makes the trains run on time may gain some measure of legitimacy, despite abuse of persons and procedures. Conversely, a democratically elected government that governs by democratic procedures but is chronically unable to solve its nation's problems may lose its legitimacy. Its citizens might lose faith in democracy as a workable form of government and demand a different system. Support for a political system is thus a combination of belief in the rightness of a system of government and satisfaction with the way it is working.

On a relatively superficial level, Americans express strong pride in their country. In response to questions in public opinion polls, 96 percent say that they are proud to be American; 89 percent say they are very patriotic; 89 percent characterize their love of America as "very strong" or "extremely strong"; and 79 percent say their feelings about the flag are "very good" or "extremely good."[7]

When people are asked about their pride in the United States, they tend to offer political factors as examples. In other countries people are much more likely to give nonpolitical reasons for their pride: their country's economy, culture, or physical beauty. They are not nearly as likely to say they are proud of their political system.[8] Americans not only give political reasons for their pride in the United States but also cite "freedom" or "liberty" as the aspect of their political system that makes them proud. Thus not only is there strong patriotic pride in the nation, but a central democratic value also is a prominent feature of that sentiment.

Pride in the nation and its democratic form of government translates into high levels of political system support. Of the respondents in a national survey, 85 percent agreed that, "whatever its faults, the United States still has the best system of government in the world." More than half of the public "would not change anything" in the American political system.[9]

Vague principles may be widely endorsed even though, at the same time, specific applications may be opposed. So it should not be surprising that respondents will agree to vague statements of system support while they endorse contradictory specifics. For example, 80 percent of the public say that the Constitution should not be amended.[10] However, majorities also believe that it should be changed to abolish the electoral college or mandate a balanced budget. Almost certainly, none of these answers reveals how people would behave if faced with real choices on amending the Constitution.

Democratic Beliefs and Values

The beliefs and values supporting the American political system are variously referred to as the *American creed,* the *American consensus,* and the *American ethos.*[11] Among the most important values making up this creed are beliefs in *freedom, equality,* and *individualism.*

Social and political theorists make a distinction between the economic system and the political system. Most would say that the United States has, as an ideal, a democratic political system and a capitalist or free-market economic system. Ordinary citizens are more likely to mix the two and view freedom as a basic value in both. The freedom to own property, fundamental to a capitalist economic system, is considered by ordinary U.S. citizens to be as important as the right to vote, for example.

Although highly valued in American culture, freedom is not considered an absolute. People accept all kinds of limitations on their freedom. For example, when given a choice between government intervention and a wholly free market, Americans are clearly in favor of government activity. In the 2008 American National Election Study (ANES), by a ratio of more than two to one, the public preferred strong government intervention to handle economic problems rather than depending solely on free-market operations. Similarly, majorities of the public support limiting the freedom to read pornography, to own guns, and to smoke cigarettes.

The widespread belief in equality similarly needs to be qualified. Americans believe in "equality before the law" and in "equal opportunity" but are largely uninterested in using government to promote economic and social equality. For example, the public agrees overwhelmingly (89 percent) with the proposition that "our society should do whatever is necessary to make sure that everyone has an equal opportunity to succeed."[12] But a substantial minority (37 percent) of the public believes "we have gone too far in pushing equal rights in this country."[13] In many respects, the value placed on individualism undermines the commitment to equality. Most social groups exhibit widespread support for the idea that people can and should get ahead by virtue of their own hard work.

Belief in Democratic Procedures

A distinction often is made between democratic *goals,* such as equality and individual freedom, and democratic *procedures,* such as majority rule; protection of the political rights of freedom of speech, press, and assembly; and due process of law. The distinction is an important one when the extent to which these ideals are supported in the political culture of a system is under consideration, because democratic goals can be pursued through undemocratic means, or democratic procedures can be used for antidemocratic ends. Likewise, mass support may exist for democratic goals but not for democratic procedures, or vice versa.

A widely held and perfectly plausible expectation is that the American public supports both these kinds of democratic values. At an abstract level this is true enough. American citizens overwhelmingly subscribe to the basic rules and goals of democracy when the commitment is kept vague. But, as discussed above, the near-unanimous support for the democratic goals of freedom and equality disappears when specific applications of these concepts are considered. The same has been true for specific applications of democratic procedures, such as protection of free speech. Majorities historically have been happy to infringe on the right to speak, to organize, and to run for office of unpopular groups such as atheists, Communists, and the Ku Klux Klan.

Rising educational levels in the United States brought an increased willingness on the part of the public to allow free speech on unpopular points of view and permit books with distasteful perspectives to remain in public libraries. Numerous studies document the shift in attitudes occurring from the mid-1950s to the 1970s, and without exception they find a strong relationship between increased tolerance and higher levels of education.[14]

Some important qualifications are in order. First, the electorate's responses are attitudes that may have little meaning for it and are not measures of its behavior or of its attitudes under crisis or threat to democratic principles. Second, people may not be more tolerant but the focus of their intolerance may have shifted. People now tolerate speeches by Marxists but object to those of fascists or racists.[15] More broadly, the desire for censorship may have shifted from political speech to other forms of expression, such as art and music, particularly when sexual or sacrilegious themes are involved.

The September 11, 2001, attacks on the United States raised questions about Americans' willingness to sacrifice rights and freedoms in waging the war on terrorism, especially regarding the 2001 USA PATRIOT Act, which expanded the government's authority to monitor and regulate citizens. Initially, the public was about evenly divided over the provisions of the act, with between a quarter and a third believing it "goes too far" in restricting people's civil liberties, and equal numbers thinking it does not go far enough.[16] By the fall of 2008, the American public was more concerned that the government would "restrict the average person's civil liberties" (51 percent) than fail to combat terrorism (31 percent.)[17] Generally, the public is not supportive of the act's provisions directed at "ordinary citizens" but is supportive of activities directed at "terrorists." For example, in 2004, 71 percent disapproved of federal agents searching a U.S. citizen's home without informing the person, yet majorities supported a range of similar activities when the targets were "terrorists."[18]

When considering public support for civil liberties and other democratic values, it is essential to keep in mind the distinction between mass attitudes and those of the political, social, and economic leaders in American society who consistently support democratic principles more strongly than the general public. Support among leaders is usually so high that it is possible to conclude that the leaders in society defend and maintain democratic procedures. Consensus among leaders on democratic rights and values makes the weakness of the general public's support less crucial. Table 1-1 compares the responses of samples of the public with those of "political influentials" to questions about support for the "democratic rules of the game" in the 1960s and in 2004. In both time periods, the political influentials were consistently more likely to support maintaining civil liberties and democratic processes than a sample of the electorate.

Presumably, leaders are recruited and educated in such a way that they come prepared with, or develop, agreement on democratic procedures. Leaders apparently make decisions that maintain democratic practices, even without widespread public support. A somewhat less comforting possibility is that political elites are simply sophisticated enough to understand what the "correct" answer is to attitude questions dealing with democratic beliefs. The seemingly greater adherence to these values by the politically active would attest to the

TABLE 1-1   Political Influentials versus the Electorate, Responses to Items
Expressing Belief in Democratic Values, 1964 and 2004

Item	Percentage agreeing with item	
	Political influentials	General electorate
There are times when it almost seems better for people to take the law into their own hands rather than wait for the machinery of government to act. (1964)	13	27
The majority has the right to abolish minorities if it wants to. (1964)	7	28
I don't mind a politician's methods if he manages to get the right things done. (1964)	26	42
Almost any unfairness or brutality may have to be justified when some great purpose is being carried out. (1964)	13	33
People ought to be allowed to vote even if they can't do so intelligently. (1964)	66	48
The true American way of life is disappearing so fast that we may have to use force to save it. (1964)	13	35
Terrorists pose such an extreme threat that governments should now be allowed to use torture if it may gain information that saves innocent lives. (2004)	8	27
In order to combat international terrorism, [I favor] restricting immigration into the United States. (2004)	36	76

Sources: The 1964 data were adapted from Herbert McClosky, "Consensus and Ideology in American Politics," *American Political Science Review* 58 (June 1964): 365, Table 1. There were 3,020 influentials and 1,484 in the public sample for 1964. The 2004 data were taken from *Global Views 2004: American Public Opinion and Foreign Policy* (Chicago: Chicago Council of Foreign Relations, 2004), available at www.ccrf.org/globalviews2004. There were 450 influentials, including 100 members of Congress or their senior staff, and 1,195 in the public sample for 2004.

Note: Because respondents were forced to make a choice on each item, the number of omitted or "don't know" responses was, on average, fewer than 3 percent and thus has little influence on the direction or magnitude of the results reported in the table.

prominence of such norms in the mass political culture but would not necessarily suggest any great commitment or willingness to abide by these values. A third possibility exists that political leaders, like ordinary citizens, are willing to violate the rights of groups and individuals whom they particularly dislike or fear. Enough incidents of undemocratic behavior by public officials have occurred in recent decades—harassment of dissidents during the Vietnam War, "dirty tricks" to undermine the electoral process in 1972, surreptitious aiding of the Nicaraguan contras in violation of the law in the 1980s, and efforts to undermine the fair counting of ballots in Florida in 2000—to suggest no great depth of appreciation of democratic principles on the part of elites of either political party. The increasing incivility in Congress and the mass media that has accompanied the increased polarization of the society along political lines suggests that the democratic virtue of tolerance of one's opponent's views is in short supply among political elites today.

Reaction to the Supreme Court's decisions on flag burning illustrates several aspects of the role of political elites in supporting democratic values. Political dissidents have occasionally burned the American flag to protest policies or governmental actions with which they disagree. In retaliation, Congress and some state legislatures have passed laws making it a crime to desecrate the flag. The Supreme Court has consistently ruled these laws to be an unconstitutional infringement on free speech—classifying flag burning as "symbolic speech" and therefore protected by the First Amendment. Inevitably, such decisions provoke a public outcry and calls to amend the Constitution as a means to circumvent the Court's rulings and punish those who would burn the flag. In these circumstances, various political elites—the Court itself and some congressional leaders—support democratic values by resisting the popular passion for punishing flag burners. At the same time, other political leaders see an opportunity to exploit an issue that plays well among the public, because polls consistently show the public believes, by majorities of three or four to one, that there should be no right to burn or deface the U.S. flag.[19] In the past, proposed constitutional amendments to ban flag burning have been defeated once the issue became rephrased as "tampering with the Bill of Rights," thus demonstrating the generalized, if vague, support the public has for democratic values and the critical nature of elite leadership.

The widespread interest of political analysts in public opinion and democratic beliefs has been based partly on a somewhat mistaken impression. Stable democratic political systems have been assumed to rest on a nearly universal commitment to fundamental principles and their application, but the evidence is inconclusive. A democratic system cannot long survive widespread, intense hostility to democratic values, but positive belief in particular operating procedures among the public is probably unnecessary. Hostility to democratic procedures is fatal, whether among the leaders or the public, but support of specific procedures may prove essential only among leaders. Perhaps the public need not agree on basic principles so long as it does not demand disruptive policies and procedures.

Declining Trust in Government

In general, the public has considerable confidence in the *institutions* of government but not much in the *individuals* charged with operating these institutions. Thus virtually no popular support is found for abolishing the presidency, the Supreme Court, or Congress, although disenchantment is widespread with the way the nation's political leadership is performing in the major branches of government. In early 2009, about 10 percent of the public had "a great deal" of confidence in Congress, and roughly one-third had "a great deal" of confidence in the presidency and the Supreme Court.[20] Such low levels of confidence, with some variations, have existed since the early 1970s and represent a noticeable drop from those of earlier years.

John R. Hibbing and Elizabeth Theiss-Morse argue, in their book *Congress as Public Enemy,* that it is the very openness to public scrutiny of congressional activities that generates distaste.[21] This may explain the higher level of confidence in the more secretive executive and Supreme Court decision making. In short, when the people see democracy in action, they do not like it very much.

Figure 1-1 shows another indicator of declining public confidence in the political system. For years, the ANES has asked respondents whether they thought "the government in Washington could be trusted to do the right thing." Figure 1-1 shows an overall decline from high levels in the 1950s and early 1960s to the point in the early 1990s where only a third of the public believed the government would do what is right "all of the time" or "most of the time." Short-term reversals in this downward trend have been associated with policy successes or popular incumbents. President Ronald Reagan created an upbeat mood in the 1980s that translated into a modest restoration of confidence in government, as did the booming economy in the mid-1990s. After September 11, 2001, a *Washington Post* poll reported an upward spike in the level of trust in government, shown toward the right on Figure 1-1. Of the people questioned, 64 percent of the public said they trusted the government all or most of the time—a level that had not been seen since the early 1960s.[22] But commercial polls show that a month later the percentage dropped from 64 percent to 55 percent, with continuing decline thereafter.[23] By the fall of 2008, unhappiness with the Bush administration had sent the level of trust back to its previous low levels.[24]

Because the most dramatic decline in trust in government officials occurred between 1964 and 1976, it is easy to blame the Vietnam War and the Watergate scandal. Although no doubt these were contributing factors, the decline in trust had already begun before Vietnam became an issue and continued after Richard M. Nixon's resignation from office.

FIGURE 1-1   Attitudes toward Politics and the Political System, 1952–2009

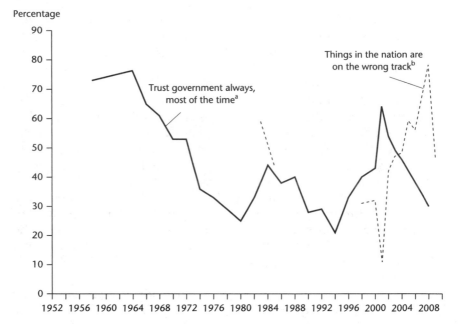

Percentage

Sources: Trust data from American National Election Studies, available at www.election studies.org. Wrong track data from NBC News/ *Wall Street Journal* Poll, available at www .pollingreport.com. Wrong track data for the 1980s from CBS News/ *New York Times* Poll, available from the Roper Center for Public Opinion Research.

[a]"How much of the time do you think you can trust the government in Washington to do what is right—just about always, most of the time, or only some of the time?"

[b]"All in all, do you think things in the nation are generally headed in the right direction, or do you feel that things are off on the wrong track?"

Furthermore, the pattern of declining trust extends to many nongovernmental institutions, such as the news media, schools, the professions, and people in general. It is paralleled by similar trends outside the United States in many of the developed nations of the world.

In recent years, commercial polling organizations have begun to track trust and confidence in government another way, by asking whether respondents "think things in the nation are generally headed in the right direction, or do you feel that things are off on the wrong track?" Although comparison with the years of high confidence in the 1950s and early 1960s cannot be made, responses to this question, also shown in Figure 1-1, indicate the increased support for government in the aftermath of September 11, followed by mounting concern over the direction of the country later in the Bush years, and—at the very end of the time series—the hope represented by the early days of the Obama administration. Political strategists have come to use the responses to the "right track/wrong track" question as a kind of leading indicator of the electoral chances of the party in power; one can judge for oneself how well it reflects the closeness of the 2000 election, Bush's bigger victory in 2004, and the Democratic victories in 2006 and 2008.

The Role of the Citizen

Questions about "trust in government" or whether the country is moving in the right direction are attempts to measure individuals' *external political efficacy*, or the extent to which citizens believe that their government is working the way it should—which, in a democratic system, involves responding to the will of the people. In contrast, the concept of *internal political efficacy* refers to the degree to which individuals see themselves as capable of influencing the political process because of their own abilities and competence. The two may sometimes be difficult to disentangle in practice, but in theory they are distinct. A person may think, "I'm a capable, knowledgeable person, but the system is so corrupt that I don't get a fair hearing" (high internal efficacy but low external efficacy). Another person might have the opposite set of feelings: "This is the greatest country in the world; if only I had an education I could run for office, too" (high external efficacy but low internal efficacy). A democratic system requires confidence in its institutions and processes. It also requires citizens who feel competent to involve themselves in politics.

Agreement or disagreement with statements such as "Politics and government are too complicated for people like me to understand," or "I feel that I have a pretty good understanding of the important political issues facing our country" are used as indicators of internal political efficacy. In the 2008 ANES, 70 percent of the respondents agreed that "politics is too complicated for people like me to understand," indicating a low sense of political efficacy, whereas 75 percent agreed that they felt they had "a pretty good understanding" of the issues of the day, which would indicate a higher level of internal efficacy. Obviously, different indicators produce different results. In any case, these indicators have yielded similar numbers over the years, so we can conclude that there have not been significant increases or decreases in citizens' sense of their own political competence. Internal political efficacy, however measured, is highly related to education, as one might expect.

Despite some apparent misgivings about their own political competence and the willingness of officeholders to listen, most Americans understand the basic obligations of citizens in a democracy. About 85 percent of all adults believe that good citizens have a duty to vote in "every national election," although many do not act on that commitment.[25] Although Americans also believe in the importance of informing themselves about political and governmental affairs, they readily concede that in most cases they personally are not as well informed as they should be.

The most common form of political participation is exercising the right to vote. (We will discuss voter turnout in chapter 2, including the impact of declining levels of trust on citizens' willingness to participate.) Maintaining a representative democracy involves more than voting, however. Because the message or mandate of an election is seldom clear, specific policy concerns must be communicated to one's elected representatives. Organizing with like-minded individuals increases the chances that one's interests will be heard. Participation in voluntary associations—political and nonpolitical—has long been noted as an important contributor to democratic politics. Alexis de Tocqueville, writing in the nineteenth century, commented on Americans' proclivity toward joining organizations of all sorts. Not only do participants in voluntary associations learn useful political skills, but the existence of many organizations with overlapping memberships also tends to moderate conflict. People whose interests conflict on one set of issues may find themselves working as allies on another. Membership in organizations links people to each other and to their communities. For example, in his study of Italian states Robert D. Putnam shows that the most significant difference between those with effective democratic politics and those without is the existence of a strong associational life.[26]

Putnam also raises an alarm over what he refers to as the "declining social capital" in the United States. Americans, he argues, are now less likely to join organizations of all kinds—from bowling leagues to labor unions to political parties. He attributes this change to women in the workforce, increased residential mobility, and technological innovations such as television, the personal computer, and the videocassette recorder, all of which allow individuals to work and play in isolation.[27] Putnam also finds, in a later and more controversial study, that people living in more heterogeneous communities—ethnically, racially, and religiously—are more fearful, less trusting, and less likely to volunteer.[28]

In a major study of political participation in the United States, Sidney Verba, Kay L. Schlozman, and Henry E. Brady seem to counter Putnam's claim, finding organizational participation in America "lively and varied."[29] In a comparison with a similar study in 1967, they find a decline in some forms of political activity, such as voting and membership in political clubs, but similar levels of participation in community activities and sizable increases in political contributions and contacting

public officials about issues. Putnam would agree with the last contention, also noting increases in the membership in tertiary—or mass membership—organizations. Such organizations, however, usually do not
involve the face-to-face interaction that fosters cooperation and builds
community. The opportunities for networking via the Internet are only
beginning to be explored in the context of community-building.
Although the Internet doubtless brings together like-minded people for
a variety of purposes, early impressions suggest that these contacts are
more likely to reinforce prejudices and incite intolerance against the
un-like-minded, rather than moderate conflict and build bridges
through cross-cutting interests, as envisioned by pluralist theorists.

Verba, Schlozman, and Brady also conclude that the pattern of
participation in America distorts the voice of the people. Those with
education and money participate; the poor and uneducated do not.
As a consequence, the interests of the affluent are well represented in
government, and those of the less advantaged are not. Participation in
religious institutions does not have this social class bias, and Verba,
Schlozman, and Brady conclude that religious organizations are an
important mechanism for developing political skills among the less
advantaged citizenry.[30] In ongoing research, Putnam and David Campbell also cite the importance of religious communities in encouraging
participation, finding that people active in religious networks are "better citizens" who vote more often, volunteer more, and give more to
charitable purposes.[31]

More intense forms of political activity, such as working on political
campaigns, have remained much the same over this time period—
although the levels of involvement have never been high. Many individuals who contribute financially to campaigns are not involved in any
other way. When all forms of campaign activity—including financial
contributions—are counted, somewhat more than 10 percent of the
electorate is involved in some way.

Childhood Socialization

Most social groups, particularly those with distinctive sets of norms
and values, make some effort to teach appropriate attitudes and expected
behaviors to their new members. In a democracy, this would include
teaching beliefs and values supportive of majority rule, tolerance for
diverse opinions, and an understanding of the role of citizens as
participants in the political process.

In most societies the process of socialization is focused primarily on
the largest group of new members: children. Through the process of
political socialization the political culture of a society is transmitted

from one generation to the next, but this socialization is also an important mechanism through which change in the political culture can take place.

At a time when most learning about politics occurred in the home, the prevailing political culture probably changed no faster than the attitudes of the adult population as a whole, in response to varied personal experiences and changing circumstances in the environment. In modern societies other agents of political socialization also are involved, particularly the educational system and, increasingly, the mass media. To the extent that these institutions instill a different set of values and norms compared with those held by the adult population as a whole, an opportunity exists for changing the political culture. The prevalence of middle-class values among both teachers and the media in the United States has guaranteed that these orientations became and remain widespread in the population as a whole. As a more extreme example, under the Communist regimes in the People's Republic of China and, formerly, the Soviet Union, the official ideology dominated both the schools and the mass communications system. Massive changes in values took place within the span of a generation. (The fact that contrary attitudes survived the indoctrination attests to the multiplicity of agents of socialization, even in totalitarian states.) The worldwide availability of the Internet and the points of view it conveys mean that changes in political culture can occur rapidly even in traditional and authoritarian societies. The ideological movement that became the 1979 Islamic Revolution in Iran was spread via smuggled audiocassette tapes; challenges to that regime in 2009 were similarly organized through Internet communications.

Given the importance of the socialization process in the transmission of the fundamental beliefs and values of the political culture, it is surprising that socialization studies have not paid more attention to the development of attitudes supportive of democratic goals and procedures. Data collected in the 1950s by David Easton, Robert D. Hess, and others show that children develop an affective attachment to the term *democracy* early (by about the third grade), but the concept acquires meaning much more slowly.[32] The progress of learning from the fourth grade to the eighth grade is shown for several concepts in Figure 1-2. Perhaps the most interesting aspect of the data in the figure is the high level of disagreement among teachers over the correctness of including the right of dissent in the meaning of democracy.

In 1999 an elaborate cross-national Civic Education Study directed by Judith V. Torney explored attitudes toward democratic culture among teenagers in twenty-eight countries.[33] The data in Table 1-2 display knowledge of the concept of democracy among American ninth graders. The top of Table 1-2 shows one-sided agreement that it is very good

FIGURE 1-2 Children's and Teachers' Understanding of the Concept of
Democracy

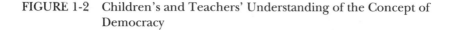

Percentage agreeing that the phrase
is part of the definition of democracy

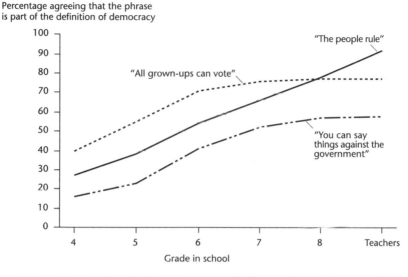

Grade in school

Source: Adapted from Robert D. Hess and Judith V. Torney, *The Development of Political Attitudes in Children* (New York: Anchor Books, 1968), 75, Table 13.

for democracy "when everyone has the right to express their opinions freely" and "when citizens have the right to elect political leaders freely." Fifty-five percent believe the first item is "very good for democracy" and only 2 percent think it is "very bad for democracy." (When the "very good" and "somewhat good" responses are added together, the total is 83 percent, as shown in parentheses in the table.)

Collectively, ninth graders are not nearly so sure of other tenets of democracy listed in Table 1-2. For example, only 24 percent believe it is very good for democracy for political parties to have different positions on issues or for newspapers to be free of government control. Young people may absorb the ambivalence that many adults, especially their teachers, feel toward political parties and a free press—a situation also reflected in the Easton and Hess studies forty years before. (In the 1999 study, teachers divided half and half in thinking participation in political parties was a good idea in a democracy.) Ninth graders were fairly evenly divided on preventing newspapers from printing stories that might offend ethnic groups. They were even less supportive of the idea that the separation of church and state is a good idea in a democracy. All of this suggests the schools are stronger in teaching some principles of democracy than others.

TABLE 1-2   Ninth Graders' Views on What Is Good and Bad for Democracy, 1999

	Percentage saying	
	Very bad for democracy	Very good for democracy
When everyone has the right to express their opinions freely	2 (9)	55 (83)
When citizens have the right to elect political leaders freely	5 (12)	61 (81)
When political parties have different positions on important issues	6 (25)	24 (59)
When newspapers are free of all government control	10 (37)	24 (51)
When people participate in political parties in order to influence government	10 (29)	22 (55)
When newspapers are forbidden to publish stories that might offend ethnic groups	19 (38)	27 (50)
When there is a separation between the church and the state	24 (49)	15 (32)

Source: U.S. Department of Education, National Center for Education Statistics, Civic Education Study, 1999, available at www.wam.umd.edu/~iea.

Note: The percentages in parentheses combine "very bad for democracy" responses with the "somewhat bad" and the "very good" with the "somewhat good."

The development of children's thinking about the institutions of government and about their own roles as citizens has also been studied. A child's first view of government and governmental leaders casts the leaders as all-powerful and benevolent, undoubtedly the result of the twin objectives of parents and teachers to instill an acceptance of authority and to shield young children from the harsher realities of political life. Gradually, the child acquires a more realistic and more cynical view of the world. Children also begin with a personalized view of government. Government means the president or, for some, the police officer. In time these images are replaced or supplemented with more abstract ideas about Congress and the election process.[34]

During the elementary grades, children develop a set of attitudes toward their own roles as citizens. Initially, the emphasis is on obedience: the good citizen obeys the law, just as good children obey their parents. In the American socialization process, this is gradually replaced by a view of oneself as a more active participant in the political system: the good citizen is one who votes. Still later, the child adds the notion that the government can be influenced through the voting process.

As with other attitudes, the development of confidence in one's own ability to influence government is related to social class and intelligence among children, just as it is related to social class and education in adults. Some other aspects of the view of the citizen's role that children develop in the later elementary years might conceivably hinder their effectiveness or willingness to participate in the real world of politics later. The role of the individual in influencing government is stressed; the role of organized group activity in politics is downgraded. In the same way, American children develop a low tolerance for conflict, believing, for example, that it hurts the country when political parties disagree.

In the past, the youngest voters were typically the most trusting of government—a tendency one would expect, given their recent exposure to an educational process that tries to build support for the system. In the 1950s and early 1960s, when most of the major socialization studies were undertaken, young people entered adulthood with a strong affective feeling toward the government and a positive orientation toward themselves as participants in it.

A study of high school seniors and their parents, carried out in 1965 by M. Kent Jennings, showed that trust and confidence in government were fairly high among the students.[35] As learning continues into adulthood, substantial modification of attitudes can occur through a variety of personal experiences with politics, new group membership, and the like. The original students in the Jennings study have been reinterviewed at intervals over the years. Their level of trust in government declined from 93 percent in 1965, to 67 percent in 1973, 51 percent in 1982, and 49 percent in 1997.

Maintaining a Democracy

Belief in democratic ideals is essential to the preservation of a democratic system, both because such beliefs inhibit citizens from undemocratic actions and because the public will demand proper behavior on the part of political leaders. Belief that the system and its leaders meet democratic expectations in adhering to democratic procedures and responding to the wishes of the public is also important. A third factor is perhaps less obvious. A democratic system must meet some standard for effectiveness in solving societal problems. If not, the public may conclude that democracy does not work, that some other form of government—such as a dictatorship—is needed to maintain order, fend off an enemy, or provide economic well-being.

When people's expectations are not met in the behavior of political leaders or in the experiences they have in the political process, disappointment, cynicism, or hostility may result. Americans hold high expectations for the political system and, as a consequence, are subject to considerable disenchantment with the performance of government and their own role in politics. Although no direct evidence on this point is available, nothing has been found to suggest that the value they place on the ideals of democracy, majority rule, or the importance of participation in politics has declined. Instead, events over the past thirty years have led to a larger perceived discrepancy between the specific American political institutions (and their incumbents) and the ideal.

Ideals, combined with the generally high expectations Americans hold for the political system, can lead to cynicism and mistrust of political leadership when scandals occur or policies fail to work. But another form of disenchantment operates at the individual level. The American ethos and the content of the political culture lead individuals to expect a wide range of conditions and values. They expect to enjoy freedom, justice, and equality; they expect to enjoy personal economic success; and they expect to be safe from violence.

If individuals find that what is happening to them is far different from these expectations, they may react with resentment. Many individuals, to be sure, respond to adversity in personal terms and do not view their problems from a collective or political perspective. Others, however, may engage in disruptive political activities. In a society such as the United States, the people who suffer economic hardship or are victims of social injustice are oftentimes minorities that are isolated by race, ethnicity, sexual orientation, or some other identifiable characteristic. Under these circumstances such a group may develop a set of distinct subcultural values, passively withdraw from political activity, or become actively disruptive of the system. The bombing of the federal building in Oklahoma City in 1995 and the discovery of "home-grown" terrorist cells in the years since 2001 illustrate that a disruptive, antisystem sentiment can emerge. The rioting in Seattle, Washington, at the World Trade Organization meetings in 2000 indicated the capacity to mobilize large numbers of people with different agendas. The Internet has created an unprecedented opportunity for communication and mobilization of individuals who would not have been so well connected in the past.

Given the lack of sophistication in the public's understanding of democratic values and procedures, along with the declining levels of trust in government and its leaders, some uneasiness emerges about public support for American democracy—and perhaps for any democratic regime. The United States can be seen as a democratic system that has survived without a strong democratic political culture because governmental policies have gained continual, widespread acceptance. If that satisfaction erodes, however, the public has no deep commitment to democratic values and processes that will inhibit support of antidemocratic leaders or disruptive activities.

The near-collapse of the financial system in the fall of 2008, with its attendant scandals and bailouts and the deep recession that commenced, is the kind of crisis that tests both the efficacy of our political and economic institutions and their adherence to such fundamental democratic values as fairness and equality. Like Franklin D. Roosevelt during the Great Depression of the 1930s, Barack Obama has the task of bolstering the legitimacy of American institutions by demonstrating that they can work effectively to restore some semblance of the American dream to the average citizen.

Democratic theory implies that the public should demand values and procedures embodying democratic principles. The hope or expectation is that the public in a democratic society will insist on certain values and processes. A mass public demanding democratic values and procedures would provide strong support for a democratic regime. However, a democratic system could survive with much lower levels of support, given other conditions.

In our view, a distinction should be made between the factors necessary for establishing a democracy and those contributing to maintaining one. The example of contemporary Russia, to mention only one case, suggests that stronger public support probably is required for the successful launching of a new democracy than it is for maintaining an already established one. Possibly, preserving a regime simply requires that no substantial proportion of the society be actively hostile to the regime and engage in disruptive activities. In other words, absence of disruptive acts, not the presence of supportive attitudes, is crucial.

However, leaders' positive support for a political system is essential to its existence. If some leaders are willing to oppose the system, it is crucial that there be no substantial number of followers to which such leaders can appeal. The followers' attitudes, as opposed to their willingness to act themselves, may provide a base of support for antisystem behavior by leaders. In this sense, unanimous public support for democratic principles would be a firmer basis for a democratic system.

High levels of dissatisfaction, accompanied by lack of strong commitment to democratic values in the American public, appear to create some potential for public support of undemocratic leaders. However, as shown in subsequent chapters, many Americans feel an attachment to one or the other of the established political parties—an attachment that inhibits their embracing new political leaders. The parties and the public's attachment to them are often seen as preventing political change. They can also be seen as encouraging stability and preserving a democratic system by lessening the likelihood of a demagogue's rise to power.

Notes

1. U.S. Commission on Civil Rights, "Voting Irregularities in Florida during the 2000 Presidential Election," available at www.usccr.gov/vote2000/stdraft1/main.htm. See especially chap. 5.
2. In party primary elections voting in both primaries invalidates up to one-third of the ballots.
3. Arguably, 1960 is another case. See note to Figure 3-1.
4. Gallup Poll, April 20–22, 2001, Roper Center for Public Opinion Research.
5. 2004 American National Election Study.
6. Pew Research Center for the People and the Press, www.people-press.org.
7. "Opinion Roundup," *Public Perspective* 3 (May/June 1992): 7–9; and 2004 American National Election Study.
8. Gabriel Almond and Sidney Verba, *The Civic Culture* (Princeton: Princeton University Press, 1963). These patterns have been evident in cross-national public opinion polls since Almond and Verba first recorded them in 1963.
9. ABC News/*Washington Post* Poll, December 14–15, 2000, Roper Center for Public Opinion Research.
10. Ibid.
11. For a major effort to capture this fundamental aspect of political culture, see Herbert McClosky and John Zaller, *The American Ethos* (Cambridge, Mass.: Harvard University Press, 1984).
12. 2008 American National Election Study.
13. Ibid.
14. For the major study of the 1950s, see Samuel Stouffer, *Communism, Conformity, and Civil Liberties* (Garden City, N.Y.: Doubleday, 1955). For a later work, see C. Z. Nunn, H. J. Crockett, and J. A. Williams, *Tolerance for Nonconformity* (San Francisco: Jossey-Bass, 1978).
15. John L. Sullivan, James Piereson, and George E. Marcus, *Political Tolerance and American Democracy* (Chicago: University of Chicago Press, 1982); and George E. Marcus, John L. Sullivan, Elizabeth Theiss-Morse, and Sandra L. Wood, *With Malice toward Some* (Cambridge, England: Cambridge University Press, 1995).
16. Gallup Poll, November 2003, Roper Center for Public Opinion Research.
17. CBS News/*New York Times* Poll, September 21–24, 2008, Roper Center for Public Opinion Research.
18. Gallup, CNN, *USA Today* Polls, February 2004, Roper Center for Public Opinion Research.
19. In April 2000 the Freedom Forum found 25 percent agreed that "people should be allowed to burn or deface the American flag as a political statement" and 74 percent disagreed. The public was evenly divided on amending the

Constitution to prohibit desecration of the flag. In a 2006 poll, a majority of the public (54 percent) opposed amending the Constitution to make it illegal to burn the flag. Gallop/*USA Today* Poll, June 2006. Both polls are available from the Roper Center for Public Opinion Research.

20. Harris Poll, February 2009, Roper Center for Public Opinion Research.
21. John R. Hibbing and Elizabeth Theiss-Morse, *Congress as Public Enemy* (Cambridge, England: Cambridge University Press, 1995), chap. 3.
22. Stephen Barr, "Trust in Government Surges during Crisis," *Washington Post,* September 30, 2001, C02.
23. CBS News/*New York Times* Poll, October 25–28, 2001, Roper Center for Public Opinion Research.
24. 2008 American National Election Study.
25. Ibid.
26. Robert D. Putnam, *Making Democracy Work: Civic Traditions in Modern Italy* (Princeton: Princeton University Press, 1993).
27. Robert D. Putnam, "Bowling Alone: America's Declining Social Capital," *Journal of Democracy* 6 (January 1995): 65–78.
28. Robert D. Putnam, "E Pluribus Unum: Diversity and Community in the Twenty-First Century—the 2006 Johan Skytte Prize Lecture," *Scandinavian Political Studies* 30, no. 2 (2007): 137–174.
29. Sidney Verba, Kay L. Schlozman, and Henry F. Brady, *Voice and Equality: Civic Voluntarism in American Politics* (Cambridge, Mass.: Harvard University Press, 1995), 509.
30. Ibid., chap. 17.
31. Robert D. Putnam and David Campbell, *American Grace,* forthcoming, 2010.
32. The results of this study have been reported in several articles and in Robert D. Hess and Judith V. Torney, *The Development of Political Attitudes in Children* (New York: Anchor Books, 1968); and David Easton and Jack Dennis, *Children in the Political System: Origins of Political Legitimacy* (New York: McGraw-Hill, 1969).
33. See Stephane Baldi, Marianne Perie, Dan Skidmore, Elizabeth Greenberg, Carole Hahn, and Dawn Nelson, *What Democracy Means to Ninth-Graders: U.S. Results for the International IEA Civic Education Study,* National Center for Education Statistics, U.S. Department of Education, 2001, at nces.ed.gov/pubscarch/pub sinfo.asp?pubid=2001096.
34. David Easton and Jack Dennis, "The Child's Image of Government," in *Socialization to Politics: A Reader,* ed. Jack Dennis (New York: Wiley, 1973), 67.
35. The findings of this study are most extensively reported in M. Kent Jennings and Richard G. Niemi, *The Political Character of Adolescence: The Influence of Families and Schools* (Princeton: Princeton University Press, 1974); and M. Kent Jennings and Richard G. Niemi, *Generations and Politics* (Princeton: Princeton University Press, 1981).

Suggested Readings

Almond, Gabriel, and Sidney Verba. *The Civic Culture.* Princeton: Princeton University Press, 1963. A classic study of political culture in five nations, including the United States.

Baldi, Stephane, Marianne Perie, Dan Skidmore, Elizabeth Greenberg, Carole Hahn, and Dawn Nelson. *What Democracy Means to Ninth-Graders: U.S. Results From the International IEA Civic Education Study.* National Center for Educational Statistics, U.S. Department of Education, 2001. An interesting political socialization study as part of a multination project. For more information, see nces.ed.gov/pub search/pubsinfo.asp?pubid=2001096.

Dalton, Russell J. *The Good Citizen: How a Younger Generation Is Reshaping American Politics.* Revised Edition. Washington, D.C.: CQ Press, 2009. An exploration of how young Americans are creating new norms of citizenship and engagement, including evidence from the 2008 election.

Hibbing, John R., and Elizabeth Theiss-Morse. *Stealth Democracy: Americans' Beliefs about How Government Should Work.* Cambridge, England: Cambridge University Press, 2002. A provocative analysis of the public's attitudes toward American political processes.

Marcus, George E., John L. Sullivan, Elizabeth Theiss-Morse, and Sandra L. Wood. *With Malice toward Some.* Cambridge, England: Cambridge University Press, 1995. An innovative study of the public's tolerance of unpopular groups.

McClosky, Herbert, and John Zaller. *The American Ethos.* Cambridge, Mass.: Harvard University Press, 1984. An analysis of the public's attitudes toward democracy and capitalism.

MacKuen, Michael B., and George Rabinowitz, eds. *Electoral Democracy.* Ann Arbor: University of Michigan Press, 2003. A wide-ranging set of essays from a conference to honor Philip E. Converse.

Putnam, Robert D. *Bowling Alone: The Collapse and Revival of American Community.* New York: Simon and Schuster, 2000. An analysis of the decline of participation in civic affairs.

Rosenstone, Steven J., and John Mark Hansen. *Mobilization, Participation, and Democracy in America.* New York: Macmillan, 1993. An analysis of the interaction among the strategic choices of political elites and the choices of citizens to participate in politics.

Skocpol, Theda, and Morris P. Fiorina, eds. *Civic Engagement in American Democracy.* Washington, D.C.: Brookings Institution, 1999. A collection of readings on civic engagement in historical perspective.

Stimson, James A. *The Tides of Consent: How Public Opinion Shapes American Politics.* Cambridge, England: Cambridge University Press, 2004. Mainly about policy views and their impact, but also an interesting discussion of trust in government.

Verba, Sidney, Kay L. Schlozman, and Henry E. Brady. *Voice and Equality: Civic Voluntarism in American Politics.* Cambridge, England: Cambridge University Press, 1995. A survey of various forms of political participation, their determinants, and their impact on representative democracy.

Internet Resources

The Web site of the American National Election Studies, www.electionstudies .org, offers extensive data on topics covered in this chapter. Click on "Guide to Public Opinion" and then choose "Support for the Political System." Some of the attitudinal data cover 1952 to the present. For all items, additional information is presented on numerous social groupings in each election year.

If you have access through your school, click on "The Roper Center for Public Opinion Research." Click on "iPOLL Databank" and then follow the sign-in instructions, which have a keyword search capability. You will find hundreds—perhaps thousands—of items related to political culture from surveys taken from the 1930s to the present.

For a rich collection of data on American ninth graders, see the Civic Education Study, www.terpconnect.umd.edu/~jtpurta/.

chapter two

Suffrage and Turnout

IN 2008 THE VOTING turnout rate in the presidential election was 62 percent, one of the highest in ninety years and up several percentage points from 2004.[1] Turnout in 2008 continued an upward trend in recent elections, reversing a long downward trend after 1960.

The decline in the voting turnout rate after 1960 was accompanied by a great deal of commentary and concern about the future of American democracy. The decline appeared paradoxical, because it occurred at a time when the legal impediments to voting had been eliminated or eased and the education levels of American citizens were reaching all-time highs. Despite greater opportunities to vote, Americans seemed to be doing so less frequently. A favorite theme among editorial writers was the declining turnout rate as a symbol of the growing disenchantment of voters with the political system.

Whether the recent upturn represents a permanent reversal in the overall decline in turnout is too soon to tell. In this chapter, we will put the downward trend in turnout—along with the recent reversal—into a broader historical context, as well as consider some arguments that suggest the decline was not as significant as previously assumed. We will look at the factors that make some individuals more likely to vote than others and examine how changes in the political environment can affect whether people vote. We will also look at the way in which voting turnout is estimated and, in doing so, raise some questions about whether the concern over declining turnout is justified.

Extensions of Suffrage

Suffrage, or the *franchise,* means the right to vote. Originally, the U.S. Constitution gave the determination of who should have the right to vote entirely to the states. Later, amendments were added to the Constitution that restricted the states' abilities to deny the right to vote on the basis of such characteristics as race, gender, or age. However, the basic constitutional provision that gives states the right to set the qualifications for voting remains, and over the years states have used such things as property ownership, literacy, and length of residency as criteria for granting or withholding the right to vote.

During the colonial period and the early years of the Republic, suffrage was commonly restricted to white males possessing varying amounts of property. In effect, only a small proportion of the adult population was eligible to vote. The severity of the impact of property requirements varied from state to state, and their enforcement differed perhaps even more. Gradually, the required amount of property held or the amount of taxes paid to obtain suffrage was reduced. Sometimes these changes were hard-won reforms enacted by state legislatures or by state constitutional amendment; at other times practical considerations led to substantial reforms. For example, delays in acquiring final title to land holdings in the western frontier areas during the 1800s made establishing property requirements for suffrage impractical. Often during the early years of American history, candidates in local elections would simply agree among themselves that all white males could vote instead of trying to impose complicated restrictions on the electorate. Only in more settled communities could complex restrictions on suffrage be effectively enforced. In sections of the East, however, wealthy landlords sometimes supported the enfranchisement of their poorer tenants with the expectation of controlling their votes.[2]

After the eventual granting of suffrage to all white males, the next major change was the enfranchisement of black males by constitutional amendment following the Civil War. Even though the change was part of a set of issues so divisive that it had led to war, the numerical impact of adding black males was slight in the nation as a whole. However, unlike other changes in suffrage, it had a geographical bias: the impact of enfranchising black males was felt almost entirely in the South. (Their subsequent disfranchisement in the South will be discussed later.) The next major constitutional extension of voting rights was suffrage for women in 1920. It created by far the most dramatic increase in the number of eligible voters, roughly doubling the size of the potential electorate. In the early 1970s, through a combination of federal statutory law and state laws followed by constitutional amendment, the definition of citizenship for purposes of voting was lowered to age eighteen, accomplishing another major extension of suffrage.

These extensions of suffrage, which have not been easy or inevitable, may be explained by the existence of certain political forces. In stable political systems such as the United States, the extension of suffrage will result from (1) a widely shared commitment to moral principles that entail further grants of suffrage, and (2) the expectation among political leaders that the newly enfranchised will support the political preferences of the leaders.

As we discussed in chapter 1, the political culture and political rhetoric of America carry strong themes of individualism and equality. As a result, the commitment most Americans have to equality, individualism, and democracy has provided a basis for supporting extensions of voting rights.

But more than idealism contributed to the expansion of the electorate. In the two most dramatic extensions of suffrage, to blacks and to women, political leaders expected the newly enfranchised to support certain policies. Republicans—the party of abolition—anticipated that black voters in the South after the Civil War would band with poor whites and help to secure Republican domination of the southern states. The intense prejudice of whites and the difficulty in maintaining the enfranchisement of blacks kept the strategy from working under most circumstances, but a significant element in Republican enthusiasm for black suffrage was the knowledge that Republican voters were being added to the rolls. The same mixture of idealism and self-interest appears to have supported suffrage for women as well. Women voters were seen optimistically as the cure for corruption in government, as unwavering opponents of alcohol, and as champions of virtue in the electorate. Reformers of all sorts encouraged the enfranchisement of women as a means of promoting their own goals. No doubt, similar factors were at work in the most recent extension of suffrage to those between the ages of eighteen and twenty. But perhaps more important was the widespread feeling that a system drafting young people to fight in the unpopular Vietnam War ought to extend to them the right to participate in the electoral process.

A unique aspect of the extension of suffrage in the United States was the addition of states in the frontier expansion across the continent. During the decades immediately preceding the Civil War, the politics of slavery dominated political decisions about additions of states, with accompanying expectations about the policy impact of expansion. Here too the question of the enlargement of the electorate was dominated mostly by concern over the political persuasion of the newly enfranchised voters.

Because different state and local election practices have existed throughout American history, no single set of eligibility requirements can be used as a basis for deciding who belonged to the electorate at any one time. For example, individual states had granted suffrage to blacks, women, and young voters, either in law or in practice, before these groups' nationwide enfranchisement. In some states, women had previously been allowed to vote in local and school elections but not in statewide or federal contests. Thus many different eligible electorates existed with different characteristics.

Restrictions on Suffrage

Under the provisions of the U.S. Constitution, the states set the qualifications for voters. The three extensions of suffrage by constitutional amendment did not alter this, but they prohibited the states from using certain criteria—race, gender, or age—to deny the right to vote. Because states retained the right to impose other restrictions, they have at times used these restrictions to prevent whole classes of people from voting. The most notorious of these efforts was the effective disfranchisement of blacks in the southern states during the late nineteenth and early twentieth centuries.

Several techniques for disfranchising blacks were used after Reconstruction in the South, and from time to time some of these techniques were applied in the North on a more limited basis to restrict the electoral participation of immigrants. The most common methods included white primaries, the poll tax, literacy tests, discriminatory administrative procedures, and intimidation. In some southern states only whites were allowed to vote in the party primary (the crucial election in one-party states), under the rationale that primaries to nominate candidates were internal functions of a private organization. In 1944 the U.S. Supreme Court ruled such white primaries unconstitutional on the ground that the selection of candidates for election is a public function in which discrimination on the basis of race is prohibited. The now-illegal poll tax, whereby each individual was charged a flat fee as a prerequisite for registration to vote, was used for years and no doubt disfranchised both poor blacks and poor whites. The poll tax eventually became unpopular with the white voters who had to pay it, whereas the blacks—disfranchised by other means—did not. The literacy test gave local officials a device that could be administered in a selective way to permit registration of whites and practically prohibit that of blacks. The standards of literacy applied to blacks in some cases—for example, reading and interpreting the state constitution to the satisfaction of the white registrar—made it impossible for even highly educated blacks to register, whereas whites might be required to know only how to sign their names. To remain effective over long periods of time, these and other similar administrative devices probably depended on intimidation or the use of violence against blacks. Detailed analysis by Jerrold D. Rusk and John J. Stucker of the impact of the poll tax and literacy tests from 1876 to 1916 suggests that the poll tax was the more effective device, and its efficacy was greatest where the tax rate was highest and its application most cumulative.[3]

A study of black registration in 1958 by Donald R. Matthews and James W. Prothro indicated that southern states using poll taxes and literacy tests still inhibited black voter registration after World War II.[4] The poll tax has since been outlawed by amendment to the U.S. Constitution, and the use of federal voting registrars in the South under the terms of the Voting Rights Act of 1965 eliminated the worst excesses in the application of literacy tests. Registration rates in the South for whites and blacks were approximately equal by 1980, and turnout rates have concurrently increased to the point that little difference in turnout is evident now between the North and South in presidential voting.

The outlawing of the poll tax through constitutional amendment and the suspension of literacy tests by the Voting Rights Act of 1965 and its extensions have eliminated two important restrictions on the right to vote. Other state restrictions on suffrage remain, although there is great variation from state to state. In all but four states, prison inmates cannot vote. In many states, convicted felons cannot vote until they have served their entire sentence—in other words, completed probation or parole; in some, a felony conviction entails a permanent forfeiture of voting rights. With the prison population growing, this amounts to a sizable restriction of the franchise. The United States Election Project estimates that in 2008 over three million citizens were ineligible felons.[5] Because of longer sentences and higher rates of incarceration among blacks, this restriction falls more heavily on the black population. A study by the Sentencing Project in 1998 estimated that 13 percent of black males were disfranchised under these requirements.[6]

Residency requirements are another common restriction on suffrage. In the past such requirements were often highly restrictive. Some states mandated up to two years of residence in the state before one was eligible to vote, thus effectively disfranchising highly mobile segments of the population. In the 1970s the Middle Atlantic states, with their mobile populations and traditionally rigorous residency requirements, had as high a rate of unregistered citizens as did the states of the former Confederacy, with their legacy of racial discrimination. In 1972 the Supreme Court linked the imposition of a residency requirement to the length of time needed to prepare lists of registered voters before an election, suggesting that thirty days were sufficient to do this. Since then the Court has allowed state laws requiring fifty days to stand.

By the early 1990s the legal barriers to voting had been reduced, for the most part, to the requirement that voters be registered to vote in advance of an election. The inconvenience of administrative arrangements for voter registration and the frequent need to reregister have offered greater obstacles to voting than have other eligibility standards.

Several states have moved toward same-day registration, early voting, and vote by mail in an effort to remove impediments to voting and to increase electoral turnout. The Help American Vote Act of 2002 provided a federal mandate to the states to adopt a system of provisional ballots and a statewide electronic database of registered voters in an effort to overcome glitches in registration procedures.

Nevertheless, as we discussed in chapter 1, the close presidential elections of 2000 and 2004 showed that at least as many forces are at work trying to use suppression of turnout for partisan advantage as there are efforts to increase turnout. The presidential election in Florida in 2000 and, to a lesser extent, Ohio in 2004 revealed an impressive array of means whereby voters were denied the right to vote. After its investigation following the election in Florida, the U.S. Commission on Civil Rights wrote that its "findings make one thing clear: widespread voter disenfranchisement—not the dead-heat contest—was the extraordinary feature in the Florida election."[7] Despite fears to the contrary before the election, and a massive Voter Protection project launched by the Democrats, Barack Obama's comfortable margin quieted any charges of vote suppression in 2008.

Turnout in American Elections Historically

One of the most persistent complaints about the current American electoral system is its failure to achieve the high rates of voter turnout found in other countries and common in the United States in the nineteenth century. U.S. voter turnout was close to 80 percent before 1900 (see Figure 2-1); modern democracies around the world frequently record similarly high levels. Turnout in the United States since the start of the twentieth century, in contrast, has exceeded 60 percent only in presidential elections.

These unfavorable comparisons are somewhat misleading. The *voting turnout rate* is the percentage of the eligible population that votes in a particular election. It is ideally calculated as the number of votes cast divided by the total number of eligible adult citizens. The definition of *eligible adult* takes into account the historical changes in eligibility occasioned by the extension of suffrage to blacks, women, and eighteen-year-olds, but it often does not take into account state barriers to eligibility, such as residency requirements or the restrictions on felons. As discussed, these may be substantial. Even worse, no official count of citizens exists, because the decennial census no longer asks about citizenship. Thus all noncitizens are counted as if they were eligible to vote. Because a considerable number of those included in

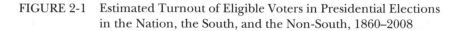

FIGURE 2-1   Estimated Turnout of Eligible Voters in Presidential Elections
in the Nation, the South, and the Non-South, 1860–2008

Sources: Robert Lane, *Political Life* (New York: Free Press, 1965), 20; Walter Dean Burnham, "The Changing Shape of the American Political Universe," *American Political Science Review* 59 (March 1965): 11, Figure 1; Center for the Study of the American Electorate, available at www1.american.edu/ia/cdem/case; and United States Election Project, available at elections.gmu.edu.

the eligible population are not legally able to vote, the turnout rate appears lower than it actually is. And in some states, blacks, women, and eighteen-year-olds were given the right to vote before suffrage was extended to them by amendment to the U.S. Constitution. Not including them in the denominator before nationwide suffrage makes the turnout rate in earlier years appear higher than it actually was.

Determining the numerator in the turnout rate is also difficult. The total number of ballots cast throughout the country is unknown; some states only report the total vote for particular races. For example, not included are those who went to the polls but skipped the presidential race, or who inadvertently invalidated their ballots. This "undercount" of votes cast also reduces the estimate of turnout.

Given these problems with calculating turnout, various attempts have recently been made to provide more accurate estimates. Ruy A. Teixeira's analysis of turnout in the 1988 election suggests an underestimate of turnout of about 4 percent.[8] The U.S. Census Bureau has published recalculated estimates of the turnout rate since 1978, using citizenship and reported vote from its Current Population Survey. The estimates are considerably higher than the "official rate," in part because they are based on reported vote—which may be inflated, because individuals are reluctant to admit they did not vote—and in part because they are able to exclude noncitizens, who are ineligible to vote, from the denominator. (The Census Bureau estimates the number of noncitizens at eighteen million.[9]) Two academic projects—the United States Election Project, run by Michael McDonald at George Mason University, and the Center for the Study of the American Electorate, headed by Curtis Gans at American University—attempt to more accurately figure turnout by correcting both the numerator and the denominator of the official figures on a state-by-state basis. McDonald's turnout rate is two to five points higher than the official rate during the period studied, although the two trend lines run roughly parallel.[10] Gans's estimates for the past three decades are almost identical to McDonald's.[11]

Despite the difficulties in estimating turnout, the data in Figure 2-1 show that some dramatic changes occurred historically in the rate of voter turnout. Each major extension of suffrage—in 1868, 1920, and 1971—was marked by a drop in the proportion of the electorate voting. Perhaps this is not surprising, because the newly eligible voters might be expected to take some time to acquire the habit of exercising their right to vote. Furthermore, the drop in the turnout rate occasioned by the extension of suffrage was, in each case, the continuation of a downward trend.

During the nineteenth century, national turnout appears to have been extremely high—always more than 70 percent. The decline in national turnout from shortly before 1900 to 1916 is in part attributable to the restriction of black voting in the South. This decline in voting in the South also resulted from the increasing one-party domination of the region. In many southern states the real election was the Democratic primary, with the Republicans offering only token opposition, or none at all, in the general election. Turnout was often extremely low in the general election—far lower than can be accounted for simply by the disfranchisement of blacks.

Explaining the voting record shown in Figure 2-1 for the northern states presents a more difficult problem. Turnout declined substantially in the first two decades of the twentieth century and has not returned to its previous levels. The disfranchisement of blacks and whites in the South cannot account for northern nonvoting.

Two different explanations have been offered for the decline in voting in the North that commenced in the late 1890s. A persuasive set of arguments has been made by E. E. Schattschneider and Walter Dean Burnham in their individual studies of this period.[12] They contend that a high level of party loyalty and political involvement during the last quarter of the nineteenth century caused high turnout and great partisan stability. Then, during the 1890s, electoral patterns shifted in such a way that the South became safely Democratic, and most of the rest of the nation came under the domination of the Republican Party. Schattschneider's analysis emphasizes the extent to which this alignment enabled conservatives in both regions to dominate American politics for many years. According to this line of argument, one consequence of declining competition and greater conservatism throughout the electoral system was a loss of interest in politics accompanied by lower turnout and less partisan loyalty in the early twentieth century. Burnham emphasizes the disintegration of party voting with more ticket-splitting and lower turnout in off-year elections.

Some elements of this account are undeniably accurate. Electoral patterns did change somewhat around the turn of the century, with many regions of the nation changing from competitive to one-party areas. Throughout areas previously characterized by high turnout, straight-ticket voting, and stable voting patterns, turnout and partisan stability suffered greater fluctuations.

An alternative set of arguments gives these patterns a different interpretation.[13] The high rate of turnout in the nineteenth century may not have resulted from political involvement by an interested, well-informed electorate. On the contrary, it may have been possible only because of low levels of information and interest. During the last half of the nineteenth century, a largely uninformed electorate was aroused to vote by means of extreme and emotional political appeals. Presumably, in the absence of more general awareness of the political situation, these alarmist arguments produced firm commitments to vote. By and large, the parties manipulated the electorate—a manipulation possible because the electorate was not well informed.

Furthermore, proponents of this argument allege that the party organizations "delivered" or "voted" substantial numbers of voters during this period, by party loyalists casting multiple votes, "voting tombstones" (dead people), or buying votes. Thus the remarkable stability of party voting may be a testimony to the corruption of the party organizations. The decline of stable party voting in the early twentieth century coincides with attacks on political corruption and party machines. The resultant weakening of party machines and increased honesty in electoral activities could have reduced turnout. In fact, the apparent hostility of the electorate to the parties throughout this period seems inconsistent with strong party loyalty.

A study by Jerrold D. Rusk shows dramatic changes in voting patterns associated with electoral reform laws, especially the introduction of the secret, or Australian, ballot.[14] Before the introduction of electoral reforms, the political parties each prepared distinctively colored ballots with only their own candidates listed on them. The parties distributed the ballots to their potential voters, who then openly placed them in the ballot box. The Australian ballot provided for secret voting and an official ballot with all candidates' names appearing on it. Another of the reforms instituted during the early twentieth century to combat corruption was the imposition of a system of voter registration. Besides limiting the opportunity for fraudulent voting, registration requirements created an additional barrier to the act of voting that had the effect of causing the least-motivated potential voters to drop out of the electorate. Many states introduced permanent or semipermanent forms of registration that involved only a one-time effort by the voter. However, in others—such as New York, where annual registration was required in many cities—the barrier to voting could be formidable.

After reaching an all-time low in the early 1920s, turnout in national elections increased steadily until 1940. A substantial—though temporary—drop in turnout occurred during World War II and its aftermath, and another decline took place from 1960 through the 1980s, before the recent uptick in the early years of the twenty-first century. Great differences in turnout among the states are concealed within these national data. Rates of voting in the South, as shown in Figure 2-1, were consistently low until recently, when they nearly converged with northern turnout. Regional differences in turnout in presidential voting have almost disappeared. State variation within regions, however, is still considerable.

High- and Low-Stimulus Elections

Elections vary in the amount of interest and attention they generate in the electorate. As Figure 2-2 demonstrates, presidential elections draw higher turnout, whereas off-year congressional elections are characterized by lower levels of turnout. Even in a presidential election year, fewer people vote in congressional elections than vote for president. The most dramatic decline in turnout is the 10 to 20 percent drop in voting experienced in off-year elections. Primaries and local elections elicit still lower turnout. Most of these differences in turnout can be accounted for by the lower visibility of the latter elections: when less information about an election is available to the voter, a lower level of interest is produced.

FIGURE 2-2   Estimated Turnout of Eligible Voters in Presidential and
Congressional Elections, 1868–2008

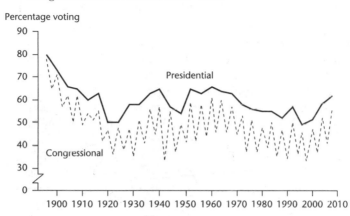

Sources: Walter Dean Burnham, Jerome M. Clubb, and William Flanigan, *State-Level
Congressional, Gubernatorial, and Senatorial Election Data for the United States, 1824–1972*,
Inter-university Consortium for Political and Social Research; Center for the Study of the
American Electorate, available at www1.american.edu/ia/cdem/casc; and United States
Election Project, available at elections.gmu.edu.

The differences in level of interest from presidential to congressional to local elections are generally the result of five factors:

1. Differences in media coverage given the election
2. Significance attached by voters to the office
3. Importance of issues raised in the campaign
4. Attractiveness of the candidates
5. Competitiveness of the contest

Variation in these factors leads to what Angus Campbell called *high-
stimulus* and *low-stimulus* elections.[15]

Newspapers and television give far more coverage to the activities
and speeches of presidential candidates than to those of congressional
candidates. Such bombardment through the mass media awakens the
relatively uninterested and often provides them with some reason to
vote. This is not nearly so likely to happen in other election campaigns,
where only the motivated citizens will become informed and concerned
to any degree. Even so, a week or so after the election, a substantial
proportion of the voters will not recall the name of the congressional
candidate for whom they voted.

The factors of media coverage, the significance of the office, and the
importance of the issues do a better job of explaining the differences in

the levels of turnout in presidential elections versus other kinds of elections than they do among presidential elections themselves. Media coverage and campaigning through the media have steadily increased regardless of the ups and downs of turnout; no evidence suggests that the significance attached to the presidency has changed. Although it is easy to attribute the increased turnout in 2004 and 2008 to the critical issues of the wars in Iraq and Afghanistan and to the economic crisis of 2008, we need to keep in mind that other presidential elections have featured intensely debated issues, such as civil rights and the Vietnam War in 1968, the Vietnam War again in 1972, and the Iranian hostage crisis and inflation in 1980. Yet turnout was steadily eroding during those years.

The lack of attractiveness of the presidential candidates has often been cited as a possible explanation for low turnout, contrasting the enormously popular Dwight D. Eisenhower in 1952 and 1956 with the lesser-of-two-evils contests of some other years. Certainly, low-turnout elections have taken place in which both candidates were viewed unfavorably (the Michael S. Dukakis–George H. W. Bush contest in 1988 and the Bill Clinton–Bob Dole matchup in 1996, for example). But a candidate viewed very negatively by a portion of the electorate may also increase turnout by bringing large numbers of voters to the polls to vote in opposition. George W. Bush's polarizing presidency had that effect in 2004. In 2008 Barack Obama was greeted with greater enthusiasm than any presidential candidate of either party in the last six elections, while his opponent, John McCain, was viewed less favorably.[16] It is impossible to know whether the enthusiasm for Obama increased turnout more or less than the lack of enthusiasm for McCain depressed it.

A somewhat different factor appeared to increase turnout in 1992. Although none of the three candidates—the senior Bush, Clinton, or Ross Perot—was viewed particularly favorably in personal terms by the electorate, the fact that there were three alternatives brought more people to the polls. If some people do not vote because they do not like either of the candidates, then having more candidates in the race increases the chances that one candidate will be deemed worthy of a vote.

Another factor often thought to raise the level of turnout in an election, perhaps by increasing the level of interest, is the degree of competition between the parties. Presumably, the closer and more uncertain the outcome, the more people will see their vote as potentially decisive. Undeniably, the virtual absence of party competition in the South during the period of black disfranchisement was associated with extremely low levels of turnout, even among white voters. Both competition and turnout in the South have increased since blacks joined the electorate. However, the elections of 1968, 1976, 1980, and 1988 suggest that the expectation of a close race does not invariably lead to heightened turnout, whereas the 1984 election that reelected the popular

Ronald Reagan shows that the expectation of a landslide does not necessarily depress turnout. Conversely, the expectation that Clinton would easily win in 1996 is widely interpreted as having depressed turnout in that election. The high turnout in 2004 surely resulted in part from the competitiveness of the race nationwide, but issues such as the war in Iraq, along with Democrats' sense that the 2000 election had been unjustly taken from them, also contributed to turnout.

Although the pre-election polls in 2008 suggested that the race would be less close, there were plenty of factors to make supporters of the front-runner nervous and to give hope to the opposition. Among them was the possibility of a "Bradley Effect." This hypothesis, launched after Thomas Bradley's surprisingly narrow win as mayor of Los Angeles in the 1980s, suggested that white voters would misrepresent their intended vote against a black candidate in public opinion polls in order not to appear racist. The Bradley Effect, if it ever existed, did not make an appearance in 2008.

Another aspect of competitiveness also has a relationship to the level of turnout, especially in congressional and state elections. A hotly contested race with strenuous activity by party organizations is likely to get more voters to the polls on election day, even though the final outcome may not be particularly close. In this regard, both 2004 and 2008 are noteworthy, as the political parties and the campaigns poured unprecedented resources into their Get Out the Vote (GOTV) efforts.

The Republican Party moved first to computerize information about the electorate and use it to coordinate phone calling with literature drops and mailings. By 2006 the Democratic Party had caught up and maybe surpassed the Republicans in the size and quality of their GOTV operation. Both parties use phone calls and publicly available data to create a database of voters that (ideally) indicates their likelihood of voting, their partisan leaning, and their main issue concerns. Early in the election year, a party recruits activists to work on these information-gathering and mobilizing activities. As the campaign unfolds, targeted issue appeals are directed at the undecided and less partisan members of the electorate. A special effort is made to contact unregistered potential supporters. (Strong partisans of either party who are certain to vote are ignored by both sides.) With sufficient volunteers or paid staff in the last days before the election, a party can call and door-knock potential supporters who otherwise could not be counted on to turn out. Even with large numbers of volunteers these efforts are expensive, and they require considerable organizational capabilities and data analysis expertise. In both 2006 and 2008 the enthusiasm among Democrats created a distinct advantage in recruiting volunteers for these activities. Evidence of this grassroots enthusiasm can be found in data collected by the Pew Research Center. These data show that contacts with voters by the Obama campaign were much more likely to have been in person (rather than by telephone) than those made by the McCain campaign.[17]

Most organizations concentrate their efforts in the so-called "battleground states" where both sides have a chance to win. In 2004, in addition to using its GOTV campaign in states that were expected to be competitive, the Republican Party made a big effort to turn out supporters in safe Republican states. The strategy was so successful that safe southern states—some of which had their highest turnout ever—were the engine behind the popular vote victory for Bush. Without this boost in turnout from safe southern states, Bush would once again have won the electoral college vote while losing the popular vote—an outcome he wanted very much to avoid.

Voters and Nonvoters

All but a small proportion of the eligible electorate vote at least occasionally, but individuals vary in the regularity with which they cast their ballots. Individual interest in politics is one factor creating such differences. In the previous section, the level of interest in a campaign was treated as a characteristic of the political environment, generated by the importance of the office at stake, the amount of media coverage, and so on. But interest and involvement in politics are also characteristics of individuals, and individuals vary substantially in the attention they pay to politics, their involvement in politics, and the amount of information about candidates and issues they acquire. As one would expect, the probability of voting increases at each level of expressed interest and involvement in political campaigns. This relationship is illustrated in Figure 2-3. The highly interested, involved, and informed citizens (a combination of characteristics highly valued in the belief system of a democratic society) turn out to cast their ballots on election day, whereas the apathetic, uninvolved, and ill-informed stay at home.

FIGURE 2-3   Relationship between Electoral Participation and Interest, Involvement, and Information

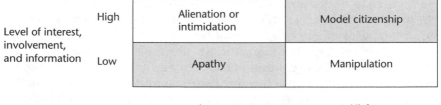

Two deviant cases that run contrary to the expected pattern can also be seen in Figure 2-3. The first deviant condition, *alienation,* describes voters characterized by high interest and low turnout. The situation may be one of voluntary alienation, in which individuals withdraw from political participation purposefully. Their high level of interest and information implies some reason for their withdrawal. They are dissatisfied with, or offended by, the political system. *Nonvoluntary alienation* refers to situations in which interested potential voters are prevented from participating, perhaps through intimidation. Both situations are dangerous to the political system because highly interested and informed citizens who do not participate have the potential for extremely disruptive activities. Alienation in this form is thought to be uncommon in American politics. In the United States, the interested and informed are consistently the most likely to participate, even though they are somewhat more cynical about the political system. Studies have consistently shown no relationship between cynicism or alienation and nonvoting in elections.[18]

The second deviant case, *manipulation,* describes voters characterized by low interest and high turnout. It refers to a situation in which individuals with little information or interest become involved in voting. Presumably, this manipulation is achieved by getting individuals to vote either through coercion or by highly stimulating and arousing appeals. Coercive methods for ensuring turnout may range from police-state orders to fines for failing to vote. More common in the American political system are exceptionally moving or alarming appeals, bringing to the polls people so unsophisticated that they are easily swayed. Very high levels of turnout can be inspired by emotional, inflammatory appeals—which offer one possible explanation for the high turnout levels in the United States for many years after the Civil War. Campaigns were marked by extreme appeals, and, because education levels were low, it is reasonable to suspect that there were lower levels of interest, involvement, and information than during the campaigns of the twentieth century and beyond.

Even though interest in politics is strongly correlated with voting, about half of those who say they have hardly any interest do vote in presidential elections, suggesting that other factors are also at work. One of these is a sense of civic duty—the attitude that a good citizen has an obligation to vote. Because such feelings are usually a prime focus of the political socialization fostered by the American educational system, turnout is the highest among those with the longest exposure to this system. Length of education is one of the best predictors of an individual's likelihood of voting.

Because education is so closely associated with relative affluence and social status, people who vote are usually slightly better off in

FIGURE 2-4   Percentage of the Electorate Reporting Having Registered and
Voted in the 2008 Election, by Age

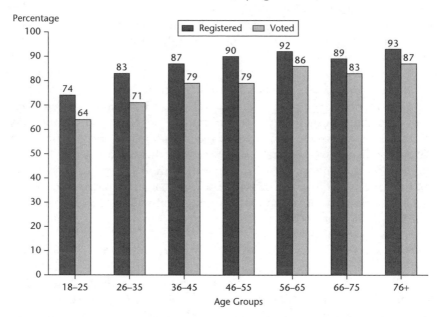

Source: 2008 American National Election Study, available at www.electionstudies.org.

socioeconomic terms than the population as a whole. This bias is likely to increase in low-stimulus elections, as greater numbers of occasional voters drop out of the electorate and leave the field to the better educated and more affluent, who rarely miss an election. In analyzing voting in presidential primaries in 1980 and 1988, Barbara Norrander found voters to be older, better educated, and wealthier than their counterparts who did not vote, but with no substantial ideological or issue differences.[19] In the 2008 presidential primaries, those who voted in the Republican primaries were somewhat more conservative than Republican voters in the general election. No parallel ideological difference was found between Democratic primary and general election voters.[20]

Another important factor contributing to nonvoting is age. A relatively large proportion of young people pass up their first opportunities to vote. The extension of the franchise to eighteen-year-olds in 1972 enlarged the pool of eligible voters, but these young, new voters voted at lower rates than their elders, causing turnout to decline. Figure 2-4, based on survey data from the 2008 presidential election, shows that the likelihood of voting increases from young adulthood through middle age. In most presidential years—but not in 2008—a slight decline in

FIGURE 2-5   Turnout in the 2008 Election, by Age and Education

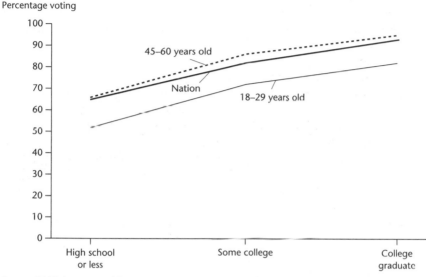

Source: 2008 American National Election Study, available at www.electionstudies.org.

turnout is evident among the most elderly portion of the population. The tendency of young people not to vote is partially offset by their generally higher levels of education. Although the turnout of middle-aged people is higher at each educational level than that of young adults, the gap narrows among the better educated (see Figure 2-5).

Reported turnout increased in all age groups in 2004 and 2008, in comparison with earlier years. The increase was most impressive among the youngest group of eighteen- to twenty-five-year-olds, whose turnout increased from 48 percent in 2000 to 64 percent in 2008. But the overall increase in turnout over these two elections should not be construed solely as youthful enthusiasm for Obama or distaste for Bush; older people also turned out in greater numbers.

Much of the nonvoting among young people may be attributed to the unsettled circumstances of this age group rather than to simple disinterest in politics, although young people are slightly less interested than older people of similar educational levels. Military service, being away at college, geographic mobility with the possible failure to meet residence requirements, and the additional hurdle of initial registration all create barriers to voting for young citizens that are less likely to affect older ones. Efforts to promote voter registration have affected the young; as of 2008, about three-fourths of the youngest members of the electorate had registered to vote.

By age thirty-five, most people have joined the voting population at least on an occasional basis. A small proportion of the middle-aged and older group remains outside the voting public. These habitual nonvoters, who have passed up several opportunities to vote, make up less than 5 percent of the total electorate, according to current survey research estimates.*

This group has steadily decreased in size, and the social forces that brought about the decrease will likely reduce it still further. In the past, habitual nonvoters were disproportionately southern, black, and female. Restrictions against black suffrage, coupled with a traditional culture that worked against active participation of women in civic life, meant that fifty years ago in the South large proportions of blacks of both genders, as well as white women, had never voted in a presidential election. Figure 2-6 shows the historic changes that took place as a result of the civil rights movement of the 1950s and 1960s. In 1952 large percentages of black women and men and, to a lesser extent, white women in the South had never voted. These percentages fell dramatically in the next two decades. By the late twentieth century, turnout patterns were similar in the North and South.

With the first African American candidate on a major-party ticket in 2008, black turnout increased dramatically. The Pew Research Center estimated that black turnout increased 4.9 percent in 2008 in comparison with 2004, with black women voting at the highest rate of any racial or gender group. Young black voters also voted at a much higher rate in 2008, an 8.7 percent increase over 2004, and voted at a higher rate than young white voters.[21]

Registration as a Barrier to Voting

Registration requirements are the last major legal impediment to voting. Registration poses barriers to voting in several ways. In most parts of the country, an unregistered citizen must go to the courthouse several weeks before the election, during working hours, and fill out a form. Although not a horrendous burden, it does take time and some ability to deal with a governmental bureaucracy. Regulations also typically cancel the registration of people who fail to vote in a few consecutive

---

* The reported vote obtained in surveys, including surveys by the U.S. Census Bureau, is consistently higher than that of official statistics. Validation studies suggest that more than 10 percent of the respondents claim to have voted when they did not. Bias in survey samples—that is, interviewing disproportionate numbers of voters—is also a factor contributing to the difference. See U.S. Census Bureau, "Current Population Reports," *Studies in the Measurement of Voter Turnout*, Series P-23, no. 168 (Washington, D.C.: U.S. Government Printing Office, 1990).

FIGURE 2-6   Percentage of Adults Who Have Never Voted, by Race and
Gender, for the South and the Non-South, 1952–1980

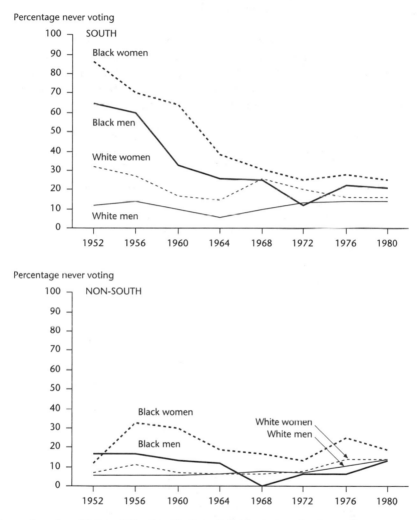

Source: American National Election Studies, available at www.electionstudies.org.

Note: The states in the South are Alabama, Arkansas, Florida, Georgia, Kentucky, Louisiana, Maryland, Mississippi, North Carolina, Oklahoma, South Carolina, Tennessee, Texas, Virginia, and West Virginia. The remainder are the states in the non-South.

elections. In addition, residential mobility annually relocates millions of citizens in new precincts in which they must reregister. All of these circumstances raise the costs of political involvement, costs that a significant number of citizens will choose not to assume. Furthermore, voter registration is not always purely an electoral matter: an unknown number of Americans prefer to remain off registration lists to avoid jury duty, bill collectors, or a former spouse.

Not surprisingly, individuals with little or no interest in politics lack the motivation to overcome registration barriers on their own. Voter registration drives, in which volunteers go door to door or register voters at shopping malls and on college campuses, capture many politically uninvolved people. A certain proportion of these people will not have the interest or incentive to bear the additional costs of getting to the polls on election day. The Center for the Study of the American Electorate estimates that over 74 percent of the eligible electorate was registered to vote in 2008, the highest percentage in many decades.[22] In states with party registration, the increases in 2008 were almost entirely among Democrats and independents. Something over 10 percent of those registered did not vote.

Table 2-1 illustrates differences among unregistered citizens, registered nonvoters, and registered voters in terms of their level of interest in the election campaign and their partisanship. The registered nonvoters generally fall between the two other groups. In most years, a partisan impact is visible in the failure of potential voters to vote, with Republicans having greater representation among voters than they do in the

TABLE 2-1   Interest and Partisanship of Registered Voters and Nonvoters and Unregistered Citizens, 2008

		Registered	
	Unregistered	Nonvoters	Voters
Very much interested	16%	33%	52%
Somewhat interested	41	40	40
Not interested at all	44	26	8
Total	101%	99%	100%
Strong Democrat	7%	11%	22%
Weak Democrat	15	16	15
Independent Democrat	23	25	14
Independent	29	22	7
Independent Republican	14	12	12
Weak Republican	8	8	14
Strong Republican	2	5	16
Other, don't know, or apolitical	2	1	1
Total	100%	100%	101%
(*Weighted N*)	(277)	(177)	(1,627)

Source: 2008 American National Election Study, available at www.electionstudies.org.

electorate as a whole. This did not happen in 2008. The nonvoters—
both registered and unregistered—were disproportionately independents and the uninterested. If anything, Democrats in 2008 were more
likely to turn out to vote than their Republican counterparts.

In recent years, various plans have been introduced to boost voter
turnout by reducing difficulties in registration. Some state governments
have implemented same-day registration, whereby individuals can register at the polls on election day. In 1993 Congress passed the "motor
voter" bill, which provides that registration forms will be available at
various governmental agencies that citizens visit for other purposes.
These include agencies where motor vehicles are registered and driver's
licenses are obtained; however, because of a Republican-sponsored
amendment, states are not required to provide them at unemployment
and welfare offices. The purpose of the bill is clearly to make it easier for
all citizens to exercise their right to vote, but Democratic support and
Republican concerns point to a potential side effect. Because the unregistered tend to be poorer and less well educated, Democrats, who traditionally represent such groups, hoped (and Republicans feared) that
reducing registration obstacles would increase the number of Democratic voters.

Many of the same political considerations were at play in the passage of the Help America Vote Act of 2002, which mandated that states
provide provisional ballots for those citizens who believe they are registered to vote but whose names are not on the registration rolls. Much of
the debate in Congress involved the form of identification that voters
seeking to cast provisional ballots would need to produce at the polls.
Republican legislators sought more rigid standards to prevent voter
fraud; Democrats generally argued for keeping the barriers to a minimum.[23] In 2008 partisan concerns again emerged when Republicans
charged that the Association of Community Organizations for Reform
Now (ACORN), an activist community organization with ties to Obama,
was submitting fraudulent voter registration cards as part of its voter
registration drive. In fact, it appears that it was ACORN who was being
defrauded by some of its own paid workers, who submitted obviously
invalid cards (registering Mickey Mouse, among others) in order to
receive per-card payments. Any organization distributing and collecting
voter registration cards is required by law to submit them to the registration office. ACORN did so, but flagged fraudulent ones as suspicious,
thereby making it highly unlikely that "Mickey" or his colleagues would
actually be able to cast a ballot on election day.

Registration requirements are one reason why the United States
has significantly lower turnout rates than other Western democracies, where governments maintain registration lists instead of placing
the burden of registration on the individual.[24] Reducing registration

requirements is a logical and fairly easy means to increase the turnout rate, but it should not be expected to have an astounding effect. The Federal Election Commission estimates that the 1993 motor voter law resulted in an increase of less than 2 percent in registration in 1996 over 1992.[25] In part, the impact was so small because many states had already implemented aspects of the law, so their practices and procedures did not change. During 1995 and 1996, almost one-third of all registrations were by mail and one-third came through some form of motor voter program. Public assistance offices were the source of a little more than 6 percent of the registrations, even though not all states provided registration forms in these offices.

Despite Republican fears that easing registration requirements would bring more Democrats to the polls, the main impact of making it easier to register seems to have been a decline in the proportion of the officially registered who vote. Failure to register prohibits voting, but registering does not ensure turnout. More of those only casually interested in politics and government register—because it is so easy. But when election day arrives, it takes the same amount of energy to get to the polling place as it always did.

The minimal impact of lessening registration requirements has led some states to experiment with easing the act of voting itself—by mailing ballots to registered voters and allowing them to vote by mail. Other states have loosened the conditions under which voters can request absentee ballots. Still other states have set up systems for in-person early voting in the weeks prior to the election. Oregon has pursued these possibilities most aggressively, with the entire electorate receiving mail-in ballots in statewide elections beginning in 2004. Interest in using absentee ballots rose in many states in 2004, in part because of fears of long lines, concern about the absence of a paper trail with electronic ballot arrangements, and other issues. In 2008, 31 percent of the voters in the American National Election Study reported voting early in person or by mail. Although an unprecedented number of early ballots were cast in 2008, the procedure apparently is more a convenience or safeguard for voters who would have voted anyway than a means to draw the marginal voter to the polls, according to Curtis Gans of the Center for the Study of the American Electorate.[26]

Is the Level of Turnout in the United States a Cause for Concern?

A great deal of editorial ink has been spilled to lament, and academic analysis undertaken to explain, the generally low level of turnout in the United States. Even the recent level of around 60 percent is low by international and historical standards. In this section we will look at some of the explanations that have been offered for the generally low level of turnout and then suggest some alternative ways of looking at the issue.

Part of the difficulty analysts have had in understanding the decline in turnout after 1960 is that it happened at the same time that legal restrictions on voting were being eased and education levels were increasing. These circumstances should be expected to increase turnout. One explanation for the decline in the face of these factors has focused on the expansion of the electorate in 1971 to include eighteen-year-olds. Because young people are less likely to vote than older people, their inclusion in the electorate would be expected to decrease turnout, other things being equal. However, this can account for only a small portion of the ensuing decline.

Another possibility, raised by political commentators in 1972, 1980, and 1984, was that calling the election early in the evening, before the polls closed in all states—especially western states—reduced turnout. Once potential voters learned that a television network had declared a winner in the race for president, the argument went, they would no longer be interested in voting for president or any other office. However, the 1976 and 2000 elections were so close that the winner was not known until long after the polls had closed in all fifty states, and no appreciable impact was seen on turnout. Public concern about calling the election too early, together with congressional threats of regulation, led the networks to restrict their reporting voluntarily in 1988 and thereafter. However, if public opinion polls before the election all point to a clear winner, as they did in 1996, the impact on turnout may be the same. Persuasive as the idea is, the evidence on this matter is inconclusive, and no one has clearly demonstrated that these factors have influenced turnout in a significant way.[27]

A somewhat more sweeping form of this argument—and one harder to test—suggests that the style of media coverage of campaigns has turned elections into a spectator sport that voters watch with varying degrees of interest but in which they feel no need to engage. The prediction of the winners in polls, the focus in presidential debates on who "won" instead of on substance, the attention to the "horse-race" aspects of the primary campaigns, and the networks' competition to call the election first are all alleged factors in the withdrawal of the voter from active participation. If one were to pursue this argument further, one might conclude that the GOTV efforts of the two parties and the grassroots organizing of the Obama campaign have helped to turn spectators back into participants.

In a major study of nonvoting, Ruy Teixeira offers two general explanations for the decline in turnout after 1960.[28] First, he cites a set of circumstances that he calls *social connectedness*—that is, the extent to which individuals are socially integrated into their community. This is similar to Robert D. Putnam's idea of *social capital*, which we discussed in chapter 1. Older people, married people, and those who attend religious services and are settled in their communities are more socially connected than young, single, and mobile people who do not belong to community organizations. Over the past few decades, the proportion of socially unconnected people has increased. Teixeira estimates that about one-third of the decline in turnout is associated with the decline in social connectedness.

The second factor is the extent of *political connectedness*—that is, the degree to which people feel interested and involved in government and believe government is concerned and responsive to them. The decline in political connectedness paralleled a loss of trust in government, a lower sense of political efficacy, a decline in interest in politics, and a diminished sense of civic duty—many of the trends we noted in chapter 1. These changing attitudes toward government and politics account for more than half of the decline in turnout, according to Teixeira.

Turnout rose sharply in 1992, and examining the possible reasons for it would be worthwhile. Ross Perot's candidacy in the 1992 presidential race led to an atypically high level of turnout among the young, the nonpartisan, and those disenchanted with government and political leadership. These groups, in fact, are the socially and politically disconnected whose increased numbers, Teixeira argues, were responsible for the decline in turnout. Perhaps Perot's candidacy gave these voters an alternative that allowed them to connect with the political world. (By 1996 Perot looked less like the outsider who could fix the system, and he drew fewer of the unconnected into the electorate.) Beyond this, the 1992 campaigns of Perot, Clinton, and, to a lesser degree, George H. W. Bush used new means for reaching the voters. Talk-show appearances, Perot's "infomercials," town meetings, and MTV's Rock the Vote initiative were all efforts to establish connections with the public in the age of cable television. Presidential candidates clearly differ in how well they come across in these venues, but none can now avoid them.

Steven J. Rosenstone and John Mark Hansen make the point that another aspect of participation is *mobilization*.[29] If candidates and parties fail to mobilize potential voters—or fail to find appropriate means to reach them—then it is not surprising that people do not vote. The declining turnout rate may have been more a failure of party elites than of citizens. The mobilization efforts of both parties as well as other organizations in 2004 and 2008 surely contributed to the sharp increase in turnout in those elections.

Throughout our discussion of turnout, we have implied that nonvoting needs to be explained. We have assumed that voting is normal or to be expected. However, the topic could be approached differently. The question could be asked, "Why do people bother to vote?"—as if nonvoting were the natural pattern or expected behavior and voting required explanation. The answer that one vote can determine the outcome of an election and that most people vote anticipating that their vote may be crucial is not reasonable, even after an extremely close election such as in 2000. One vote rarely decides an election, although many races are close; no voter should expect to cast the deciding vote in an election. However, "votes count" in an election in another sense—as an expression of preference for a candidate or for a party, regardless of whether that candidate ultimately wins or loses. Elections are more than simply a mechanism for selecting public officials; they are also a means for communicating, albeit somewhat dimly, a set of attitudes to the government. For most Americans, voting remains the only means of influence regularly used. Many see it as the only avenue open to ordinary citizens to make the government listen to their needs. The desire to be counted on one side of the fence or the other and the feeling that one ought to be so counted are perhaps the greatest spurs to voting. If this is true, then perhaps the most disturbing lesson that comes from examining electoral procedures in Florida in 2000 was the realization that your vote may not even get counted—let alone make a difference.

Our discussion—and most such discussions—also assumes that a high level of turnout is a good thing, and low turnout is something to be concerned about. Exercising one's right to vote is seen as support for the political system, embrace of one's role as a citizen, and willingness to endorse one or another of the candidates. Failure to vote is taken as alienation from politics or apathy about the fate of the nation. Over the years, a few commentators have pointed out another possibility. Some people may not vote because of basic satisfaction with the way things are going or a feeling that things will be all right no matter which candidate is elected. While hardly model citizens, such people do not pose much of a problem for the political system. But then suppose that these people begin to feel that the outcome of the election will impact their lives, that one of the candidates will take the country in a direction they do not want to go. With their comfortable existence being threatened, they might decide to vote. If enough people felt this way, turnout would go up.

Something like this may have happened in 2004 and 2008. The issues facing the country were urgent, but just as important, significant portions of the politically active public took a polarized view of politics. They distrusted and disliked those with whom they disagreed on a variety of issues. They did not want to see government in the hands of their opponents. They worked hard to mobilize like-minded people to get them to the polls to prevent the other side from winning. And turnout went up.

The point is twofold. Rising turnout is not an unmixed blessing. Although more engaged citizens may be good from a civics perspective, it can also mean that people are angry, worried, or threatened by events or by the prospect of one or another candidate holding office. Second, whether turnout remains elevated in the future or settles back to its recent lower levels will depend in great part on whether the current deep division in the politically active segment of the society remains.

Notes

1. This estimate of turnout is from the United States Election Project, available at www.elections.gmu.edu. This estimate includes state data, where available, on the more than one million people who cast ballots but did not vote for president. Also included are the nearly five million eligible voters living overseas. Another authoritative estimate of turnout in 2008 is 63 percent, by the Center for the Study of the American Electorate, available at www1.american.edu/ia/cdem/case/.
2. Chilton Williamson, *American Suffrage from Property to Democracy: 1760–1860* (Princeton: Princeton University Press, 1960), especially 131–181.
3. Jerrold D. Rusk and John J. Stucker, "The Effect of the Southern System of Election Laws on Voting Participation," in *The History of American Electoral Behavior*, ed. Joel Silbey, Allan Bogue, and William Flanigan (Princeton: Princeton University Press, 1978). For a treatment of these and many additional topics, see also J. Morgan Kousser, *The Shaping of Southern Politics* (New Haven: Yale University Press, 1974).
4. Donald R. Matthews and James W. Prothro, "Political Factors and Negro Voter Registration in the South," *American Political Science Review* 57 (June 1963): 355–367.
5. See www.elections.gmu.edu.
6. "Losing the Vote: The Impact of Felony Disenfranchisement Laws in the United States," Sentencing Project, October 1998, available at www.sentencing project. org.
7. U.S. Commission on Civil Rights, "Executive Summary," in "Voting Irregularities in Florida during the 2000 Presidential Election," available at www.usccr .gov/vote2000/stdraft1/exsum.htm.
8. Ruy A. Teixeira, *The Disappearing American Voter* (Washington, D.C.: Brookings Institution, 1992), 10.
9. U.S. Census Bureau, available at www.census.gov/population/www/socdemo/voting.html#hist.
10. See www.elections.gmu.edu; and Michael McDonald and Samuel Popkin, "The Myth of the Vanishing Voter," *American Political Science Review* 95, no. 4 (2001): 963–974.
11. The Center for the Study of the American Electorate, available at www1.american. edu/ia/cdem/case.
12. E. E. Schattschneider, *The Semisovereign People* (New York: Holt, Rinehart, and Winston, 1960), especially chap. 5; and Walter Dean Burnham, "The Changing Shape of the American Political Universe," *American Political Science Review* 59 (March 1965): 7–28.
13. The most general statement of this argument is found in Philip E. Converse, "Change in the American Electorate," in *The Human Meaning of Social Change*,

ed. Angus Campbell and Philip E. Converse (New York: Russell Sage Foundation, 1972), 263–337. For an analysis that alters the estimates of turnout, see Ray M. Shortridge, "Estimating Voter Participation," in *Analyzing Electoral History,* ed. Jerome M. Clubb, William H. Flanigan, and Nancy H. Zingale (Beverly Hills, Calif.: Sage Publications, 1981), 137–152.

14. Jerrold D. Rusk, "The Effect of the Australian Ballot Reform on Split-Ticket Voting: 1876–1908," *American Political Science Review* 64 (December 1970): 1220–1238.

15. Angus Campbell, Philip E. Converse, Warren E. Miller, and Donald E. Stokes, eds., *Elections and the Political Order* (New York: Wiley, 1966), 40–62.

16. See the Pew Research Center for the People and the Press survey, October 29–November 1, 2008, available at www.people-press.org.

17. Pew Research Center, November Post-Election Survey, available at www.people-press.org.

18. Arthur T. Hadley, *The Empty Polling Booth* (Englewood Cliffs, N.J.: Prentice-Hall, 1978), 20, 41.

19. Barbara Norrander, *Super Tuesday: Regional Politics and Presidential Primaries* (Lexington: University of Kentucky Press, 1992); and Barbara Norrander, "Ideological Representativeness of Presidential Primaries," *American Journal of Political Science* 33 (August 1989): 570–587.

20. The 2008 American National Election Study.

21. Mark Hugo Lopez, "Dissecting the 2008 Electorate: Most Diverse in U.S. History," Pew Research Center Publications, April 30, 2009.

22. The Center for the Study of the American Electorate, available at www1.american.edu/ia/cdem/case.

23. *CQ Almanac Plus 2002* (Washington, D.C.: Congressional Quarterly Inc., 2003), 143.

24. G. Bingham Powell Jr., "American Voter Turnout in Comparative Perspective," *American Political Science Review* 80 (March 1986): 17–44.

25. "Executive Summary of the Federal Election Commission's Report to the Congress on the Impact of the National Voter Registration Act of 1993 on the Administration of Federal Elections," available at www.fec.gov/votregis/nvra sum.htm.

26. Quoted in "Much Hyped Turnout Record Fails to Materialize; Convenience Voting Fails to Boost Balloting," *AU News,* American University, November 6, 2008.

27. See Laurily K. Epstein and Gerald Strom, "Election Night Projections and West Coast Turnout," *American Politics Quarterly* 9 (October 1981): 479–491; and Raymond Wolfinger and Peter Linquiti, "Tuning In and Turning Out," *Public Opinion* (February–March 1981): 56–60.

28. Teixeira, *The Disappearing American Voter.*

29. Steven J. Rosenstone and John Mark Hansen, *Mobilization, Participation, and Democracy in America* (New York: Macmillan, 1993).

Suggested Readings

Conway, M. Margaret. *Political Participation in the United States,* 3rd ed. Washington, D.C.: CQ Press, 2000. A good introduction to the study of turnout and other forms of political participation.

McDonald, Michael P., and Samuel L. Popkin. "The Myth of the Vanishing Voter," *American Political Science Review* 95, no. 4 (December 2001): 963–974.

Patterson, Thomas E. *The Vanishing Voter: Public Involvement in an Age of Uncertainty.* New York: Alfred A. Knopf, 2002. An analysis of political participation based on a huge, year-long survey in 2000.

Rosenstone, Steven J., and John Mark Hansen. *Mobilization, Participation, and Democracy in America.* New York: Macmillan, 1993. An analysis of the interaction among the strategic choices of political elites and the choices of citizens to participate in politics.

Rusk, Jerrold D., and John J. Stucker. "The Effect of the Southern System of Election Laws on Voting Participation." In *The History of American Electoral Behavior,* ed. Joel Silbey, Allan Bogue, and William Flanigan. Princeton: Princeton University Press, 1978. A sophisticated analysis of the disfranchisement of voters in the South in the nineteenth century.

Teixeira, Ruy A. *The Disappearing American Voter.* Washington, D.C.: Brookings Institution Press, 1992. A sophisticated and thorough analysis of the factors that have contributed to the decline in turnout in the United States and a discussion of the impact of proposed reforms.

U.S. Census Bureau. *Voting and Registration in the Election of November 1992.* Series P-20, no. 466. Washington, D.C.: U.S. Government Printing Office, April 1993. A report of findings on turnout and registration based on a huge survey that allows complex analysis of many subgroups within the U.S. population.

Internet Resources

There are two important Web sites for the analysis of aggregate turnout data. One is the Center for the Study of the American Electorate, www1.american.edu/ia/cdem/case, and the other is the United States Elections Project, elections.gmu.edu. Both use strategies for reducing the error in turnout estimates as well as commentary on turnout.

The Web site of the American National Election Studies, www.electionstudies.org/, offers data on turnout in both presidential and off-year elections since 1952. After clicking on "Guide to Public Opinion," click on "Political Involvement and Participation in Politics." You also can examine turnout of numerous social groups from 1952 to the present.

Turnout and registration data for the nation and the states are available at the U.S. Census Bureau Web site, www.census.gov. Click on "V" under the subject headings and then find "Voting."

Charles Franklin of the University of Wisconsin, Madison, has a blog, politicalarithmetik.blogspot.com, that touches on many political topics including turnout. He also produces commentary for a public opinion Web site, pollster.com.

Partisanship

I N CONTEMPORARY POLITICAL commentary, candidates and officeholders are often assessed in terms of how well they appeal to their party's "base." Sen. John McCain, R-Ariz., is said to have picked Gov. Sarah Palin of Alaska as his running mate in 2008 because she compensated for his lack of appeal to the Republican base. Democratic strategists worry that President Barack Obama will have difficulties with the Democratic base as he searches for common ground on the abortion issue or goes slowly in implementing his campaign promise of rescinding the "don't ask, don't tell" policy on gays in the military. Candidates and officeholders need to retain the approval of their most loyal supporters while reaching out to others at the same time.

This discussion involves *partisanship*—the sense of attachment or belonging that an individual feels for a political party. In this and the next two chapters we will explore the concept of partisanship and its implications for political behavior. In this chapter we will discuss the meaning of partisanship and how the partisanship of Americans has changed over the course of the country's political history. In chapter 4 we will examine the impact of partisanship on the way people act politically and how partisanship changes over the lifetime of the individual and between generations. In chapter 5 we will consider the social characteristics of partisans and independents.

Party Loyalty

For almost a century and a half the U.S. electorate has supported a two-party system in national politics. Such remarkable stability is unknown in other democracies. Within this stable party system, however, voter support for Republicans and Democrats has fluctuated

FIGURE 3-1   Partisan Division of the Presidential Vote in the Nation, 1824–2008

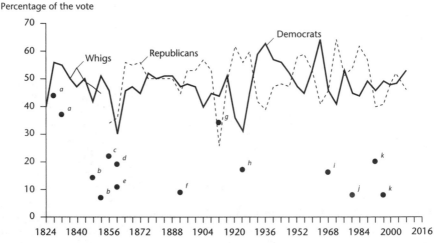

Percentage of the vote

Sources: Walter Dean Burnham, Jerome M. Clubb, and William H. Flanigan, *State-Level Congressional, Gubernatorial, and Senatorial Election Data for the United States, 1824–1972,* Inter-university Consortium for Political and Social Research; U.S. Census Bureau, *2009 Statistical Abstract,* Tables 380 and 381, available at www.census.gov.

Note: In presenting these data, we have not drawn attention to the wide range of errors that may exist. Errors are made in collecting and recording data, as well as in computation. The presidential election of 1960 provides an illustration of another form of uncertainty that enters into these data—choices made among alternative ways of presenting the data. The popular vote is customarily listed in such a way that John F. Kennedy appears a narrow winner over Richard M. Nixon in 1960. To reach this distribution of the total vote, the Kennedy vote from Alabama must be exaggerated, because uncommitted electors were on the slate of Democratic electors in Alabama. Eventually six of the uncommitted electors voted for Harry F. Byrd; five electors voted for Kennedy. If the Kennedy popular vote in Alabama is reduced to a proportion, say five-elevenths in this case, of the vote for Democratic electors and if only this reduced popular vote is added to his national total, then Nixon, not Kennedy, has the larger popular vote total nationally in 1960. In percentages these are negligible changes, but symbolically such differences can become important. In our tables and figures we have followed the usual practice of presenting the augmented Kennedy total.

Other parties gaining at least 5 percent of the vote: [a]National Republican; [b]Free Soil; [c]American; [d]Southern Democratic; [e]Constitutional Union; [f]People's; [g]Bull Moose; [h]Progressive; [i]American Independent; [j]Anderson Independent Candidacy; [k]Perot Independent Candidacy, Reform Party. Ralph Nader's 2.7 percent in 2000 falls below this minimum and is not shown.

widely, and significant numbers of voters occasionally, as in 1992, abandon the traditional parties to support third-party or independent candidates. The aggregate vote totals for presidential elections, shown in Figure 3-1, reveal a wide range of party fortunes, even in elections close together in time. Some of the more dramatic fluctuations have involved the appearance of strong third-party candidates, such as Theodore Roosevelt in 1912, George C. Wallace in 1968, and Ross Perot in 1992 and, to a lesser degree, 1996. Perot's 1992 showing of 19 percent was the largest percentage won by a third-party candidate since 1912. Although Ralph Nader's votes denied the presidency to Al Gore in 2000, his 2.7 percent of the popular vote was an unimpressive figure for a third-party candidate in recent years. (He did even less well in his subsequent runs—about one-half of one percent in 2004 and 2008.)

Despite these variations in election outcomes, and despite the demonstrated capacity of American voters for highly selective and differentiated support for candidates offered them by the political parties, most voters have a basic and stable loyalty to one party or the other. This tendency of most individuals to be loyal to one political party makes the idea of partisanship, or *party identification* as it is often called, one of the most useful concepts for understanding the political behavior of individuals. After good survey data became available in the late 1940s, party identification assumed a central role in all voting behavior analysis.[1]

Party Identification

Party identification is a relatively uncomplicated measure determined by responses to the following questions:

- Generally speaking, do you usually think of yourself as a Republican, a Democrat, an independent, or what?

- [If Republican or Democrat] Would you call yourself a strong [Republican/Democrat], or a not very strong [Republican/Democrat]?

- [If independent] Do you think of yourself as closer to the Republican Party or to the Democratic Party?

Leaving aside for the moment the people who do not or cannot respond to such questions, this yields seven categories of participants in the electorate according to intensity of partisanship.

Strong Democrats	Weak Democrats	Independent Democrats	Independents	Independent Republicans	Weak Republicans	Strong Republicans

Partisanship

Because this self-identification measure of party loyalty is the best indicator of partisanship, political analysts commonly refer to *partisanship* and *party identification* interchangeably. While many other influences are at work on voters in U.S. society, and partisanship varies in its importance in different types of elections and in different time periods, partisanship is the single most important influence on political opinions and voting behavior.

Partisanship represents the feeling of sympathy for and loyalty to a political party that an individual acquires—sometimes during childhood—and holds through life, often with increasing intensity. This self-image as a Democrat or a Republican is useful to the individual in a special way. For example, individuals who think of themselves as Republicans or Democrats respond to political information partially by using party identification to orient themselves, reacting to new information in such a way that it fits in with the ideals and feelings they already have. A Republican who hears a Republican Party leader advocate a policy has a basis in party loyalty for supporting that policy, apart from other considerations. A Democrat may feel favorably inclined toward a candidate for office because that candidate bears the Democratic label. Partisanship orients individuals in their political environment, although it may also distort their picture of reality.

This underlying partisanship is also interesting to political analysts because it provides a base against which to measure deviations in particular elections. In other words, the individual voter's long-standing loyalty to one party means that, "other things being equal," or in the absence of disrupting forces, he or she can be expected to vote for candidates of that party. However, voters are responsive to a great variety of other influences that can either strengthen or weaken their tendency to support their usual party. Variations occur from election to election in such factors as the attractiveness of the candidates, the impact of foreign and domestic policy issues, and purely local circumstances. These current factors, often called *short-term forces,* may move voters away from their usual party choices.

The concepts of partisanship and short-term forces can also be used in understanding the behavior of the electorate as a whole. If the political predispositions of all the individuals in the electorate were added up, the result would be an "expected vote" or "normal vote."[2] This is the electoral outcome that would be expected if all voters voted their party identification. Departures from this expected vote in elections represent the impact of short-term forces, such as issues or candidates.

In assessing the partisanship of the American electorate historically, we will not be able to add up individual party identifications to find an expected vote. Survey data of this type have been available only for the past seventy years or so. For the period from 1824 to 1968, we base

FIGURE 3-2   Democratic Expected Vote in Presidential Elections,
1840–1968

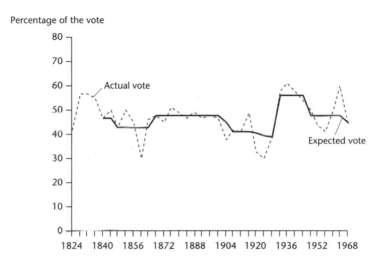

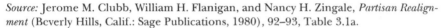

Source: Jerome M. Clubb, William H. Flanigan, and Nancy H. Zingale, *Partisan Realignment* (Beverly Hills, Calif.: Sage Publications, 1980), 92–93, Table 3.1a.

our estimates on the only available data—election returns for aggregate units.[3] These data cannot reveal voting patterns of individuals, but they do allow one to make assessments of party loyalty and temporary deviations from party by collections of voters. Even though the same set of individuals does not turn out to vote in each election, we use the election returns over the years to indicate the collective partisanship of the electorate. From these data an estimate is made of the expected vote for the Democratic and Republican Parties. It is then possible to say, for example, that the electorate deviated from its normal voting pattern in favor of the Republican Party in 1904 or that the voters departed from their normal Democratic loyalty in 1952.

Our estimates of the expected vote nationwide in presidential voting for the Democratic Party from 1840 to 1968 and for the Republican Party from 1872 to 1968 are shown in Figures 3-2 and 3-3, respectively. The actual vote in these elections is also shown to indicate the amount of departure from underlying partisan patterns that occurred in each election.

For the more recent period, something similar to the normal vote technique developed by Philip E. Converse, which depends on individual-level survey data, can be used to create an expectation about vote choice in the absence of short-term forces. This technique uses party identification, expected defection rates, and turnout to generate

FIGURE 3-3   Republican Expected Vote in Presidential Elections,
             1872–1968

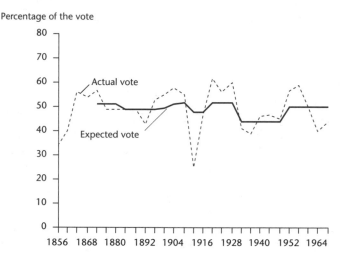

Source: Jerome M. Clubb, William H. Flanigan, and Nancy H. Zingale, *Partisan Realignment* (Beverly Hills, Calif.: Sage Publications, 1980), 92–93, Table 3.1a.

an estimate of the normal vote. Using a simplified calculation method, the Democratic and Republican normal votes—along with the actual vote for president, from 1968 to 2008—are shown in Figures 3-4 and 3-5, respectively. (Note that because normal vote calculations depend on party identification, and identifications with third parties are trivial, the Republican normal vote is a mirror image of the Democratic normal vote.) The deviation of the actual Democratic vote meanders under the Democratic normal vote line, meaning that Democratic presidential candidates since 1968 have rarely done as well as would be expected, given the distribution of party identification. The elections of 2004 and 2008 were exceptions, as the Democratic candidates' performances matched Democratic partisan strength in the electorate. In elections in which a third-party candidate won a significant number of votes—1968, 1992, and 1996—both the Democratic and Republican candidates performed below what the normal votes would predict.

Types of Electoral Change

As we have said, the utility of the concept of the expected vote in part lies in providing a base against which to measure and analyze departures from the expected pattern. One type of departure is usually

FIGURE 3-4   Democratic Normal Vote with Presidential Vote, 1968–2008

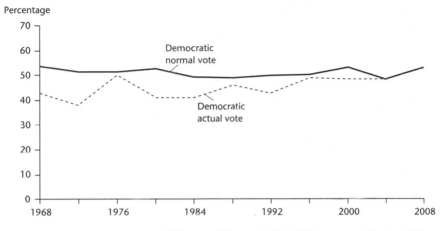

Sources: U. S. Census Bureau, *2009 Statistical Abstract,* Table 380; American National Election Studies, available at www.electionstudies.org.

Note: The normal vote calculations are a simplified version of Philip E. Converse's original analysis. See Philip E. Converse, "The Concept of a Normal Vote," in *Elections and the Political Order,* ed. Angus Campbell, Philip E. Converse, Warren E. Miller, and Donald E. Stokes (New York: Wiley, 1966), 9–39.

referred to as *deviating change:* the temporary deviations from normal party loyalty attributable to the short-term forces of candidate images or issues.[4] The amount of deviating change in an election tells how well a candidate or party did relative to the party's normal performance. In these terms, the Dwight D. Eisenhower victories in 1952 and 1956 and the Richard M. Nixon landslide in 1972 appear even more dramatic because they represent big Republican margins during a time when the Democratic Party held an advantage in party loyalists. These deviating elections involved substantial departures from the underlying strength of the two parties in the electorate.

Temporary deviating changes may be dramatic and reflect important electoral forces, but another type of change is of even greater interest. On rare occasions in American national politics, a permanent or *realigning change* in voting patterns occurs. In such instances, the electorate departs from its expected voting pattern but does not return to the old pattern afterward. The changes sometimes are large enough to alter the competitive balance between the parties, with significant consequences for the policy directions of the government. Such a period of change is usually referred to as a *partisan realignment.*[5]

Electoral analysts usually discuss three major realignments in American history. One occurred during the time of the Civil War and

FIGURE 3-5   Republican Normal Vote with Presidential Vote, 1968–2008

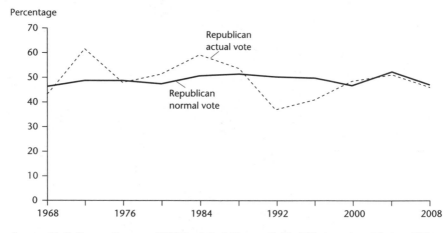

Sources: U. S. Census Bureau, *2009 Statistical Abstract,* Table 380; American National Election Studies, available at www.electionstudies.org.

Note: The normal vote calculations are a simplified version of Philip E. Converse's original analysis. See Philip E. Converse, "The Concept of a Normal Vote," in *Elections and the Political Order,* ed. Angus Campbell, Philip E. Converse, Warren E. Miller, and Donald E. Stokes (New York: Wiley, 1966), 9–39.

the emergence of the Republican Party; another followed the depression of 1893 and benefited the Republicans; and the most recent followed the depression of 1929 and led to Democratic Party dominance. These abrupt changes in the expected votes of the parties can be seen in Figures 3-2 and 3-3 (see pages 71 and 72). Each realignment of partisan loyalties coincided with a major national crisis, leading to the supposition that a social or economic crisis is necessary to shake loose customary loyalties. But major crises and national traumas have not always led to disruptions of partisanship, suggesting that other political conditions must also be present for a crisis to produce a realignment. The nature of the realignment crisis has political significance, however, because it generally determines the lines along which the rearrangement in partisan loyalties will take place, as different segments of the electorate respond differently to the crisis and to attempts to solve it.

In general, realignments appear to happen in the following way. At a time of national crisis, the electorate rejects the party in power, giving a decisive victory to the other party—a victory that includes not only the presidency but also large majorities in both houses of Congress. Armed with a political mandate, the new party in office acts to meet the crisis, often with innovative policies that are sharp departures from the past. *If* the administration's policy initiatives are successful in solving the nation's problems (or at least if they are widely perceived as successful), then significant numbers of voters will become partisans of the new administration's party and continue voting for this party in subsequent elections, thus causing a lasting change in the division of partisan strength in the electorate. If the administration in power is *not* perceived as successful in handling the crisis, then in all likelihood the voters will reject that party in the next election, and its landslide victory in the previous election will be regarded, in retrospect, as a deviating election.

In a realignment the people who become partisans of the new majority party likely are independents and previously uninvolved members of the electorate, not partisans of the other party. In other words, in a realignment few Democrats or Republicans switch parties. It appears more likely that independents drop their independent stance and become partisan. Thus, for a realignment to occur, a precondition may be a pool of people without partisan attachments who are available for realignment. This, in turn, suggests a longer sequence of events that forms a realignment cycle.

First there is the crisis that, if successfully handled, leads to a realignment. This initiates a period of electoral stability during which the parties take distinct stands on the issues that were at the heart of the crisis. Party loyalty is high during this period, both within the electorate and among the elected political leaders in government. However, as time passes, new problems arise and new issues gradually disrupt the old alignment and lead to greater electoral instability. During this period, often referred to as a *dealignment*, voters are much more susceptible to the personal appeals of candidates, to local issues, and to other elements that might lead to departures from underlying party loyalty. As the time since the last realignment lengthens, more and more new voters come into the electorate without attachments to the symbols and issues of the past that made their elders party loyalists. This group of voters, who have no strong attachments to either party, may provide the basis for a new realignment should a crisis arise and one or the other of the parties be perceived as solving it.

Party Systems and Realignments

Political historians often divide American electoral history into five *party systems*—eras that are distinguished from each other by the different political parties that existed or by the different competitive relationships among the parties.[6] The transition from one party system to another has usually been marked by a realignment.

The first party system, which extended from the 1790s until about 1824, saw the relatively rapid formation of two parties, the Federalists and the Jeffersonian Republicans. The issue that divided the parties most clearly was their attitude toward the power of the central government. The commercial and financial interests supported the Federalist position of increasing the authority of the central government, whereas Jeffersonian Republicans distrusted the centralizing and, in their view, aristocratic tendencies of their rivals. The parties began as factions within Congress, but before long they had gained organizations at the state and local level and had substantially broadened the base of political participation among the voting population. After 1815, competition between the two parties all but ceased as the Jeffersonian Republicans gained supremacy, moving the country into the so-called Era of Good Feelings.

The second party system is usually dated from 1828, the year of the first presidential election with substantial popular participation, which marked the resurgence of party competition for the presidency. Emerging ultimately from this renewed competition were the Democrats and the Whigs, parties that competed almost evenly for national power until the 1850s. Mass political participation increased and party organizations were strengthened as both parties sought electoral support from the common people. Although the Democratic Party had come to prominence led by frontiersman Andrew Jackson, by the 1850s both Democrats and Whigs had adherents in all sections of the nation. Thus, when the issue of slavery broke full-force on the nation, the existing parties could not easily cope with the sectional differences they found within their ranks. As the Whigs and Democrats compromised or failed to act because of internal disagreements, a flurry of minor parties appeared to push the cause of abolition. One of these, the Republican Party, eventually replaced the floundering Whigs as one of the two major parties that would dominate party systems thereafter.

The intense conflicts that preceded the Civil War led to the basic regional alignment of Democratic dominance in the South and Republican strength in the North that emerged from the war and that characterized the third party system. But the extreme intensity and durability of the partisan loyalties were also significantly dependent on emotional attachments associated with the war. The strength of partisan attachments after the Civil War was not lessened by the sharp competitiveness of the two parties throughout the system. Electoral forces were so evenly balanced that the Republican Party could effectively control the presidency and Congress only by excluding the southern Democrats from participation in elections. Once Reconstruction relaxed enough to permit the full expression of Democratic strength, the nation was narrowly divided, with the slightest deviation determining the outcome of elections.

The most dominant characteristic of the Civil War realignment was the regional division of party strongholds, but considerable Republican vote strength was found throughout much of the South and Democratic strength in most of the North. Especially in the North, states that regularly cast their electoral votes for Republican presidential candidates did so by slim margins. Within each region persistent loyalty to the minority party was usually related to earlier opposition to the war. The intensity of feelings surrounding the war overwhelmed other issues, and the severity of the division over the war greatly inhibited the emergence of new issues along other lines. Thus a significant feature of the Civil War realignment is its "freezing" of the party system.[7] Although later realignments have occurred and a fourth and fifth party system can be identified, after the Civil War the same two parties have remained dominant. New parties have found it impossible to compete effectively (although they may affect electoral outcomes). The subsequent realignments changed only the competitive position of these two parties relative to each other. Thus, although the choices were frozen following the Civil War, the relative strength of the parties was not.

Toward the end of the nineteenth century, Civil War loyalties weakened enough to allow new parties, particularly the Populists in the Midwest and South, to make inroads into the votes of both major parties. Following the economic recession of 1893, for which the Democrats suffered politically, the Republican Party began to improve its basic voting strength. In 1896 the formation of a coalition of Democrats and Populists and the unsuccessful presidential candidacy of their nominee, William Jennings Bryan, resulted in increased Republican strength in the East and a further strengthening of the secure position of the Democratic Party in the South. Republican domination was solidified in the Midwest by the popularity of Theodore Roosevelt in the election of 1904. By the early twentieth century, competitive areas were confined to the border states and a few mountain states.

The realignment of 1896 and the fourth party system that followed are appropriately viewed as an adjustment of the Civil War alignment. Few areas shifted far from the previous levels of voting; most individuals probably did not change their partisanship. The issue basis of the alignment was economic. The Republicans advocated development and modernization while opposing regulation of economic activity. The Democrats supported policies intended to provide remedies for particular economic hardships. At a minimum these issues led the more prosperous, more modern areas in the North to shift toward the Republicans and the more backward, more depressed areas in the South to shift toward the Democrats. These tendencies are based on normal vote patterns and should not obscure the considerable variation in the vote for president during these years, particularly in the elections of 1912 and 1916.

Following the onset of the Great Depression in 1929 under a Republican president, Democrat Franklin D. Roosevelt rode the reaction to economic hardship to a landslide victory in 1932. In his first administration, Roosevelt launched a program of economic recovery and public assistance called the New Deal. The Democrats emerged as the majority party, signaling the start of the fifth party system. The New Deal realignment resulted in far greater shifts than the earlier realignment of 1896, because it moved many of the northern states from Republican to Democratic status. Because the policies of the Democratic administration during the New Deal appealed more to the working class than to the middle class, more to poor farmers than to prosperous farmers, these groups responded differently to Democratic candidates. The New Deal and the electorate's response to Roosevelt's administration considerably sharpened the social class basis of party support. Especially for younger voters during these years, class politics was of greater salience than it had been before or has been since.

This realignment resulted in adjustments in previous loyalties, but it did not override them completely. The New Deal coalition was based on regional strength in the South, which was independent of social class, and further reinforced an already overwhelming dominance in the region. The most incompatible elements in the New Deal coalition were southern middle-class whites, mainly conservative, and northern liberals, both white and black, and this incompatibility led to the later unraveling of the New Deal alignment. The disintegration of the New Deal coalition occurred first in presidential voting with the departure of southern white voters from the Democratic Party. In 1964 the states of the Deep South were the only states carried by Republican candidate Barry Goldwater, a stark reversal of one hundred years of history. This pattern continued for the next four decades. Only when the Democratic candidate was a southerner (Jimmy Carter in 1976 and Bill Clinton in 1992 and 1996) did the Democrats have a chance to carry some southern states. In 2000 Gore, also a southerner, was given a chance of winning only two southern states—Florida and his home state of Tennessee. Ultimately, he won neither. (Of course, he was running against another southerner, George W. Bush.) Obama's success in winning three southern states—Florida, North Carolina, and Virginia—in 2008 needs to be viewed against this recent history.

The departure of the South from the Democratic fold is the major reason for the end of the New Deal coalition. To a degree, working-class whites in the North also have been attracted to the Republican Party on occasion, and middle-class voters—particularly those in service professions—have shifted toward the Democrats.

Survey data on party identification over the past fifty years also yield evidence of the New Deal alignment, as well as its later deterioration (see Table 3-1). In the early years of this period, the advantage that the Democrats enjoyed nationwide was largely a result of having an overwhelming Democratic majority in the South, as shown in Table 3-2. The increased

TABLE 3-1 Party Identification of the Electorate, 1952–2008

Party identification	1952	1956	1960	1964	1968	1972	1976	1980	1984	1988	1992	1996	2000	2004	2008
Democrats	47%	44%	46%	51%	45%	40%	39%	41%	36%	35%	35%	38%	36%	32%	34%
Independents	22	24	23	22	29	35	36	35	34	36	38	32	42	38	40
Republicans	27	29	27	24	24	23	23	22	28	28	25	29	20	29	25
Nothing, don't know	4	3	4	2	2	2	2	2	2	2	2	1	2	2	1
Total	100%	100%	100%	99%	100%	100%	100%	100%	100%	101%	100%	100%	100%	101%	100%
(N)	(1,799)	(1,762)	(1,954)	(1,571)	(1,557)	(2,705)	(2,403)	(1,614)	(1,948)	(2,040)	(2,485)	(1,714)	(977)	(1,212)	(2,323)

Source: American National Election Studies, available at www.electionstudies.org.

TABLE 3-2 Party Identification of the Electorate for the Nation, the Non-South, and the South, 1952–2008

The Nation

	1952	1956	1960	1964	1968	1972	1976	1980	1984	1988	1992	1996	2000	2004	2008
Strong Democrats	22%	21%	20%	27%	20%	15%	15%	18%	17%	17%	18%	19%	19%	16%	19%
Weak Democrats	25	23	24	25	25	26	25	23	20	18	17	20	17	15	15
Independents	22	23	22	22	29	35	36	34	34	36	38	32	42	38	40
Weak Republicans	14	14	14	13	14	13	14	14	15	14	14	16	10	12	12
Strong Republicans	13	15	15	11	10	10	9	8	13	14	11	13	10	16	13
Apolitical, other	4	4	5	2	2	2	2	2	2	2	2	1	2	2	1
Total	100%	100%	100%	100%	100%	101%	101%	99%	101%	101%	100%	101%	100%	99%	100%
(N)	(1,799)	(1,762)	(1,954)	(1,571)	(1,557)	(2,705)	(2,872)	(1,614)	(1,989)	(2,040)	(2,485)	(1,714)	(977)	(1,212)	(2,323)

The Non-South

	1952	1956	1960	1964	1968	1972	1976	1980	1984	1988	1992	1996	2000	2004	2008
Strong Democrats	18%	17%	18%	23%	17%	13%	12%	15%	15%	16%	16%	17%	18%	15%	19%
Weak Democrats	22	19	20	23	24	22	22	22	18	16	17	20	17	14	17
Independents	26	26	25	25	28	37	38	37	33	36	39	32	44	42	40
Weak Republicans	16	16	16	16	17	16	17	14	17	16	15	17	11	12	13
Strong Republicans	17	18	17	12	12	12	10	9	14	15	12	14	9	16	10
Apolitical, other	2	2	4	1	1	1	2	2	2	2	1	1	1	1	1
Total	101%	98%	100%	100%	99%	101%	101%	99%	99%	101%	100%	101%	100%	100%	100%
(N)	(1,290)	(1,249)	(1,293)	(1,087)	(1,076)	(1,799)	(1,623)	(1,050)	(1,352)	(1,322)	(1,650)	(1,123)	(642)	(793)	(1,328)

The South

	1952	1956	1960	1964	1968	1972	1976	1980	1984	1988	1992	1996	2000	2004	2008
Strong Democrats	31%	29%	23%	36%	26%	17%	19%	23%	19%	21%	21%	22%	21%	18%	18%
Weak Democrats	32	32	33	30	28	32	30	25	23	21	18	19	15	19	12
Independents	14	15	17	15	30	29	32	29	35	35	37	32	38	32	39
Weak Republicans	8	9	8	8	8	10	11	13	11	10	12	14	10	13	12
Strong Republicans	6	8	12	8	4	9	7	7	9	11	9	13	12	17	17
Apolitical, other	9	9	6	3	2	2	2	3	3	2	3	0	4	2	1
Total	100%	102%	99%	100%	98%	99%	101%	100%	100%	100%	100%	100%	100%	101%	99%
(N)	(509)	(513)	(661)	(484)	(481)	(906)	(780)	(564)	(596)	(718)	(835)	(591)	(335)	(419)	(995)

Source: American National Election Studies, available at www.electionstudies.org.

strength of the Republicans in the South after 1964 led to a number of years of fairly even balance nationwide between Democrats and Republicans. Since 2006, the Democrats have gained an advantage over the Republicans, as Democrats increased their strength in the North.

Another important element in the breakup of the New Deal alignment, also reflected in these tables, was the increase beginning in 1966 in the proportion of independents. Supporters of George Wallace in the South represented part of this increase initially, but an even larger portion is composed of young voters who, since the early 1970s, have not chosen sides in politics as quickly as their elders did. The increase leveled off in the 1970s, and although the proportions have fluctuated, the number of independents remains near its highest point since the era of survey research began. The 42 percent independent in 2000 is the largest proportion of independents in the history of the American National Election Studies.

The New Deal partisan realignment established in the 1930s remained intact longer in congressional voting. However, by the 1970s additional shifts in the New Deal alignment became evident, as conservative Republicans began to show strength in races for other offices in many parts of the South. Long-standing southern Democratic incumbents in Congress were safe from competition. As they stepped down, though, their seats were won more often than not by Republicans. Conversely, in some areas of the North moderate Republicans were replaced by liberal Democrats. In the 2008 congressional elections, not one Republican was elected to the House of Representatives from New England. These trends are shown in Figure 3-6, plotting the Democratic vote for Congress in the North and South since 1936. Clearly, Democratic strength in the South was crucial for the Democrats' control of the House of Representatives for much of this historical period.

We should be clear about what is changing and what is not. White southerners have always been conservative, especially on matters concerning race. From the Civil War until the 1960s, the Democratic Party was at least as conservative as the Republican Party on the crucial issue of race. When the national Republican Party took the more conservative position on race in 1964, white southerners began to vote for Republican presidential candidates; they continued to vote for southern conservative Democratic candidates in state and local races. Meanwhile, for the same reasons in reverse, newly enfranchised black southern voters were moving into the Democratic Party. Over the years, the positions of the two parties have become more clearly distinguished—the Democratic Party as the more liberal party on racial as well as economic issues, the Republican Party as the more conservative party. Particularly in the South, voters have changed their partisanship

FIGURE 3-6   Democratic Vote for Congress, North and South, 1936–2008

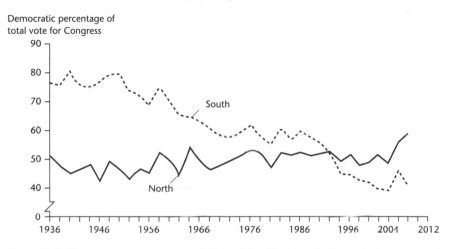

Democratic percentage of
total vote for Congress

Source: U.S. House of Representatives, Office of the Clerk, available at clerk.house.gov/ member_info/electionInfo/index.html.

and their votes accordingly. Figure 3-7, showing the party identification of white voters, North and South, from 1952 to 2008 shows the dramatic shift in the partisanship of white southerners over this period. The congressional elections of 1994 were perhaps the culmination of this process. When the Republicans took control of the House of Representatives and Senate, their leadership was predominantly southern.

Are Conditions Right for a Realignment?

The unraveling of the New Deal coalition is best seen, we believe, as a long process of dealignment.[8] Voter movement and electoral volatility have been in evidence since the 1960s. Furthermore, much of this movement has been a sorting-out process whereby some voters are finding their natural home in a political party that shares their views on issues that concern them most. Over this same time period, however, a sizable number of voters have found neither political party a congenial place and have chosen instead to become independent, not adopt a party identification in the first place, or support independent candidates such as Perot or, to a lesser extent, Nader. Through the 1990s, neither party was able to gather the political support to take firm control of government or complete initiatives that would appear to solve societal problems and win converts to their ranks. Bill Clinton perhaps had the opportunity to do so in 1993 when the House, Senate, and

FIGURE 3-7   Democratic Identification among Southern and Non-Southern
Whites, 1952–2008

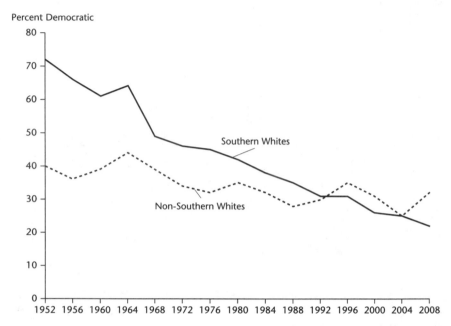

Source: American National Election Studies, available at www.electionstudies.org.

presidency were held by the Democrats. The opportunity was lost as his
health care initiative went down in defeat. The Republicans gained control of the House of Representatives in 1994—the first time in forty
years. For the remainder of that decade gridlock reigned in Washington, D.C., as the parties engaged in increasingly acrimonious battles
over the budget and Clinton's impeachment. The twenty-first century
began with a disputed election and an evenly divided and polarized
electorate. Control of the Senate depended on the allegiance of one
senator from Vermont who switched from Republican to independent.
Although the Republicans recaptured the Senate and retained the presidency and control of the House in 2004, the administration's foreign
policy faltered and the economy crashed. The number of citizens who
call themselves independent remains close to record highs.

Into this scenario rode a charismatic young candidate for president
who promised change and won election with the largest margin of victory in twenty-four years. His party increased the size of the majorities it
had recaptured in both houses of Congress in 2006, giving the new

administration control of all three branches of the federal government. Six months into the new Congress, the Democrats reached the magic number of sixty votes needed to shut off a filibuster in the Senate, after one switch of allegiance (Arlen Specter of Pennsylvania, who changed from Republican to Democratic) and one resolution to a long-running recount (Al Franken of Minnesota). Public opinion polls found fewer people who identify with the Republicans, and more identifying with the Democrats. The new administration took office amid great euphoria; sky-high approval ratings; and an ambitious agenda of health care reform, energy independence, stopping climate change, and restoring international respect and prestige. All the ingredients for a realignment were there—a crisis (or crises); an electorate willing to throw the rascals out; a pool of voters without affiliation to either party, available for conversion; and unified control of government, giving the new administration the ability, in principle, to enact its policy agenda. The opportunity is there for the new administration to capture the imagination of those available independents, turn them into Democrats, and change the partisan division in the country for the foreseeable future.

Perhaps.

As we contemplate this scenario, we need to keep in mind one further condition for a realignment—successful management of the crisis at hand, or at least the appearance of it. If the Obama administration is able to extricate the United States from Iraq, quell the turmoil in Afghanistan and Pakistan, keep the homeland safe from terrorism, resurrect the economy, and provide health care reform without destroying the budget—or appear to be making progress on all these fronts—the Democratic Party may come to enjoy a partisan advantage for many years. If his administration fails to deliver some semblance of success, however, we will likely look back at 2008 as another zig or zag in a continuing era of dealignment.

After the 2004 presidential election one might have said very similar things about the prospects for the Republicans. (In fact, we did.) In 2004 the Republicans widened their majority in the Senate and George W. Bush claimed the mandate of a popularly elected president that he had been denied in 2000. The Republicans achieved the unified control of government that gave them the opportunity to put into effect the initiatives that—if perceived as successful—could win converts to their party from the large pool of self-identified independents and produce a Republican majority for the future. In no time at all, however, that support unraveled—over Iraq, Hurricane Katrina, the use of torture on detainees, and various other perceived failings. The idea of a Republican realignment was put off for another time.

Notes

1. The most important work on party identification is in Angus Campbell, Philip E. Converse, Warren E. Miller, and Donald E. Stokes, *The American Voter* (New York: Wiley, 1960), 120–167. For an updated treatment, see Michael S. Lewis-Beck, William G. Jacoby, Helmut Norpoth, and Herbert F. Weisberg, *The American Voter Revisited* (Ann Arbor: University of Michigan Press, 2008), chaps. 6 and 7.
2. For the most important statement of these ideas, see Philip E. Converse, "The Concept of a Normal Vote," in *Elections and the Political Order*, ed. Angus Campbell, Philip E. Converse, Warren E. Miller, and Donald E. Stokes (New York: Wiley, 1966), 9–39.
3. This discussion and data presentation are based on our earlier work in William H. Flanigan and Nancy H. Zingale, "The Measurement of Electoral Change," *Political Methodology* 1 (summer 1974): 49–82.
4. This and most discussions of the classification of elections are based on the work of V. O. Key and Angus Campbell. See V. O. Key, "A Theory of Critical Elections," *Journal of Politics* 17 (1955): 3–18; and Angus Campbell, "A Classification of Presidential Elections," in *Elections and the Political Order*, ed. Angus Campbell, Philip E. Converse, Warren E. Miller, and Donald E. Stokes (New York: Wiley, 1966), 63–77.
5. This and the following discussion draw heavily on Jerome M. Clubb, William H. Flanigan, and Nancy H. Zingale, *Partisan Realignment: Voters, Parties, and Government in American History* (Boulder, Colo.: Westview Press, 1990). See especially chaps. 5 and 8.
6. See, for example, William N. Chambers and Walter Dean Burnham, eds., *The American Party Systems: Stages of Political Development* (New York: Oxford University Press, 1975).
7. This concept was developed by Seymour Martin Lipset and Stein Rokkan in their discussion of the development of the European party systems in *Party Systems and Voter Alignments* (New York: Free Press, 1967), 1–64.
8. Some analysts have argued that the movement of white southerners into the Republican Party and that of blacks and some northern whites into the Democratic Party constitutes a realignment and should be regarded as the start of a new party system. Disagreement arises about when this realignment occurred. Some date it from the 1960s, with the start of Republican dominance in presidential voting; others view it as a Reagan realignment of the 1980s.

Suggested Readings

Beck, Paul Allen. "The Dealignment Era in America." In *Electoral Change in Advanced Industrial Democracies: Realignment or Dealignment?* ed. Russell J. Dalton, Scott C. Flanagan, and Paul Allen Beck. Princeton: Princeton University Press, 1984. A good survey of post-1960s politics as an example of dealignment.

Burnham, Walter Dean. *Critical Elections and the Mainsprings of American Politics*. New York: W. W. Norton, 1970. An early, important statement of the electoral realignment perspective.

Campbell, Angus, Philip E. Converse, Warren E. Miller, and Donald E. Stokes. *The American Voter*. New York: Wiley, 1960. The classic study of public opinion and voting behavior in the United States.

Clubb, Jerome M., William H. Flanigan, and Nancy H. Zingale. *Partisan Realignment: Voters, Parties, and Government in American History.* Boulder, Colo.: Westview Press, 1990. A conceptualization of realignments that emphasizes both electoral behavior and political leadership.

Converse, Philip E. "The Concept of a Normal Vote." In *Elections and the Political Order,* ed. Angus Campbell, Philip E. Converse, Warren E. Miller, and Donald E. Stokes. New York: Wiley, 1966. This chapter established the role of party identification as a baseline for the analysis of vote choice.

Lewis-Beck, Michael S., William G. Jacoby, Helmut Norpoth, and Herbert F. Weisberg. *The American Voter Revisited.* Ann Arbor: University of Michigan Press, 2008. A rich reanalysis of the themes from the classic work using mainly 2000 and 2004 data.

MacKuen, Michael B., Robert S. Erikson, and James A. Stimson. "Macropartisanship." *American Political Science Review* 83 (December 1989): 1125–1142. A sophisticated analysis of trends in aggregate party identification, arguing that the sizable amount of instability undermines the realignment perspective.

Mayhew, David. *Electoral Realignments: A Critique of an American Genre.* New Haven: Yale University Press, 2002. A review and critique of the analytic approaches to realignments.

Internet Resources

The Web site of the American National Election Studies, www.electionstudies .org, has basic information on partisanship and party identification. Click on "Guide to Public Opinion," and then click on "Partisanship and Evaluation of the Political Parties." For information on partisan voting patterns, click on "Vote Choice."

During election years news organizations may have Web sites with election statistics in historical depth. A site with extensive historical data is David Leip's Atlas of U.S. Presidential Elections, available at www.uselectionatlas.org.

chapter four

Partisans and Partisan Change

PARTISANSHIP is a useful concept for tracing the dynamics of American political history. It is also crucial for understanding the political behavior of individuals. We begin this chapter by examining the impact of having—or not having—a party identification on the way people respond to politics. We then turn to the question of partisan change, looking first at change in individuals' partisanship over their lifetimes and then at changes across generations.

Voting Behavior

The standard party identification question, used in almost all political surveys, asks respondents whether they are Republicans, Democrats, or independents, and whether they are "strong" or "not very strong" Republicans or Democrats. The likelihood of voting loyally in support of one party varies with the strength of individuals' partisanship. The defection rates of strong and weak (not very strong) partisans in each presidential election since 1952 are shown in Figure 4-1. Declining party loyalty is apparent as the intensity of partisanship decreases. Strong partisans consistently support the candidate of their party at higher rates than do weak partisans. (In most years Republicans have been more loyal to their party than Democrats, although this is partly accounted for by southern Democrats who regularly deserted their party in presidential elections. By the end of the twentieth century, southern Democrats were no longer distinctive in this regard; previously defecting Democrats had become independents or Republicans.)

Differences in candidate appeal affect the propensity to defect. Few Republicans deserted Dwight D. Eisenhower in the 1950s, Richard M. Nixon in 1972, or Ronald Reagan in 1984; many more left Barry

FIGURE 4-1   Defection Rates by Party Identifiers in Presidential Voting,
1952–2008

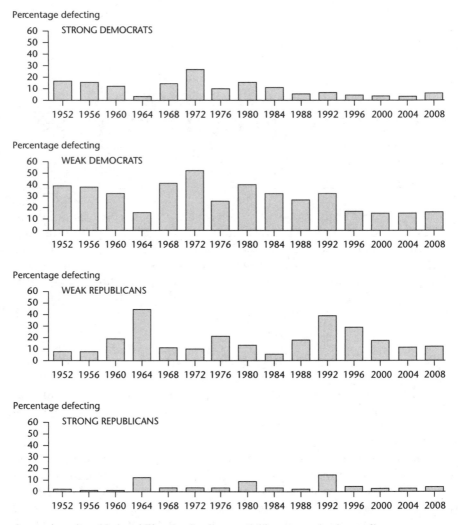

Source: American National Election Studies, available at www.electionstudies.org.

Goldwater in 1964. Similarly, most Democrats were loyal to Lyndon B. Johnson in 1964 but abandoned George McGovern in large numbers in 1972.

Another potential cause of defection is attractive third-party candidates. In 1992 Ross Perot drew defectors from both parties, although more from the Republican side. Ten percent of strong Republicans and 25 percent of weak Republicans defected to Perot. Although few strong

Democrats defected to Perot, 17 percent of the weak Democrats did. John B. Anderson in 1980 and George C. Wallace in 1968 similarly account for part of the upsurges in defections in those years.

Historically, third-party candidates often have been viewed as "halfway houses" for partisans moving from one party to another. Not as dramatic for a partisan as defection to the opposition party, a vote for such a candidate may be a first step away from party loyalty. In any event, support for third parties and an increase in defection rates have generally been symptomatic of the loosening of party ties in a dealignment.

A different pattern—one of high party loyalty on both sides—was exhibited in the presidential elections of 1976, 1988, 1996, 2000, and 2004. In these elections partisans of both parties remained loyal to candidates who were relatively balanced in their appeal. Contrary to much speculation before the election in 2008, both Barack Obama and John McCain held onto their partisan bases very effectively. In the twenty-first century, the high degree of loyalty is also a reflection of partisan polarization.[1]

Although strong partisans vary in their loyalty from year to year depending on the candidates offered by their party, this tendency is much more pronounced among weak partisans. For example, the defection rate of strong Republicans falls in a narrow range from around 2 percent in a good Republican year to 10 percent in a bad year. In contrast, weak Republicans are almost as loyal as strong Republicans when an attractive Republican candidate is on the ticket, but nearly 50 percent defected in the disastrous 1964 election. The behavior of Democrats is similar, although both strong and weak Democrats are more likely to desert their party than are Republicans. Clearly, marked departures from the expected vote of a party are accomplished by wooing away the weaker partisans of the opposite party.

The tendency of both strong and weak partisans to vote according to their party identification becomes even more pronounced as one moves down the ticket to less-visible and less-publicized offices. This is a product of the dominant two-party system nationwide. Even highly successful third-party or independent candidates down the ticket are merely local disruptions that have virtually no impact on national patterns. The voting behavior of partisans in congressional races since 1952 differs from the presidential data in two significant ways (see Figure 4-2). First, differences between the party loyalty of strong and weak partisans are usually smaller, although this was not true in 2008. Second, the defection rate does not fluctuate from year to year nearly as much as in the presidential elections, particularly among weak partisans. Both differences are attributable to the lower visibility of congressional races. In a presidential election, the flood of available information means that a particularly attractive candidate or a stirring issue may touch the

FIGURE 4-2   Defection Rates by Party Identifiers in Congressional Voting,
1952–2008

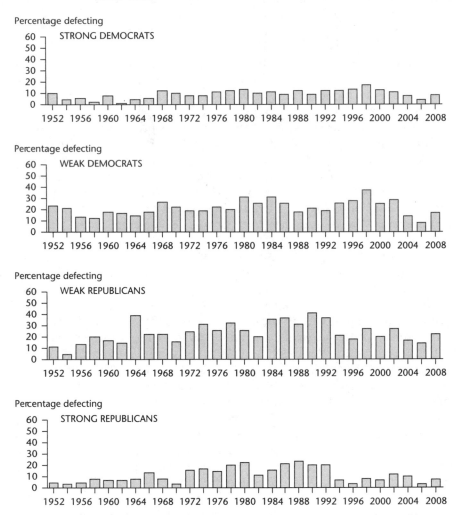

Sources: American National Election Studies, available at www.electionstudies.org; 2006 data from Pew Research Center, November 2006 Post-Election Survey, available at people-press.org.

consciousness of the weak partisans, causing them to defect from traditional party ties; the firmly attached, strong partisans are more likely to resist. In the less-publicized congressional races, the information that might cause weak partisans to defect is less likely to even reach them. In the absence of information about the candidates and issues, weak partisans vote their party identification.

In congressional voting, unlike presidential voting, Democrats were regularly more party loyal than were Republicans until 1994. This was both cause and effect of the recent disjuncture of national politics, whereby Republicans were stronger in presidential politics and Democrats dominated in congressional politics. Throughout the 1970s and 1980s the Republicans were able to field more attractive presidential candidates than the Democrats, leading more Democratic partisans to defect in presidential races. In contrast, congressional races saw Republican partisans often defecting to vote for a long-term Democratic incumbent running against token Republican opposition. The situation changed dramatically in 1994, when the Republicans gained control of the House of Representatives in large part by fanning the flames of anti-incumbent, anti-Democratic sentiment. Thereafter, with more Republican incumbents for whom to vote, Republican partisans were noticeably more party loyal than they had been in previous congressional elections. The uptick in Republican defections in 2008 is probably attributable to the Democrats' return to the majority in the House of Representatives in 2006 and the pro-Democratic tide in 2008. (The similar uptick in Democratic defections is harder to explain.)

The intensity of partisanship affects political behavior beyond its influence on the likelihood of voting for or defecting from a party's candidate. Strong partisans are also more likely to vote in all kinds of elections than are either weak partisans or independents. In fact, one explanation sometimes offered for the low turnout in the late twentieth century was the declining partisanship of the American public.[2] The turnout rates of the various categories of partisans and independents for three types of elections—presidential, off-year congressional, and primary—are illustrated in Figure 4-3. Presidential primaries, despite all their accompanying publicity and frenetic campaigning, typically have a lower average turnout than off-year congressional elections. Turnout declines in all categories as the presumed importance of the race decreases, but the rate is much steeper among the less partisan. As a result, the less salient the election, the more the electorate will be dominated by the intense partisans, who are also less likely to defect from party ties in casting their ballots.

These ideas led Angus Campbell to suggest an intriguing theory of electoral change to explain the often observed phenomenon in American politics whereby the party winning the presidency almost always loses seats in the legislature in the next congressional election.[3] Because, the argument goes, presidential elections are usually accompanied by a high level of interest, large numbers of weak partisans and independents are drawn to the polls. Because weak partisans and independents are more easily shifted from one party to another, they add

FIGURE 4-3   Voting by Partisans and Independents in Presidential, Congressional, and Presidential Primary Elections

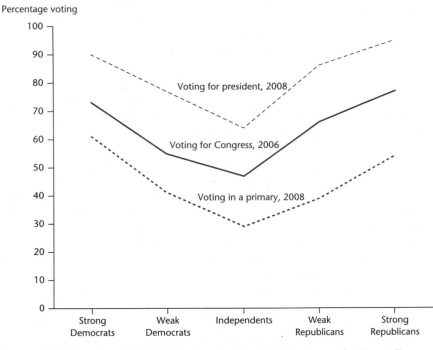

Sources: 2008 American National Election Study, available at www.electionstudies.org; 2006 data from Pew Research Center, November 2006 Post-Election Survey, available at people-press.org.

disproportionately to the vote for one presidential candidate, usually the winner. In congressional elections these less-committed voters do not turn out, whereas relatively large numbers of intense partisans do. The strong party identifiers are not so likely to shift their vote away from their party. As a consequence, support declines in off-year congressional elections for the party that won the previous presidential election with disproportionately large numbers of less-interested voters.

Persuasive as Campbell's argument may be, it rests on some assumptions that may be questionable. First, it assumes that high-stimulus elections will be landslides—that is, it assumes that the short-term forces bringing the less-interested voter to the polls will work to the advantage of only one candidate. Even though this has often been the case, and it appears to have been so in 2008, it is not invariable. The extremely close 1960 presidential election, with its emphasis on the religion (Catholicism) of Democratic candidate John F. Kennedy, was a high-turnout election, but different groups of voters were affected in different ways.

Similarly, both George W. Bush and John Kerry benefited from the high turnout in 2004.

Second, Campbell's argument suggests that the less-interested voters who come to the polls to vote for the attractive presidential candidate will also vote for that party's candidate in congressional elections. In fact, the evidence shows that in many cases weak partisans who defect in presidential elections return to their own party in congressional elections or, in the case of Perot voters in 1992 and 1996, have no congressional candidates on the same ticket for whom to vote. In addition, independents often split their tickets instead of voting for the congressional candidate of the same party as their presidential choice. To some extent, the argument also rests on the assumption that independents are not only less partisan but also less informed, concerned, and interested in politics, a view that is frequently called into question.

Are Independents Apolitical?

Independents, who now account for more than one-third of the national electorate, are the most obvious source of additional votes for either party. Although partisans, especially weak partisans, sometimes abandon their party, year after year independents are the largest bloc of uncommitted voters available to both parties. Indeed, in the current closely divided electorate, the vote of the independents can easily determine the outcome of an election.

The independents' capacity for shifting back and forth between the major parties is shown in Table 4-1. Each party has, on occasion, successfully appealed to the independents, winning over a large majority to its side. In 1984 the independents voted almost two to one for Reagan over Walter F. Mondale, and Johnson held a similar advantage over Goldwater in 1964. During the years in which the Democrats had a clear advantage in partisan identifiers, Republicans had to win a healthy majority of the independent vote even to stay in close contention. This was the case in the elections of 1976 (Jimmy Carter versus Gerald R. Ford) and 1960 (Kennedy versus Nixon). The election of George W. Bush in 2000 depended on, among other things, the substantial advantage he enjoyed over Al Gore among independents. Bush's reelection in 2004 was a different story as Democratic candidate Kerry handily carried the independent vote.[4] Obama matched Kerry's appeal to independent voters in 2008.

Third-party or independent candidates find unaffiliated voters a major source of votes. In 1992, 27 percent of the independents voted for Perot. His failure to hold those votes in 1996 turned his earlier, impressive showing into a minor story. In 1968 more than 20 percent of the

TABLE 4-1   The Distribution of Votes for President by Independents, 1948–2008

	1948	1952	1956	1960	1964	1968	1972	1976	1980	1984	1988	1992	1996	2000	2004	2008
Democratic	57%	33%	27%	46%	66%	32%	33%	45%	26%	34%	46%	42%	49%	43%	55%	56%
Republican	43	67	73	54	34	47	65	55	56	66	53	30	37	50	40	40
George C. Wallace[a]						21										
John G. Schmitz[b]							2									
John B. Anderson[c]									14							
Ross Perot[d]												27	14			
Pat Buchanan[e]														1		
Ralph Nader[f]														6	1	
Other									4		2				4	4
Total	100%	100%	100%	100%	100%	100%	100%	100%	100%	100%	101%	99%	100%	100%	100%	100%
(N)	—	(263)	(309)	(298)	(219)	(228)	(908)	(532)	(306)	(334)	(364)	(573)	(304)	(194)	(255)	(519)

Source: American National Election Studies, available at www.electionstudies.org.

[a]American Independent Party candidate in 1968.
[b]American Party candidate in 1972.
[c]Independent candidate in 1980.
[d]Independent candidate in 1992 and 1996.
[e]Reform Party candidate in 2000.
[f]Green Party candidate in 2000, independent candidate in 2004. (Combined with "other" in 2008.)

independents gave their votes to Wallace; and in 1980, 14 percent voted for Anderson. Put another way, more than half of a third-party candidate's votes typically come from independents. Furthermore, independents may shift dramatically in voting for president and remain stable in voting for Congress.

On what basis do independents make their vote choices? Two views of independents have competed for popularity. The civics textbook view is of an intelligent, informed, dispassionate evaluator of candidates and issues who, after careful consideration, votes for "the person, not the party." An alternate view—often attributed to campaign strategists—is of an uninformed and uninterested voter on whom intelligent, issue-oriented appeals and reasoned debate would be lost.

To pursue the analysis of independents, we need to make two distinctions that have not intruded on the discussion to this point. We will note these distinctions and then drop them because they complicate the analysis and are usually ignored. First, important differences exist between nonpartisans who identify themselves as independents and those who lack any political identification. A sizable segment of the electorate answers the party identification question by saying that they identify themselves as nothing or that they do not know what they are. According to the coding conventions used by the American National Election Studies, most nonidentifiers are included with the independents, but important conceptual distinctions may exist between them and self-identified independents.[5] The two types of nonpartisans are highlighted in the box in Table 4-2. Those in one set identify themselves as *independents;* the others do not think of themselves in terms of political

TABLE 4-2 Party Identifiers, Self-Identified Independents, and People Claiming No Preference, 1968–2008

	1968	1972	1976	1980	1984	1988	1992	1996	2000	2004	2008
Identify with a party	69%	64%	64%	64%	64%	63%	60%	66%	57%	61%	59%
Identify as independents	27	28	30	24	25	31	32	26	29	33	33
Have no preference	3	8	5	12	10	6	7	8	13	5	6
Don't know	a	0	a	0	0	0	1	a	1	1	1
Not ascertained	a	a	1	a	1	a	a	a	a	a	1
Total	99%	100%	100%	100%	100%	100%	100%	100%	100%	100%	100%
(N)	(1,557)	(2,702)	(1,320)	(1,614)	(1,989)	(2,040)	(2,485)	(1,714)	(981)	(1,212)	(2,323)

Source: American National Election Studies, available at www.electionstudies.org.

[a]Less than 0.5 percent.

labels. Since 1972, between about one-sixth and one-third of the non-partisans failed to identify themselves as independents. Even though the electorate generally has become more nonpartisan, it is not necessarily more independent. These situations present different implications for the political parties. Self-identified independents think of themselves as having a political identity and are somewhat antiparty in orientation. The nonidentifying nonpartisans have a less clear self-image of themselves as political actors, but they are not particularly hostile to the political parties. They are less self-consciously political in many ways.

Second, within the large group of people who do not identify with either the Democratic or the Republican Party are many who say they "lean toward" one or the other. These leaners make up two-thirds of all nonpartisans, and they complicate analysis in a significant way. On crucial attitudes and in important forms of political behavior, the leaning independents appear partisan. Independents who lean toward the Democratic Party behave somewhat like weak Democratic partisans, and independents who lean toward the Republican Party behave like weak Republicans.[6] As can be seen in Figure 4-4, independent leaners are more similar to weak partisans than strong and weak partisans are to each other.

How appropriate, then, is it to include all independents in one category? On some characteristics, such as ideological self-identification and interest in public affairs, much more variation is evident within the three independent categories than between the several partisan categories. The differences between leaners and pure independents are often greater than those among Republicans or Democrats. Because the concept of "independent" embraces these three dissimilar groups, there is little wonder that some disagreement exists over what the true independent is like.

As a consequence of including various types of people under the label "independent," making generalizations about the degree of political interest and information of independents is difficult. Some independents have considerable interest in politics, and others are apathetic. There are more informed, concerned voters among the leaning independents than among other nonpartisans, and the leaning independents are more likely to register and to vote. So are independents attentive or apathetic toward politics? The answer is, they are both.

To the student of contemporary American politics, these characteristics of the independent remain important because they determine the independent's susceptibility to political appeals. We and others have argued that the American electoral system is presently at a time when a fairly large group of potential voters has weak ties to the political parties. The argument is that, when a large portion of the electorate is either independent or exhibits more independent behavior, these

FIGURE 4-4   Percentage of Turnout, High Interest, and Democratic Vote for
President by Partisanship, 2008

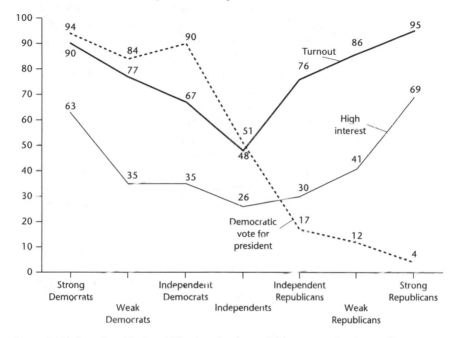

Source: 2008 American National Election Study, available at www.electionstudies.org.

people form a pool of potential recruits for one of the parties or a new
party. Between 2006 and 2008, anti-Bush and pro-Obama sentiment
combined to move some previous independents to begin calling themselves Democrats, at the same time moving some Republicans into the
independent category.

Partisan Change

Partisanship can be thought of as a basic attitude that establishes a
normal or expected vote, an estimate about how individuals or populations will vote, other things being equal. However, partisanship itself is
not unchangeable. Individuals may change not only their vote but also
their long-term party identification from one party to another. More
important, over extended periods of time the partisan composition of
the electorate may be altered as new voters of one political persuasion
replace older voters of another. When the basic partisan division of the
electorate changes, a partisan realignment occurs.

In the past the absence of survey data limited analysis of realignments, but during the current period the individual processes of partisan change that underlie aggregate shifts in the partisan division of the electorate can be studied. These processes have been a matter of some controversy. One perspective holds that individual partisans are *converted* from one party to the other during a realignment. Other analysts, noting the psychological difficulty in changing long-held and deeply felt attachments, argue that such change probably comes about through *mobilization,* not conversion. In other words, the independents or nonpolitical individuals, perhaps predominantly young voters just entering the electorate without strong partisan attachments, fuel a realignment by joining the electorate overwhelmingly on the side of one party.

Some evidence on these points comes from the New Deal era. Although survey research was then in its infancy, some scholars have creatively used data from early surveys to try to answer these questions. Research by Kristi Andersen, reported in *The Changing American Voter,* reveals high levels of nonvoting and nonpartisanship among young people and new citizens before the Great Depression.[7] Those uninvolved, uncommitted potential participants entered the electorate in the 1930s disproportionately as Democrats. Andersen's findings on the electorate of the 1920s and 1930s support the view that realignments are based on the mobilization of new, independent voters instead of on the conversion of partisans. In contrast, Robert S. Erikson and Kent L. Tedin argue on the basis of early Gallup Poll data that much of the increase in the Democratic vote in the 1930s came from voters who had previously voted Republican.[8]

In the next section we will examine the processes of partisan change in the contemporary period. Although we are in a better position to do so than we were for earlier eras, efforts are still hampered by a scarcity of panel data—that is, repeated interviews with the same individuals at different times. In most cases it will be necessary to infer individual changes from the behavior of different individuals over time.

Changes in Individuals over a Lifetime

Two types of change in partisan identification can be distinguished, both of which have significant implications for political behavior. First, an individual may change from one party to another or to independent, or from independence to partisanship. Such change is important if a large proportion of the electorate shifts in the same direction at about the same time. Second, an individual's partisanship may strengthen or weaken in intensity. A long-standing hypothesis states that the longer individuals identify with a party the stronger their partisanship will become.[9] In the electorate as a whole, the two types of change are not necessarily related to one another, so the occurrence of one form of change does not dictate or prevent the other. For example, recent decades saw an increase in the number of independents in the electorate, which can be accounted for by young people not choosing a party, or by partisans moving to independence, or both. At the same time, the remaining partisans have become more firmly committed and more party loyal, and polarization between the parties has increased.

Analysts have attempted to explain partisan change by referring to three types of causal effects: (1) *period effects,* or the impact of a particular historical period that briefly affects partisanship across all age groups; (2) a *generation effect,* which affects the partisanship of a particular age group for the remainder of their political lives; and (3) a *life-cycle effect,* which produces changes associated with an individual's age. In current political behavior all three can be illustrated: a period effect that resulted in increased independence in all age groups, a generation effect that keeps Democratic partisan loyalty high in the generation that entered the electorate during the New Deal, and a life-cycle effect that yields greater independence among the young than among their elders.

The difference between 1958, 1968, 1988, and 2008 in the proportion of independents in various age groups is shown in Figure 4-5.

FIGURE 4-5   Distribution of Independents, by Age Cohorts, 1958, 1968, 1988, and 2008

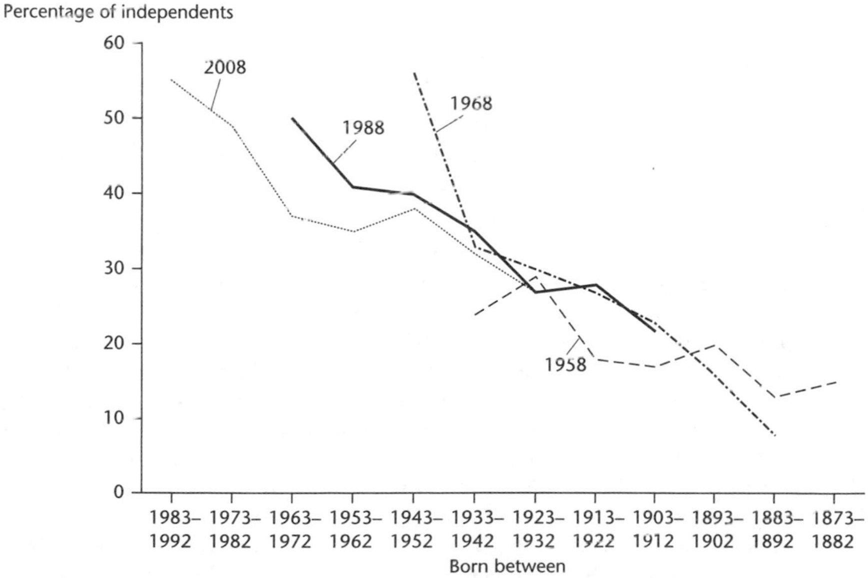

Source: American National Election Studies, available at www.electionstudies.org.

Note: The youngest cohort in each year includes only those old enough to vote.

The dotted line represents the percentage of independents in each age group in 2008, the solid line represents 1988, and the broken line represents 1968. The left end of each line reflects a higher rate of independence among the young in 1968, 1988, and 2008 when compared with 1958, the dashed line.

Each line reveals a downward slope to the right. This indicates that older individuals in each year were less likely to be independents compared with younger people in the same year (a life-cycle effect). By looking at the first point on the left of each line, the youngest respondents can be compared in each of the four years; the second point represents the second youngest group; and so on. In general, the cohorts in the 1988 and 2008 surveys have higher levels of political independence at each age than the cohorts from the 1968 and 1958 surveys (a generation effect). (An exception is the youngest cohort in 1968, who were themselves the first wave of the new, more independent generation.)

The change in particular age cohorts also can be examined using Figure 4-5.* The youngest cohort in 1968 was more than forty years old in 1988 and reveals a lower level of independence (40 percent) than it did when entering the electorate (56 percent). By 2008 the cohort was more than sixty years old and had stayed about the same in its level of independence (37 percent). At each point along the lines, the vertical distance represents an age cohort and shows the changing percentage of independents in that age cohort. Most age cohorts became more independent before 1980 and did not change much after that. This is a period effect.

Contrary to political folklore, little evidence exists that people become Republicans as they grow older—that is, that a life-cycle effect favors Republicans. Older members of the electorate were, for some years, more likely to be Republicans than younger members. The generation of young people who came of age before the Great Depression contained large proportions of Republicans, an understandable situation

---

* In the absence of repeated observations of the same individuals over time, studying many aspects of change is impossible. The use of age cohorts is an analytical technique that attempts to assess individual change through the use of surveys of different individuals over the years. Individuals of a certain age are isolated in an early survey—say thirty- to forty-year-olds in 1960—and they are compared with forty- to fifty-year-olds from a 1970 survey. Thus an age cohort can be compared at two different times. This technique has been used in several studies of partisanship. See, for example, Paul R. Abramson, "Generational Change in American Electoral Behavior," *American Political Science Review* 68 (March 1974): 93–105; David Butler and Donald Stokes, *Political Change in Britain: Forces Shaping Electoral Choice* (New York: St. Martin's Press, 1969), especially chaps. 3 and 11; and Philip E. Converse, *The Dynamics of Party Support: Cohort-Analyzing Party Identification* (Beverly Hills, Calif.: Sage Publications, 1976).

given the advantage the Republicans enjoyed nationally at that time. Relatively few members of this generation changed partisanship over the years, and these individuals constituted the older, more heavily Republican segment of the electorate. By the same token, the generation that entered the electorate during the New Deal was disproportionately Democratic. Because they also remained stable in partisanship, older voters looked increasingly Democratic as this generation aged.

The tendency of individual partisanship to strengthen with age is the subject of some controversy.[10] During periods of stable party voting, increased partisanship is likely the longer individuals identify with and vote for their party. In a multiwave panel study by M. Kent Jennings, the proportion of respondents who called themselves "strong Democrats" or "strong Republicans" increased from 15 percent in 1973 (when the respondents were about twenty-five years old) to 26 percent in 1997 (when they were around fifty).[11]

However, when party voting is frequently disrupted, this reinforcement of partisanship may not occur. Even if the strength of partisanship does not increase with age, older partisans are less likely to abandon their party and become independents. This explains in part why older partisans are less likely to vote for independent or third-party candidates than are younger partisans. In 1992, 19 percent of the Republican and Democratic partisans aged twenty-five and younger voted for Perot, but only 11 percent of partisans aged forty-five and older voted for him. In 2000 Nader's vote, although small, was greatest among the young.

Gradual changes in individual partisanship have not been assessed satisfactorily for the entire public because the few election studies based on repeated interviews of the same individuals have covered at most four years. Nevertheless, the possibility that individuals change their partisanship over longer time periods is of considerable interest. Speculation has focused on the possibility that the large number of young independents will become identified with one party or the other, thus creating a substantial shift in the overall partisan balance of the electorate. Obama's appeal to young people makes this appear a current possibility.

The best evidence of this type of change in the past comes from a major study of political socialization conducted by M. Kent Jennings. He surveyed a national sample of high school students and their parents in 1965, with follow-up interviews in 1973, 1982, and 1997.[12] This study provides a before-and-after picture of young people during the political traumas of the late 1960s and early 1970s, as well as later snapshots after a more quiescent period.

Table 4-3 shows the amount of change in partisanship between each wave of the study. As can be seen by looking at the highlighted cells, partisanship was least stable when the respondents were youngest,

TABLE 4-3   Stability and Change of Partisanship, 1965–1997

		1973					1982		
		Dem.	Ind.	Rep.			Dem.	Ind.	Rep.
	Dem.	24	14	3		Dem.	23	9	3
1965	Ind.	7	24	5	1973	Ind.	8	32	7
	Rep.	3	9	10		Rep.	2	4	13
	Total = 99%		N = 952			Total = 101%		N = 924	

		1997		
		Dem.	Ind.	Rep.
	Dem.	23	7	2
1982	Ind.	5	27	5
	Rep.	4	10	17
	Total = 100%		N = 896	

Source: Youth-Parent Socialization Panel Study, 1965–1997, Youth Wave. Data provided by Inter-university Consortium for Political and Social Research.

Note: Dem. = Democrat; Ind. = Independent; Rep. = Republican. The highlighted cells (along the diagonal) represent those individuals who remained stable in their partisanship from one time period to the next. The off-diagonal cells represent individuals who changed their partisan identification.

between 1965 and 1973. About two-thirds of the sample reported the same partisanship when interviewed in 1982 as in 1973 and, again, between 1982 and 1997. Most of the changes that did occur were between partisanship and independence; relatively few reported switching from Democrat to Republican or vice versa.

Changes across Generations

A shift in the partisan composition of the electorate owing to generational change is ordinarily a gradual one, because political attitudes, including partisanship, tend to be transmitted from parents to their children. Normally, more than two-thirds of the electorate identify with their parents' party if both parents had the same party identification. Adoption of parents' partisanship by their children is consistent with the notion of family socialization. Children pick up the partisanship of their parents while young, but the parents' influence diminishes as the child comes into contact with other political and social influences

FIGURE 4-6   Party Identification of High School Seniors and Their
                      Parents, 1965

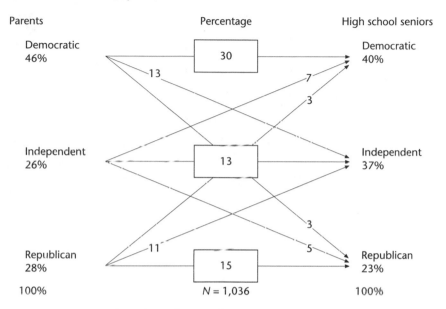

Source: Adapted from Paul A. Beck, Jere W. Bruner, and L. Douglas Dobson, *Political Socialization* (Washington, D.C.: American Political Science Association, 1974), 22.

Note: On the left of the figure is the distribution of the parents' party identification and on the right is their children's. The numbers in the three boxes highlight the percentages of the children who had the same party identification as their parents. The numbers on the remaining arrows show various amounts of change from their parents' partisanship by the children. For example, 7 percent of the total number of children had independent parents but became Democrats.

during the teenage years. For most individuals the political influence of their surroundings will be consistent with their family's political leanings, so the similarity between parents' and offspring's partisanship remains strong. In contrast, people who remember their parents as having conflicting loyalties are more likely to be independents than either Democrats or Republicans. This is even more true of the children of parents without any partisan attachments. Thus in each political generation a sizable number of voters lacks an inherited party loyalty.

The Jennings study also permits the examination of the process of generational change because it allows a comparison of party identification for parents and their children. As can be seen in Figure 4-6, 58 percent of the seventeen-year-olds in 1965 had adopted the party

FIGURE 4-7   Party Identification of High School Seniors and Their
Parents, 1997

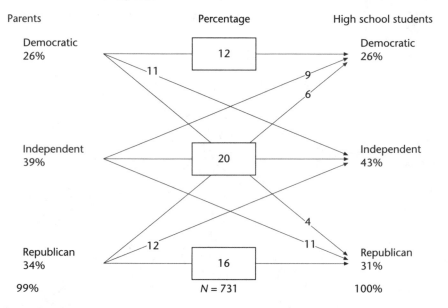

Source: Youth-Parent Socialization Panel Study, 1965–1997, Youth Wave. Data provided by Inter-university Consortium for Political and Social Research.

identification of their parents. Of the high school seniors, 30 percent were Democratic and came from Democratic families. Another 10 percent of the seniors were Democratic but came from independent or Republican families. Although not explicitly shown in Figure 4-6, Democrats had a somewhat higher transmission rate than either Republicans or independents. Despite the higher transmission rate, there were so many more Democratic parents that their children also contributed substantial numbers to the independent ranks.

The latest wave of the Jennings study allows an examination of generational change in a more recent time, by comparing the partisanship of the 1965 high school seniors, now parents, with the partisanship of their high school–age children (see Figure 4-7). (Not all the original 1965 students had children of that age in 1997, so the focus is on only a subset of those in the original sample reinterviewed in 1997. Therefore the distribution of partisanship of these parents will not be the same as for the whole 1997 sample covered in Table 4-3. The group of parents is somewhat less Democratic and more Republican than the full group.) Figure 4-7 suggests that parents transmitted their partisanship to their children at a lower rate in the 1990s than they had a generation earlier.

Hidden in these numbers, however, are traces of a modest recovery in partisanship. Unlike 1965, the younger generation is only slightly more independent than the parents, and the number of children leaving their parents' parties for independence is about equally offset by the children of independents adopting a partisanship. In 1965 twice as many children opted for independence as moved toward partisanship.

The Future of Parties and Partisanship

Since the 1970s some political observers have commented on the weakness of political parties, citing especially the overall increase in independents and the appeal of independent candidates, such as Anderson in 1980 or Perot in 1992 and 1996. These factors, combined with declines in trust and confidence in government, turnout, and attention to political news, have suggested to some that the American public has lost its capacity to identify with political parties in a meaningful way. A corollary would suggest there would likely never be another realignment because political parties would not be able to attract new partisans to their camps.

A contrary point of view argues that many of these trends slowed or stopped in the late 1970s, that partisan stability and party loyal behavior since then have been nearly as high as in the 1950s. Analysts cite increases in party-line voting in Congress, sharper ideological division between the parties, and an increase in uncivil political discourse in the mass media and in Congress as evidence of the increased commitment to, as well as the polarization of, political parties.

So is partisanship becoming stronger or weaker? It seems to us that both these phenomena are occurring—in different parts of the electorate. On the one hand, among political elites and party activists, the polarization and hostility are becoming greater. On the other hand, a large pool of individuals remains who do not identify with either of the major parties and for whom the increased intensity of the partisan debate is off-putting.

The close competitiveness of recent presidential elections has raised the intensity of feelings about politics. In 2004 and again in 2008 almost half of the public reported trying to influence other people's votes. This is a substantial increase over percentages reported in any election in the past fifty years. Higher percentages than in previous elections reported having a strong preference for their presidential choice and caring who won the election. However, this does not seem to translate to stronger partisanship. The percentage of strong party identifiers has not increased in twenty years and is not as high today as it was in the 1950s and early 1960s. The percentage of people who call themselves "extremely liberal" or "extremely conservative" has not increased either, and is generally less than 5 percent of the population.

A sizable segment of the electorate distrusts political parties, even feels hostility toward them. In the 2008 American National Election Study, a majority of the public (51 percent) preferred to see divided control of government; only 20 percent said it would be better if one party controlled both Congress and the presidency.

For at least some of these nonparty people, the problem with the parties is the same partisan and ideological intensity that has been increasing. They see the party elites and activists as extreme in their views while they see themselves as moderate. They view party conflict in Washington as divisive and contributing to, instead of solving, the country's problems. These are the people attracted to McCain's record of bipartisanship and Obama's postpartisan appeal. For such people, heightened partisan debate is unlikely to move them to embrace a political party. Becoming more engaged in political discussion, turning out to vote, and trying to influence the views of others are not unimportant aspects of the public's behavior, and they may signal changes in the partisan feelings of American citizens. However, the largest changes in partisan behavior are among leaders and political actives.

Notes

1. Larry Bartels argues that partisan loyalty has been steadily increasing since its nadir in 1972, but this trend has been overlooked by analysts focusing on the weakness of the political parties. See Larry Bartels, "Partisanship and Voting Behavior, 1952–1996," *American Journal of Political Science* 44 (January 2000): 35–50.
2. Paul R. Abramson and John H. Aldrich, "The Decline of Electoral Participation in America," *American Political Science Review* 76 (September 1982): 502–521.
3. Angus Campbell, "Surge and Decline: A Study of Electoral Change," in *Elections and the Political Order*, ed. Angus Campbell, Philip E. Converse, Warren E. Miller, and Donald E. Stokes (New York: Wiley, 1966), 40–62.
4. Had Bush adviser Karl Rove not implemented his strategy to turn out the vote among Christian conservatives in safe Republican states in the South, Bush would have again lost the popular vote nationwide, while winning in the electoral college.
5. Arthur H. Miller and Martin P. Wattenberg, "Measuring Party Identification: Independent or No Partisan Preference?" *American Journal of Political Science* 27 (February 1983): 106–121.
6. John Petrocik, "An Analysis of Intransitivities in the Index of Party Identification," *Political Methodology* 1 (summer 1974): 31–47.
7. Norman H. Nie, Sidney Verba, and John R. Petrocik, *The Changing American Voter* (Cambridge, Mass.: Harvard University Press, 1976), chap. 5.

8. Robert S. Erikson and Kent L. Tedin, "The 1928–1936 Partisan Realignment: The Case for the Conversion Hypothesis," *American Political Science Review* 75 (December 1981): 951–962.
9. Philip E. Converse, *The Dynamics of Party Support: Cohort-Analyzing Party Identification* (Beverly Hills, Calif.: Sage Publications, 1976).
10. The main participants in this controversy are Philip E. Converse and Paul R. Abramson. See Philip E. Converse, *The Dynamics of Party Support;* and Paul R. Abramson, "Developing Party Identification: A Further Examination of Life-Cycle, Generational, and Period Effects," *American Journal of Political Science* 23 (February 1979): 78–96.
11. The major findings of the first two waves of this study have been reported in M. Kent Jennings and Richard G. Niemi, *The Political Character of Adolescence: The Influence of Families and Schools* (Princeton: Princeton University Press, 1974); and M. Kent Jennings and Richard G. Niemi, *Generations and Politics* (Princeton: Princeton University Press, 1981). A report on partisanship using the first three waves of interviews is contained in M. Kent Jennings and Gregory B. Markus, "Partisan Orientations over the Long Haul: Results from the Three-Wave Political Socialization Panel Study," *American Political Science Review* 78 (December 1984): 1000–1018.
12. The parents were also reinterviewed in 1973. By 1997, many of the original high school seniors were parents of high school–age students. The study also interviewed the children of the original sample, creating a second set of parent-child interviews to compare with the original data from 1965. See Figure 4-7.

Suggested Readings

Green, Donald, Bradley Palmquist, and Eric Schickler. *Partisan Hearts and Minds: Political Parties and the Social Identities of Voters.* New Haven: Yale University Press, 2004. A strong argument for party identification as a social-psychological orientation and a powerful determinant of vote choice and political attitudes.

Keith, Bruce, David B. Magleby, Candice J. Nelson, Elizabeth Orr, Mark C. Westlye, and Raymond E. Wolfinger. *The Myth of the Independent Voter.* Berkeley: University of California Press, 1992. An effort to reaffirm the importance of party identification in an era of increasing numbers of independents.

Lewis-Beck, Michael S., William G. Jacoby, Helmut Norpoth, and Herbert F. Weisberg. *The American Voter Revisited.* Ann Arbor: University of Michigan Press, 2008. A rich reanalysis of the themes from the classic work using mainly 2000 and 2004 data.

Nie, Norman, Sidney Verba, and John Petrocik. *The Changing American Voter.* Cambridge, Mass.: Harvard University Press, 1976. A major revisionist analysis of public opinion and voting behavior emphasizing the decline of partisanship.

Niemi, Richard G., and Herbert F. Weisberg eds. *Controversies in Voting Behavior.* Washington, D.C.: CQ Press, 2001. A collection of sophisticated articles on major topics in political behavior and public opinion.

Wattenberg, Martin P. *The Decline of American Political Parties: 1952–1988.* Cambridge, Mass.: Harvard University Press, 1990. A thorough analysis of the changing patterns of partisanship in recent decades.

Internet Resources

The Web site of the American National Election Studies, www.electionstudies .org, has extensive information on partisanship and party identification from 1952 to the present. Click on "Guide to Public Opinion" and then click on "Partisanship and Evaluation of the Political Parties." Elaborate data are available separately on Democrats, Republicans, and independents.

Most political parties have Web sites. Any search engine will find them; www .democrats.org and www.rnc.org will reach the respective national committees of the two major parties.

Social Characteristics of Partisans and Independents

ATTEMPTS TO EXPLAIN American voting behavior often have relied on social and economic factors to account for both stability and change in American politics. Research based on the American National Election Studies (ANES) has documented a wide range of relationships in the U.S. electorate between social and economic characteristics and political behavior. Furthermore, many descriptions of voting patterns offered by American journalists and party strategists are based on social and economic factors. Analysis regularly attributes political trends to such categories as "soccer moms" or "born-again Christians"; frequently these explanations rely on so-called bloc voting, such as "the black vote," "the senior citizens' vote," or "the Hispanic vote," implying that some social factor causes large numbers of people to vote the same way.

The social factors that underlie partisanship reflect the partisan alignment in effect at that particular time. During the New Deal alignment, partisan choices tended to fall along economic and social class lines. Blue-collar workers, those with lower incomes, those with lower education, recent immigrants, racial minorities, and Catholics were all more likely to vote Democratic. Members of the middle class, white-collar workers, the college educated, those with high incomes, whites of northern European background, and Protestants were more likely to vote Republican.

The remnants of the New Deal alignment can still be seen in the partisan choices of today. Table 5-1 displays the party identification of selected social groups in 2008. For example, income is associated with party identification, with lower-income people more likely to be Democratic than higher-income people. Blacks and Hispanics are still much more Democratic than Republican. But significant differences also have

TABLE 5-1 Party Identification, by Social Characteristics, 2008

Category (percentage of sample)	Democrats		Independents			Republicans		Total percentage
	Strong	Weak	Lean Democrat	Independent	Lean Republican	Weak	Strong	
Men (45)	16	13	18	13	14	13	13	100
Women (55)	22	17	16	10	10	12	13	100
Whites (80)	14	14	17	12	13	15	16	101
Blacks (12)	48	23	16	9	3	2	1	102
Hispanics (9)	24	21	17	16	9	6	7	100
18–25 (13)	11	18	28	14	11	10	7	99
26–35 (19)	14	16	22	13	13	14	7	99
36–45 (17)	20	12	17	11	10	16	15	101
46–55 (20)	20	17	13	10	13	13	15	101
56–65 (15)	24	14	16	11	11	10	13	99
66–75 (9)	20	15	11	9	13	17	17	102
76 + (6)	25	16	14	6	9	7	25	102
High school education or less (43)	19	17	19	15	11	9	11	101
Some college (30)	15	15	19	12	13	12	14	100
College graduate (27)	21	13	14	5	11	19	16	99
Under $12,500 (11)	22	20	21	19	9	3	6	100
$12,500–25,000 (15)	24	18	19	11	12	9	6	99
$25,000–50,000 (25)	21	16	18	10	10	11	13	99
$50,000–100,000 (31)	14	15	18	13	13	12	16	101
Over $100,000 (9)	15	10	9	7	12	26	11	100

Union households (13)	25	17	18	8	11	9	12	100
Mainline Protestants (22)	17	11	15	9	10	20	19	101
Fundamentalists, evangelicals (33)	22	17	12	11	11	11	15	99
Catholics (23)	18	17	16	10	14	13	12	100
No religion (23)	15	15	29	15	12	9	5	100
White fundamentalists, evangelicals (19)	11	15	11	13	15	16	20	101
Non-South (57)	16	16	18	11	13	15	11	100
South (43)	12	11	15	13	14	15	22	102

Source: 2008 American National Election Study, available at www.electionstudies.org.

FIGURE 5-1   Social Composition of Partisans and Independents, by Race, Ethnicity, Religion, and Education, 2008

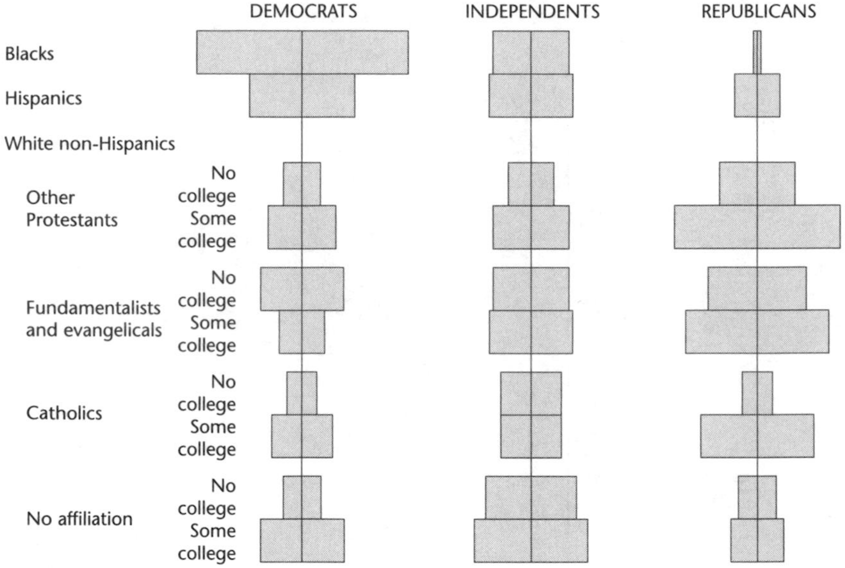

Source: 2008 American National Election Study, available at www.electionstudies.org.

emerged. Catholics were heavily Democratic when they were recent immigrants, but as later generations moved into the middle class, their disproportionate presence among Democratic partisans has faded. Religion still has an impact on partisanship, but it has become more complicated than the difference between Protestants and Catholics. The distinction between fundamentalists and evangelicals on the one hand and more traditional mainline denominations on the other has become more important politically in recent decades, with fundamentalists and evangelicals considered a part of the Republican base. This religious distinction is complicated by race, however, given that many blacks belong to fundamentalist and evangelical churches but remain overwhelmingly Democratic. The importance of religion in one's life, referred to as "religiosity," is another factor that influences one's partisanship. In Table 5-1 this can be seen most starkly in the disproportionate preference for the Democrats among those who report having no religious affiliation.

Even in the heyday of the New Deal, social and economic status was hardly a perfect predictor of partisan choice. This was most obvious in the South. White southerners were overwhelmingly Democratic—a legacy from the earlier Civil War alignment—and this traditional attachment to the Democratic Party virtually wiped out the impact of any other social or economic factor on political behavior. In the 1950s the southern middle class was about as Democratic as the working class, southern Protestants as Democratic as the relatively few Catholics in that region, and so on. Since 1956 southern whites have gone from 63 percent Democratic to 22 percent, and the social factors associated with partisanship are now not distinctively different from other parts of the country.

The percentage of the overall population that a particular group comprises has also changed since the 1950s. The proportion of Hispanics has increased dramatically; the proportions of fundamentalists, evangelicals, and people with no religious affiliations have all increased, at the expense of mainline Protestants; and the proportion of people with higher education has increased, while the percentage of union households has fallen.

The Social Composition of Partisan Groups

Another way of looking at the relationship between social characteristics and partisanship is to describe the Democratic and Republican Parties and independents in terms of the proportions of different kinds of individuals who make up their ranks. Figure 5-1 presents the social composition of Democratic, Republican, and independent identifiers, using some of the same social categories used in Table 5-1 (race and ethnicity, religion, and education). However, this way of viewing the data gives different results and answers a different set of questions. Instead of revealing to what extent particular social groups support the Democratic or Republican Parties, the data show the proportion of all Democrats who are black or Catholic. For example, the partisanship of various social groups presented in Table 5-1 shows that blacks are heavily Democratic (71 percent in 2008 identified themselves as strong or weak Democrats). But if the proportion of all Democrats who are blacks is calculated, as in Figure 5-1, blacks are found to make up just 28 percent of the total group of Democrats. Because blacks are a relatively small proportion of the population, their contribution to the total set of Democrats is not so large, despite their lopsided preference for the Democratic Party.

Studying the partisanship of social groups has generally been regarded as the more interesting way of looking at the relationship between social characteristics and political behavior, largely because of the causal connection between social characteristics and partisanship. Thus one is far more inclined to say that race and ethnicity, religion, or education cause an individual to select a particular political party than to say that political affiliation causes any of the others. Familiarity with the composition of the parties is useful, however, in understanding the campaign strategies and political appeals that the parties make to hold their supporters in line and sway the independents or opposition supporters to their side. For example, the fact that blacks constitute almost 30 percent of the Democratic partisans but make up just 1 percent of the Republican partisans is a significant factor that both parties take into account. The growing importance of the Hispanic vote for the Democrats is also reflected in Figure 5-1. In 2008 Hispanics made up 14 percent of the Democratic identifiers; eight years ago, they made up only 9 percent.

The composition of the parties affects politics in another way. In an important book on the evolution of the racial issue in the United States, Edward G. Carmines and James A. Stimson argue persuasively that the composition of the parties, particularly the composition of the party activists, influences the perceptions that less involved citizens hold about the philosophy and issue stands of the parties.[1] The fact that blacks are overwhelmingly Democratic and that vocal racial conservatives—in other words, those with a general predisposition to oppose government actions to correct racial injustices—are increasingly Republican allows the average voter to figure out which party is liberal and which is conservative on racial issues, even if race is never mentioned by candidates during the course of an election campaign.

As can be seen in Figure 5-1, the composition of the partisan identifiers is distinctively different. The Democrats are much more varied in racial and ethnic composition than the Republicans. Meanwhile, fundamentalist and evangelical Protestants and college-educated mainline Protestants make up significantly larger parts of the Republican Party than they do of the Democratic Party, although both parties contain substantial proportions of various religious groups and people with different educational levels. In other social characteristics, the partisan groupings are quite heterogeneous. They both draw substantial portions of their votes from blue-collar as well as white-collar workers, from the young, the middle-aged, the old, and so on. This diversity is also true of the independent group, as shown in Figure 5-1. As we pointed out in chapter 4, independent voters hold the balance of power between the major parties, and both must appeal to them to win elections.

Social Group Analysis

The impact of social groups on individual behavior is widely acknowledged. Social analysis of political behavior has examined three main units: primary groups, secondary groups, and social classes.

Primary groups are the face-to-face groups with which one associates, such as family, friends, and coworkers. *Secondary groups* are those organizations or collections of individuals with which one identifies, or is identified, that have some common interest or goal instead of personal contact as their major basis. *Social classes* are broad groupings based on position in society according to social status.

Primary Groups

Although investigations of the political behavior of primary groups are not numerous, all available evidence indicates that families and groups of friends are likely to be politically homogeneous. Groups of coworkers appear to be somewhat more mixed politically. Presumably, the social forces in families and friendship groups are more intense and more likely to be based on, or to result in, political unanimity; but in most work situations people are thrown together without an opportunity to form groups based on common political values or any other shared traits. Friendship groups, even casual ones, may be formed so that individuals with much in common, including political views, naturally come together.

Table 5-2 presents findings from the 2000 ANES survey that illustrate the homogeneity of primary groups. Respondents were asked the political party of the people with whom they regularly discussed politics. The table shows that agreement on voting between spouses is highest, with 90 percent of the Democrats and 92 percent of the Republicans reporting that their spouses shared their vote choice. Agreement was not so high among other groups but still reflects considerable like-mindedness. Perhaps as important is the relatively low occurrence of mismatches of Democrats and Republicans in primary groups. Sixty percent of the respondents were in agreement on presidential vote choice with all of their reported primary group contacts.

The discussion of primary groups has implications for the celebrated gender gap in the political preferences of men and women, a favorite topic of political commentators since the early 1980s. Women were less favorably inclined toward Presidents Ronald Reagan, George H. W. Bush, and George W. Bush (in 2000), and toward Republicans in general, than were men. Conversely, women were more supportive of President Bill Clinton and Vice President Al Gore than were men. The gender gap disappeared in 2004, with men and women equally likely to support George W. Bush, but re-emerged in 2008, when women were more likely to vote for Barack Obama than men by about five percentage points. Nevertheless, as evident from Table 5-1, the gender gap in partisanship is fairly small, with women more likely to call themselves "strong Democrats" and less likely to be independents than were men.

TABLE 5-2   Reported Vote Preferences of Primary Groups, by Respondent's
             Reported Vote for President, 2000

	Respondent's vote for president	
Primary group	Democrat	Republican
Reported vote of spouse		
Democrat	90%	8%
Republican	10	92
Total	100%	100%
(*N*)	(149)	(157)
Reported vote of other relatives		
Democrat	79%	22%
Republican	21	78
Total	100%	100%
(*N*)	(282)	(254)
Reported vote of coworkers		
Democrat	62%	39%
Republican	38	61
Total	100%	100%
(*N*)	(189)	(250)
Reported vote of fellow churchgoers		
Democrat	65%	17%
Republican	35	83
Total	100%	100%
(*N*)	(49)	(103)
Reported vote of neighbors		
Democrat	75%	35%
Republican	25	65
Total	100%	100%
(*N*)	(142)	(112)

Source: 2000 American National Election Study, available at www.electionstudies.org.

Note: Respondents were asked to name four people with whom they discussed political matters, after which their relationship with those mentioned was established. Reports only on those people with whom respondents talked about political matters at least occasionally.

This gender gap would be reduced further if controls were introduced for race and socioeconomic variables.[2] Given what was said about the influence of primary groups, the small size of the gender gap should not be surprising. Men and women interact with each other in primary groups throughout society. They select friends and spouses from among like-minded individuals; they respond, as family units, to similar social and economic forces. The views of men and women differ on certain issues, with women usually being less approving of military action in international affairs and more supportive of humanitarian aid, but given the general influence of primary groups, differences in overall political preferences are seldom large.

Lately, another gap, the "marriage gap," has gained some notoriety. It has been suggested that married people are more likely to gravitate to the Republican Party, while unmarried people are more likely to be Democrats. The reasons alleged for this range from commitment to traditional values to the economic position of married men versus unmarried women as heads of households. In looking at a possible marriage gap, the effects of age need to be taken into account, given that younger people are both more likely to be unmarried and to identify themselves as politically independent. Figure 5-2 shows the net difference in partisanship for white married and unmarried men and women.

FIGURE 5-2   Net Partisan Advantage among White Married and Unmarried Men and Women, 2008

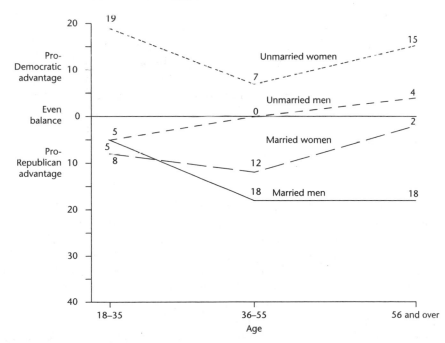

Source: 2008 American National Election Study, available at www.electionstudies.org.

Note: Values represent the percentage difference between Democrats (strong and weak) and Republicans (strong and weak) in each category.

Except for the youngest men, at every age level the married are more likely to be Republican than their unmarried counterparts, with married men being the most decidedly so. The marriage gap is large at every age among women, although it gets slightly smaller among older women. Conversely, the gap grows larger with each age category among men.

We have avoided use of the term *conformity* to describe the patterns of primary group behavior because these group processes are more casual and more a matter of give-and-take than the term implies. Most people care little about politics, and it plays a small part in their personal relationships. In few primary groups is politics of any consequence, so the things that happen in the group that lead to political homogeneity are of low salience. Individuals gradually create, evaluate, and revise their images of the world under the influence of social processes. Many of these processes are face-to-face exchanges of information or reassurances that others share views or consider them plausible, realistic, and acceptable. Most individuals are not pressured by primary groups to conform or to change politically, at least not nearly as much as they are influenced by casual, impromptu expressions of similar ideas and values. Ordinarily, primary groups do not tolerate high levels of political tension and conflict. Also, few people are subject to the social forces of only one or two primary groups, so conformity to group pressure would mean conformity to a large number of groups.

In addition to what happens within primary groups, another factor produces political similarity: the likelihood that primary group members share the same social background and experiences outside the group. Members of any primary group are apt to be socially, economically, ethnically, and racially alike, which means that the same general social influences are at work on them. Much happens outside primary group to make it politically homogeneous.

Secondary Groups

Secondary groups form around some common interest and may or may not involve personal contact among members. The term *secondary groups* covers a range of groups in society, such as labor unions, religious or fraternal organizations, and professional groups. Secondary groups are the kind of voluntary associations that form the "social capital" of a society, as discussed in chapter 1. Secondary groups are presumably composed of overlapping primary groups whose pressures toward political homogeneity spill over, tending to make the members of secondary groups alike. In addition, members of secondary groups are usually subject to the same social forces outside the group. For example, members of a labor union are likely to be in the same income group, to live in the same type of neighborhood, and to have the same social and educational background—all of which would tend to make them alike politically.

A third factor at work is the role that a secondary group may play as a reference group—in other words, as a guide in forming opinions. For example, if union members, identifying with their labor union, perceive that a particular policy is good for the union—perhaps because the union leadership says that it is—and therefore favor the policy, the union is a political reference group for those individuals. In the same way, if a union member believes that other union members support a policy and supports the policy in part for this reason, then the union members serve as a reference group. Also, if a businessperson perceives that unions favor a policy, and he or she opposes it in part for that reason, then unions serve as a negative reference group.

The most sophisticated analysis of social groups and political behavior applied to national survey data appeared in the classic work *The American Voter,* by Angus Campbell, Philip E. Converse, Warren E. Miller, and Donald E. Stokes.[3] By controlling many outside social influences with matched groups, the authors demonstrated the degree to which an individual's political behavior was influenced by secondary group membership among union members, blacks, Catholics, and Jews. They were able to show that union members, blacks, and Jews were considerably more Democratic than one would expect from the group members' other social characteristics, such as urban–rural residence, region, and occupational status. The fact that Catholics were not more Democratic in the 1950s than would be expected from their other social characteristics is consistent with what we observed earlier: as Catholics moved into the middle class, they have ceased to be disproportionately Democratic. However, union members, blacks, and Jews have remained more Democratic than expected, based on other social characteristics. In other words, group membership appears to play a role in the Democratic partisanship of union members, blacks, and Jews, but not Catholics.

The American Voter concluded that the influence was even greater if the individual identified with the group. To establish the importance of identification with the group and belief in the legitimacy of the group's involvement in politics, the authors analyzed the 1956 presidential votes of the same four social groups. The increasing impact of identification with the group and of its perceived legitimacy was associated with an increasing Democratic vote. In other words, the stronger the belief in the legitimacy of the group's political involvement and the stronger the group identification, the greater the impact of group standards on vote choice.

Among the groups usually studied, blacks and Jews are the most distinctive politically. Jews have remained strongly Democratic in their partisanship over the years in spite of social and economic characteristics more typical of Republicans. And although Jews have at times not supported the Democratic ticket, Jewish partisanship remains close to what it was in the 1950s—57 percent Democratic, 26 percent independent, and 17 percent Republican.[4] As shown in Table 5-1, blacks also are strongly Democratic in partisanship and typically vote more than 90 percent Democratic in presidential contests. The impact of group identification was dramatically revealed by increased black turnout and near unanimous black support for Obama in 2008. The percentage of blacks calling themselves "strong Democrats" jumped from 31 percent in 2004 to 48 percent in 2008 with a black candidate on the Democratic ticket.

The behavior of union members in recent years, in contrast, illustrates a decline in group identification. Despite one-sided Democratic partisanship, union members have been volatile in voting for president and willing to ignore the announced preferences of their union leaders. Despite an all-out effort by union leadership for Walter F. Mondale in 1984, Mondale barely outpolled Ronald Reagan among union households. Conversely, Bill Clinton did very well among union members, despite union leaders' general lack of enthusiasm for him. In 2008, 40 percent of union members identified with the Democratic Party versus 20 percent with the Republican Party, and Obama outpolled John McCain 61 percent to 39 percent.[5]

For many years, the partisanship of American religious groups, other than Jews, was not seen as particularly distinctive, or at least other factors were considered more important in determining political behavior. In recent years analysts have focused increased attention on religious groups in American society, especially within the highly varied Protestant category. Over recent decades the composition of the Protestant category has changed dramatically. Mainline Protestant denominations such as Methodists and Presbyterians have declined from roughly 40 percent to 18 percent of the adult population, about the same proportion as Catholics. Evangelicals and fundamentalists, on the other hand, have grown to more than one-quarter of the electorate.[6]

In a probing analysis of religious groups spanning the years 1960 to 1992, David C. Leege demonstrated the political distinctiveness of Catholics and evangelical Protestants in comparison with mainline Protestants.[7] Leege shows that for both Catholics and evangelical Protestants, significant differences in political behavior are associated with regularity of church attendance. In general, those who rarely attend church are similar to those unaffiliated with any religion. Figure 5-3 looks at some political characteristics of white fundamentalists and evangelicals in 2008. Those who attend church most regularly are considerably more Republican and conservative than those who attend less regularly. Political strategist Karl Rove's plan to utilize the evangelical churches as a way

FIGURE 5-3   Voting and Political Identification for White Fundamentalists
and Evangelicals according to Church Attendance, 2008

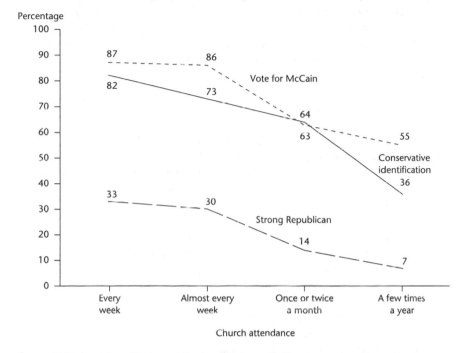

Source: 2008 American National Election Study, available at www.electionstudies.org.

to mobilize conservative votes for George W. Bush in 2004 was based on an understanding of the importance of group interaction in reinforcing opinions and motivating political activity.

It should be emphasized that Figure 5-3 looks only at whites who are fundamentalists and evangelicals. If black fundamentalists and evangelicals were considered, even greater uniformity in political behavior would be found—but in a Democratic direction, and it would not depend so much upon regularity of church attendance. A similar point can be made, however. Group identification, reinforced by social interaction, leads to distinctive political behavior. It is the interaction with like-minded individuals, represented by church attendance, that likely creates and reinforces political distinctiveness.

Social factors, such as race, religion, or union membership, vary in their relative importance from election to election. After years of dormancy a social factor may temporarily become significant during a political campaign and subsequently recede in importance. The 1960 presidential election provides a good example of this phenomenon.

John F. Kennedy's Catholicism was a major issue throughout the campaign and of great importance to both Catholics and non-Catholics. Researchers at the University of Michigan showed that Protestant Democrats who were more regular in church attendance were more likely to defect from the Democratic candidate. Among the nominal Protestants who never attended church, Kennedy's Catholicism exerted no such negative effect.[8]

Social Classes

The third major focus of analysis is social class. Some of the leading hypotheses of social and political theory link social classes and political behavior. In general, analysis of social class assumes that differences exist in the economic and social interests of social classes and that these conflicting interests will be translated into political forces. The critical variable in this view appears to be the importance of social class interests. In American society the importance of social class fluctuates but never becomes extremely high. The major political and sociological theories of social class have taken for granted the supreme importance of class interests, an assumption that seems unrealistic in American society. About one-third of all American adults say that they never think of themselves as members of a social class.

However, given a choice between "middle class" and "working class," a majority of Americans are able to place themselves in a general social position, even to the point of including themselves in the "upper" or "lower" level of a class. Even though individual self-ratings are not perfectly congruent with the positions that social analysts would assign those individuals on the basis of characteristics such as occupation, income, and education, a general social class structure is apparent. The political significance of social class varies from election to election in much the same way as that of secondary groups. In Figure 5-4 the relationship between self-identification as a member of the working or middle class and party identification is charted from 1952 through 2008 in the nation as a whole and in the South and non-South. The values shown in the graph represent the strength of the relationship between social class and party, indicated by Somer's d. If all working-class people identified with the Democratic Party and all middle-class people with the Republican Party (with independents split evenly between the two parties), the Somer's d would be +1.0; if the reverse were true, it would be –1.0. If there were no differences in the partisan preferences of middle- and working-class people, the coefficient would be 0.0. Because working-class people have been more likely to be Democratic than have middle-class people in each year since 1952, all the values in Figure 5-4 are positive.

FIGURE 5-4   The Relationship between Social Class Identification and Party
Identification, 1952–2008

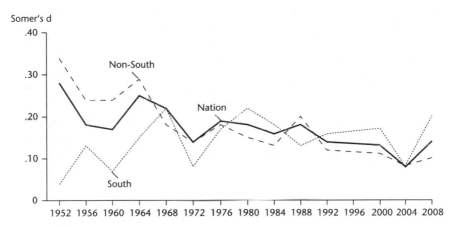

Source: American National Election Studies, available at www.electionstudies.org.

Note: The coefficients represented by points on the graph are Somer's d. The social class
identification question was not asked in 1996.

A number of points can be made about the data presented. Although
the strength of the relationship between social class and party has varied
over the years, the national trend in the relationship is downward. In
other words, since 1952 the differences in partisan preference between
working- and middle-class people have been getting smaller. In this
context, 1964, 1976, 1988, and 2008 stand out as temporary reversals of
the trend. Figure 5-4 also shows that the relationship between class and
party has followed different patterns in and outside the South. Whereas
the relationship has been declining elsewhere, the trend has been
upward in the South. During the early 1950s middle- and working-class
southerners were overwhelmingly Democratic; there were virtually no
differences between them. Later, a modest, class-based partisan alignment emerged. The middle class became increasingly Republican,
whereas the working class, particularly the black working class, remained
solidly Democratic. This class-based alignment in the South, as well as
the difference between North and South, disappeared temporarily in
2004 but was clearly evident again in 2008. This probably results from
the increase in southern blacks' identification with Obama's party. It is
perhaps surprising that the economic crisis of 2008, featuring themes of
greedy Wall Street executives and their oversized bonuses, had so little
impact on politicizing social class differences nationwide.

Another common expectation about the relationship between social
class and partisanship has to do with upward and downward social mobility.

To put it simply, the argument has been that upwardly mobile individuals abandon a Democratic identification and become Republicans, whereas the downwardly mobile abandon their Republican identification and become Democrats. Presumably the individual becomes an independent during the period of maximum social and political stress associated with this mobility. It has not been easy to assess mobility at a national level in the United States, so the surprisingly weak relationship usually found may result from inadequate measurement. In broad terms, most members of society are neither upwardly nor downwardly mobile, and the socially mobile seem no more apt to abandon their parents' party loyalty than the socially stable. Little political difference exists between the upwardly and downwardly mobile, and this appears to hold for several measures of mobility.

Along with Canada, the United States is usually regarded as an extreme case among developed democracies for the insignificance of social class in political behavior; in most European democracies social class is of greater consequence. This remains true even as the disparity between rich and poor in the United States has reached, since the 1980s, historically high levels. Two factors may depress the apparent relationship between social class and political behavior in the United States. Aggregating data for the entire population can hide stronger relationships in subgroups and in particular communities. Probably more important are the cultural values of freedom and individualism that exalt the ability and responsibility of the individual to get ahead by talent and hard work. As a result, American political leaders tend not to emphasize or exploit highly divisive social class lines and are often criticized if they do. Social class may serve as a political guide for some citizens on certain issues, but it does not appear to be extremely important in American politics.

Red and Blue States

Political commentary in recent years has often focused on the division of the country into "red" and "blue" states—red for Republican, blue for Democratic.[9] The implication is that dramatic differences in social characteristics and political culture exist between the two sets of states that lead them to vote in distinctively different ways for president. The fact that the country has been so evenly divided in presidential voting has increased the fascination.

Are there two Americas, one red and one blue? To try to answer this question, we divided the respondents in the 2008 ANES survey according to their residence in "safe red," "safe blue," or "battleground" states and compared their characteristics on a number of demographic and attitudinal dimensions.[10] The results are in Table 5-3. (Because the battleground states are presumably the most competitive, separating them in the analysis should make the remaining states appear more distinctive.)

Whether we conclude that the electorates of red and blue states are distinctly different or quite similar depends on which characteristics we consider. The top half of Table 5-3 shows characteristics in which the differences are small or nonexistent. Red and blue states appear virtually the same in some characteristics—such as level of turnout or percentage of independents, blacks, or Hispanics—as well as on attitudes toward several issues.

Some other differences are dramatic, as you can see in the bottom half of Table 5-3. The red states are overwhelmingly southern—the only southern blue state is Maryland. People in blue states are more likely to be Catholic than those who reside in red states. In comparison with blue states, those in red states are more likely to be white fundamentalists or evangelicals and to be more regular church attendees. Issue differences are in the expected direction—red states are more conservative—but the differences are not large. Even party identification is not dramatically different for red and blue states, which means there are many Democratic sympathizers in red states and many Republican sympathizers in blue states.[11]

For this analysis, we let the political campaigns define what is a "battleground state." We used where they sent the candidates during the campaign as a measure of the extent to which a state was regarded as "in play."[12] It is important to point out that the battleground states in 2008 were not necessarily the battleground states in 2004 or 2000. The nationwide shift toward the Democrats in 2008 meant that some battleground states in 2004 had become safely blue by the time the 2008 campaign was under way, and some red states of four years ago—Indiana, Missouri, North Carolina, and Virginia—had shifted to battleground status. This, by itself, is an indication that red states and blue states are hardly pure (and unchanging) political types.

The red states are distinctive in that they are primarily southern, but southern states have large percentages of black citizens whose social and political characteristics differ from the white majority. (The nonsouthern red states tend to have small populations and, therefore, do not loom large in a national sample, such as we are using here.) The blue states are primarily large, nonsouthern states with diverse populations. If anything, the movement of some border states from red to battleground status makes the remaining red states look more distinctive in cultural attributes.

TABLE 5-3   Political and Social Characteristics of Safe Red States, Safe Blue States, and Battleground States, 2008

	Blue states (Democratic)	Battle-ground states	Red states (Republican)
Number of states	18	11	21
Total electoral college votes	218	158	162
Characteristics with little or no differences between states (in percent)			
Turnout	79	78	77
Independents	40	40	40
Hispanic	10	5	12
Blacks	12	10	15
Very important to combat international terrorism	72	80	79
Government should provide many more services	46	38	40
Favor preferential hiring for blacks	19	12	13
Characteristics with noticeable differences between states (in percent)			
Democratic Party identifiers	39	36	28
Republican Party identifiers	21	23	32
Conservatives	37	45	49
Voted for Obama	65	58	40
Attend church every week or almost every week	26	30	42
Live in the South	3	40	82
College graduates	35	20	27
Catholics	34	15	20
White fundamentalists, evangelicals	11	32	23
Family income under $25,000	22	31	26
Favor governmental medical insurance	50	39	41
Approve of job Bush doing as president	19	23	36
Opposed to gay marriage	23	38	42
Pro-choice on abortion	40	33	27
Iraq war decreased risk of terrorism	20	26	31

Source: 2008 American National Election Study, available at www.electionstudies.org.

Note: The battleground states were defined as the states that both presidential and vice presidential candidates from both parties visited at least once after the conventions and where collectively they made at least ten visits. The remaining states were divided into "red" and "blue" according to their recent voting for president. The blue states are California, Connecticut, Delaware, District of Columbia, Hawaii, Illinois, Iowa, Maine, Maryland, Massachusetts, Minnesota, Nevada, New Jersey, New Mexico, New York, Oregon, Rhode Island, Vermont, and Washington. The battleground states are Colorado, Florida, Indiana, Michigan, Missouri, New Hampshire, North Carolina, Ohio, Pennsylvania, Virginia, and Wisconsin. The red states are Alabama, Alaska, Arizona, Arkansas, Georgia, Idaho, Kansas, Kentucky, Louisiana, Mississippi, Montana, Nebraska, North Dakota, Oklahoma, South Carolina, South Dakota, Tennessee, Texas, Utah, West Virginia, and Wyoming.

Social Cross-Pressures

One of the major ideas developed in the early voting studies by Paul Lazarsfeld, Bernard Berelson, and other researchers at the Bureau of Applied Social Research of Columbia University was the "cross-pressure hypothesis."[13] The cross-pressure hypothesis is simple in outline, but it can be confusing because it takes so many different forms. The hypothesis concerns the situation in which two (or more) forces or tendencies act on the individual, one in a Republican direction and the other in a Democratic direction. In the diagram below, we use the dimensions of occupation and religion, although these particular dimensions are not as politically relevant today as they were when Lazarsfeld and his colleagues introduced the concept in the 1940s.

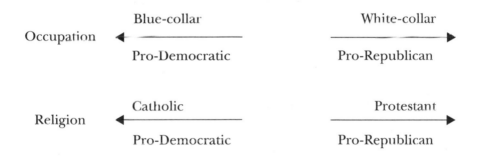

Some individuals are predisposed or pushed in a consistent way, such as white-collar Protestants, whose occupation and religion both predispose them in a Republican direction, or blue-collar Catholics, who are predisposed in a Democratic direction.

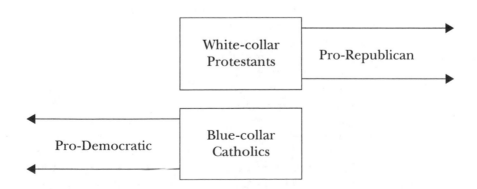

Some individuals are predisposed in both directions, or cross-pressured.

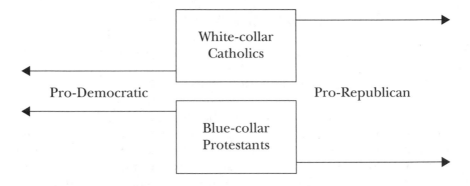

The cross-pressure hypothesis asserts that individuals under consistent pressure behave differently than individuals under cross-pressure. The predictions under the hypothesis are listed below.

Consistent pressure	Cross-pressure
Straight-ticket voting	Split-ticket voting
Early decision on vote	Late decision on vote
High interest in politics	Low interest in politics
High level of information	Low level of information
Consistent attitudes	Conflicting attitudes

These expectations about voting behavior under cross-pressure are specific applications of more general patterns investigated by sociologists and psychologists in a variety of ways. The responses to cross-pressure predicted by the hypothesis are avoidance reactions—efforts to avoid or to minimize the anxiety produced by conflict.

The cross-pressure hypothesis also has some implications for empirical political theory. According to the cross-pressure hypothesis, many large social groups are expected to be stable politically—that is, they are consistently predisposed to be Republican or Democratic by the social forces working on them. Therefore, these social pressures lead to political stability among both Republicans and Democrats because they have politically consistent social backgrounds.

Between these politically consistent social groups are cross-pressured groups predisposed toward both parties. According to the cross-pressure hypothesis, these groups are politically unstable, contributing to the voters who switch from one party to another. Thus the available voters—the voters to whom the parties must appeal to win because they hold the balance of power in elections—are in a middle position between Democrats and Republicans. These arguments lead to a reassuring view of the American electorate. A relatively stable social system produces widespread political stability. Political flexibility and sensitivity are provided by groups between the partisans who are therefore politically moderate. As long as the stable partisan groups are roughly the same size, stable competitive conditions are guaranteed. As long as social groups overlap somewhat, the necessary cross-pressures will exist to produce the switching political moderates. It appears to be an electoral system that guarantees both competition and stability.

Nevertheless, some difficulties arise with this picture of the electoral system. For one thing, the social cross-pressure hypothesis is merely a tendency and not a perfect description of the impact of social forces on political behavior. The politically stable are more heterogeneous than the previous account implies, and the politically flexible are not under dramatic social cross-pressure, according to the best data available.

Discussion supporting the cross-pressure hypothesis is most extensive in the Elmira study, *Voting*, by Bernard Berelson, Paul Lazarsfeld, and William McPhee, which surveyed residents of Elmira, New York, from June through November 1948. They found that cross-pressures affected the time when individuals decided how to vote. A slight tendency existed for cross-pressures caused by religion and socioeconomic status to be associated with late decisions on voting. Stronger relationships were associated with conflicts in primary groups.

Social cross-pressure can be conceptualized as leading to cross-pressure on political attitudes, which in turn leads to the predicted patterns of behavior. Attitudinal cross-pressure is the only form of cross-pressure that is strongly confirmed by national survey data. When attitudes toward the candidates and parties were measured by the American National Election Studies in 1952 and 1956, conflicting attitudes—those of an individual holding pro-Democratic and pro-Republican opinions—were associated with nonvoting, indecision, and indifference toward the election. These findings linking conflicting political attitudes with patterns of behavior have not always been confirmed in subsequent election studies, depending on which attitudes are examined. Nevertheless, it remains reasonable to expect conflicting political attitudes to be associated with indecision in voting behavior.

The American electoral system appears to operate in a way predicted by the cross-pressure hypothesis. Partisan stability exists among both Republicans and Democrats, with independents and political moderates contributing to the shifting of political fortunes. One should, however, be skeptical of explaining these political patterns as a result of the social forces postulated by the cross-pressure hypothesis. Neither short-run partisan stability nor independent flexibility appears to be strongly associated with social group predispositions.

Notes

1. Edward G. Carmines and James A. Stimson, *Issue Evolution: Race and the Transformation of American Politics* (Princeton: Princeton University Press, 1989).
2. Richard A. Seltzer, Jody Newman, and Melissa Voorhees Leighton, *Sex as a Political Variable: Women as Candidates and Voters in U.S. Elections* (Boulder, Colo.: Lynne Rienner, 1997).
3. Angus Campbell, Philip E. Converse, Warren E. Miller, and Donald E. Stokes, *The American Voter* (New York: Wiley, 1960), 295–332.
4. 2006 General Social Survey. The number of respondents identifying themselves as Jewish in recent ANES surveys is too small for analysis. However, the Pew Research Center for the People and the Press analyzed combined surveys from September 2001 to October 2003. The combined sample had 934 Jews out of a total of some 56,000 cases. Of the Jewish respondents, 49 percent were Democrats, 19 percent were Republicans, and presumably the rest were independents.
5. 2008 American National Election Study.
6. Ibid.
7. David C. Leege, "The Decomposition of the Religious Vote: A Comparison of White, Non-Hispanic Catholics with Other Ethnoreligious Groups, 1960–1992." Paper presented at the annual meeting of the American Political Science Association, Washington, D.C., 1993.
8. Philip E. Converse, Angus Campbell, Warren E. Miller, and Donald E. Stokes, "Stability and Change in 1960: A Reinstating Election," in *Elections and the Political Order,* ed. Angus Campbell, Philip E. Converse, Warren E. Miller, and Donald E. Stokes (New York: Wiley, 1966), chap. 5.
9. A recent, extensive analysis of divisions within the country can be found in a Pew Research Center for the People and the Press survey report, "The 2004 Political Landscape: Evenly Divided and Increasingly Polarized," November 5, 2003, available at www.people-press.org. Most of the analysis depends on differences between Democrats, Republicans, and independents, but the report also looks at partisanship within red, blue, and battleground states. Morris P. Fiorina disputes this view of polarization in *Culture War? The Myth of a Polarized America* (New York: Pearson Longman, 2005). A direct challenge to Fiorina can be found in Alan Abramowitz and Kyle Saunders, "Why Can't We All Just Get Along? The Reality of a Polarized America," *Forum* 3, no. 2, article 1, available at www.bepress. com/forum/vol3/iss2/art1.
10. Dividing states into "red" (Republican) and "blue" (Democratic) on the basis of the presidential vote winner is a more common way to classify the states. We thought that assigning the battleground states to one category or the other might obscure the distinctive qualities of the more purely red and blue states. Putting the battleground states in a separate category would thus be a better test of the idea.
11. The results are not much different if only voters are examined as opposed to the entire sample. The data in each of the three types of states are dominated by the more numerous respondents from the larger states, but that seems unavoidable.
12. Our definition of "battleground states" is based on data assembled by Gerald Pomper on visits to states during the general election campaign by the major party presidential and vice presidential candidates. His data make clear the

large differences between states that both parties fought over and the large number of safe states. See Gerald M. Pomper, "The Presidential Election: Change Comes to America," in Michael Nelson, ed., *The Elections of 2008* (Washington, D.C.: CQ Press, 2009), 65, Table 3-5.

13. Paul Lazarsfeld, Bernard Berelson, and Hazel Gaudet, *The People's Choice* (New York: Columbia University Press, 1944); and Bernard Berelson, Paul Lazarsfeld, and William McPhee, *Voting* (Chicago: University of Chicago Press, 1954).

Suggested Readings

Campbell, Angus, Philip E. Converse, Warren E. Miller, and Donald E. Stokes. *The American Voter.* New York: Wiley, 1960. A classic study of the social psychological factors influencing political behavior.

Fiorina, Morris P., with Samuel J. Abrams and Jeremy C. Pope. *Culture War? The Myth of a Polarized America.* New York: Pearson Longman, 2005.

Huckfeldt, Robert, and Carol Weitzel Kohfeld. *Race and the Decline of Class in American Politics.* Urbana: University of Illinois Press, 1989. A study arguing that racial cleavages have become more important than social class divisions in influencing electoral decisions, with serious consequences for the Democratic Party's coalition.

Huckfeldt, Robert, and John Sprague. *Citizens, Politics, and Social Communication.* Cambridge, England: Cambridge University Press, 1995. An important study examining political attitudes and behavior within their social context.

Lazarsfeld, Paul, Bernard Berelson, and Hazel Gaudet. *The People's Choice.* New York: Columbia University Press, 1944. A classic study of Erie County, Ohio, and the first study of voting to make extensive use of survey research.

Leege, David C., and Lyman A. Kellstedt. *Rediscovering the Religious Factor in American Politics.* New York: M. E. Sharpe, 1993. A collection of articles exploring the impact of religious beliefs on political behavior.

Lewis-Beck, Michael S., William G. Jacoby, Helmut Norpoth, and Herbert F. Weisberg. *The American Voter Revisited.* Ann Arbor: University of Michigan Press, 2008. A rich re-analysis of the themes from the classic work using mainly 2000 and 2004 data.

Lipset, Seymour M., and Stein Rokkan. "Cleavage Structures, Party Systems, and Voter Alignments: An Introduction." In *Party Systems and Voter Alignments,* ed. Seymour M. Lipset and Stein Rokkan. New York: Free Press, 1967. An important conceptual statement about the role of party and social cleavages in historical perspective.

Petrocik, John. *Party Coalitions: Realignments and the Decline of the New Deal Party System.* Chicago: University of Chicago Press, 1981. An analysis of American politics that emphasizes social and economic characteristics.

Stonecash, Jeffrey M. *Class and Party in American Politics.* Boulder, Colo.: Westview Press, 2000. An extensive analysis of the role of class in American politics.

Teixeira, Ruy, ed. *Red, Blue, and Purple America: The Future of Election Demographics.* Washington, D.C.: Brookings Institution Press, 2008. An in-depth treatment of the distinction between safe and battleground areas.

Internet Resources

The Web site of the American National Election Studies, www.electionstudies
.org, has extensive data on social characteristics and party identification from 1952
to the present. Click on "Partisanship and Evaluation of the Political Parties." For
every political item there is a breakdown for each social characteristic in every
election year.

For current data on partisans and independents you can find analysis on Web
sites such as the Pew Research Center for the People and the Press at www.people-
press.org and the Gallup Poll at www.gallup.com.

c h a p t e r   s i x

Public Opinion and Ideology

PUBLIC OPINION—the collective attitudes of the public, or segments of the public, toward the issues of the day—is a significant aspect of American political behavior. Public opinion polls are an ever-present feature of American journalism. The public is constantly informed about what samples of Americans think on all manner of topics. The questions then arise: Are Americans informed, issue-oriented participants in the political process? Do they view problems and issues within a coherent ideological framework? Which issues divide Democrats and Republicans? These questions address the nature and quality of American public opinion.

A *political ideology* is a set of fundamental beliefs or principles about politics and government: what the scope of government should be; how decisions should be made; what values should be pursued. In the United States the most prominent current ideological patterns are those captured by the terms *liberalism* and *conservatism*. Although these words are used in a variety of ways, generally liberalism endorses the idea of social change and advocates the involvement of government in effecting such change, whereas conservatism seeks to defend the status quo and prescribes a more limited role for governmental activity. Another common conception of the terms portrays liberalism as advocating equality and individual freedom and conservatism as endorsing a more structured, ordered society. However, these dimensions are not always joined in the political thinking of Americans. Also, some evidence indicates that after the election campaign of 1964 the terms became increasingly associated with attitudes on racial integration. To complicate the matter further, public opinion data suggest that a segment of the American electorate uses these terms to signify a set of social attitudes or lifestyles, not any particular political beliefs.

Despite these ambiguities, most commentators on the American political scene, as well as its active participants, describe much of what happens in terms of liberalism or conservatism. Political history (and current news analysis) portrays situations in terms such as a "trend toward conservatism," "middle-of-the-road policies," or "embracing liberal ideas." Furthermore, most political commentary treats the Democratic Party as the liberal party and the Republican Party as the conservative one. Although considerable ideological variation remains in both parties, the trend in recent years is toward greater ideological distinctiveness between the two parties. Candidates of both parties attempt to pin ideological labels on opposing candidates (usually candidates of the other party, but sometimes within their own). In recent years *liberal* has been portrayed more negatively than *conservative*, and some candidates for office portray themselves as "progressive" or use other such terms to avoid the liberal label.

Consideration of the ideological positions of the parties is complicated by the many dimensions of public policy: economic affairs; race relations; international affairs; and a variety of moral, social, and cultural concerns. These issue areas have many facets, and only a few themes dominate public attention at any one time. Not only does public attention to particular issues rise and fall, but the pattern of interrelationships among different sets of issues also changes over time.

Analysts of American political history pay special attention to those rare periods when a single-issue dimension dominates the public's views of governmental policy. Periods such as the Civil War or the New Deal revealed deep divisions in the public, paralleled by a distinctiveness in the issue stands of the political parties. Electoral realignments of voters are forged by unusually strong issue alignments, and during such times a close correspondence can be expected between attitudes on the relevant issues and partisanship.

At other times, highly salient issues may capture the attention of the public, but they are likely to cut across, rather than reinforce, other issue positions and party loyalties. If the parties do not take clearly differentiated stands on such issues and if party supporters are divided in their feelings toward the issues, party loyalty and the existing partisan alignment are undermined. In a complex political system such as that of the United States, new, dissimilar issue divisions accumulate until a crisis causes one dimension to dominate and obscure other issues.

The most consistent and the most distinctive ideological difference between the parties emerged during the New Deal realignment. It focused on domestic economic issues, specifically on the question of what role the government should take in regulating the economy and providing social welfare benefits. These issues still underlie the division between the parties. Since the 1930s, the Democratic Party has advocated more government activity, and the Republicans have preferred less. Historically, American political parties have not been viewed as particularly ideological, in part because other issues—such as, racial or social issues—have cut across the economic dimension and blurred distinctions between the parties. For example, in the 1940s and 1950s, the Republican Party was at least as liberal on race (i.e., supportive of civil rights legislation) as was the Democratic Party, with its strong southern base. Similarly, in the 1970s the two parties were both divided internally on the issue of abortion. Today, however, the two parties have become more ideologically polarized over a broader range of issues. The parties' supporters seem to have sorted themselves out, and now the Democratic Party takes liberal positions and the Republican Party conservative positions on racial and social issues as well as economic ones.

In this chapter we will consider public opinion on several important issues and explore the relationship of social characteristics and partisanship to these opinions. We will look at the extent to which Americans have a political ideology representing a coherent set of fundamental beliefs or principles about politics that serves as a guide to current political issues, much as partisanship does. Finally, we will briefly consider the impact of public opinion on political leaders.

The Measurement of Public Opinion

The commercial opinion-polling organizations have spent more than sixty years asking Americans about their views on matters of public policy. Most of this investigation has taken one of two forms: (1) asking individuals whether they "approve or disapprove of" or "agree or disagree with" a statement of policy, or (2) asking individuals to pick their preference among two or more alternative statements of policy. This form of questioning seriously exaggerates the number of people who hold views on political issues. People can easily say "agree" or "disapprove" in response to a question, even if they know nothing at all about the topic. If given the opportunity, many people will volunteer the information that they hold no views on specific items of public policy. For example, in 1964 more than one-third of the American electorate had no opinion on U.S. involvement in Vietnam. In contrast, in the past several decades less than 5 percent of all adults had no opinion on issues such as abortion or the death penalty. More typically, in recent years approximately 10 percent of the electorate has had no opinion on major issues of public policy. Philip E. Converse has shown, in addition, that a number of those individuals who appear to have an opinion may be regarded as responding to policy questions at random.[1]

The lack of opinion and information on topics of public policy can be explained in several ways. In general, the factors that explain nonvoting also account for the absence of opinions. Individuals with little interest in or concern with politics are least likely to have opinions on matters of public policy. Beyond this basic relationship, low socioeconomic status is associated with no opinion on issues. Low income and little education create social circumstances in which individuals are less likely to have views and information on public policies.

Some issues of public policy, such as abortion or the death penalty, are relatively easy to understand; others may be much more difficult, requiring individuals to face complex considerations. Edward G. Carmines and James A. Stimson have argued that different segments of the public respond to "hard" issues that involve calculation of policy benefits and "easy" issues that call for symbolic, "gut responses." Relatively unsophisticated, uninterested members of the electorate respond to "easy" issues; the more sophisticated, most interested citizens take positions on "hard" issues.[2]

It is no simple matter to describe the distribution of opinions in the American electorate because no obvious, widely accepted method has been established to measure these opinions. Asking different questions in public opinion polls will elicit different answers. Even on the issue of abortion, on which most people have views, the distribution of opinions can be substantially altered by asking respondents whether they approve of "killing unborn children" as opposed to "letting women have control over their own bodies." Furthermore, unlike reports of voting behavior, no direct means exist to validate measures of opinions. As a consequence, descriptions of public opinion must be taken as more uncertain and more tentative than those drawn from the discussion of partisanship.

Domestic Economic Issues

The collapse of the financial sector in the fall of 2008 and the actions of both the Bush administration and the incoming Obama administration to stimulate the economy and to bail out and then reregulate banks and insurance companies brought cries of "socialism" from conservative politicians and commentators. President Barack Obama's pledge to reform the health care system, at an unknown but certainly huge cost, reminded Democrats of the failure of the Clinton administration's health care plan in 1993. This failure led directly to the loss of the House of Representatives to the Republicans in 1994 and promises of a "conservative revolution" that would reduce government involvement in the economy and cut support for various social programs. In similar fashion, Ronald Reagan's victory in 1980 and his administration's sub-sequent slashing of taxes and social programs was portrayed as a reversal of fifty years of economic liberalism. Elections have consequences, and in policy terms there have certainly been consequences of Republican or Democratic victories. In terms of public opinion, however, broad and continuing public support remains for many governmental initiatives, regardless of election outcomes. As George W. Bush discovered when he proposed privatizing Social Security after winning reelection in 2004, long-standing programs that appear to benefit "deserving" segments of the population are difficult to "reform" because they enjoy widespread support.

The responses to public opinion questions, and public opinion itself, can be affected by political rhetoric and election slogans. For example, the General Social Survey asks a long series of questions on whether spending on various programs is "too much, not enough, or about right." Over the years, sizable proportions of the public have said that too much is being spent on "welfare." At the same time, even larger proportions have said not enough is being spent on "assistance to the poor."[3] Clearly, years of anecdotes about "welfare queens" and promises to "end welfare as we know it" have had their effect on the way particular programs are perceived, if not on the public's general willingness to use government as an instrument for social purposes.

Figure 6-1 shows the distribution of attitudes toward spending for different governmental purposes, using data collected by the General Social Survey from 1973 to 2008. The form of these questions—whether too much or too little is being spent on a problem—elicits answers that reflect the attitude of the respondents, the wording of the question as noted previously, and the current state of public policy. Thus a period of cutbacks in public spending, such as in the 1980s, would be expected to produce more responses of "too little" even if public attitudes about the ideal level of such spending had not changed. Figure 6-1 shows a drop in negative attitudes toward welfare spending after the Reagan administration slashed these programs, as well as a rise in proportions saying "too much" was being spent in the 1990s, when both political par-ties promised welfare reform. The implementation of those reforms, in turn, led to a sharp drop since 1996 in the proportion believing too much is being spent. Attitudes favorable toward spending on the envi-ronment showed a steady increase during the 1980s, as environmental programs were being curtailed, and then a gradual increase in the late 1990s and the first decade of the twenty-first century, which paralleled increased attention to climate change concerns. Support for more spending on health care has been high for several decades. Overall, Figure 6-1 shows fairly widespread willingness to support government spending on domestic social programs.

FIGURE 6-1   Attitudes toward Domestic Spending, 1973–2008

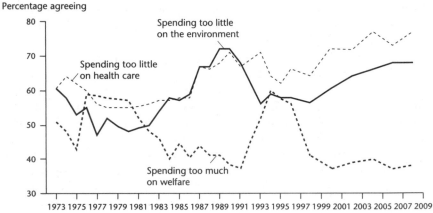

Source: National Opinion Research Center, *General Social Surveys, 1972–2008, Cumulative File,* available at www.norc.org/GSS/GSS+Resources.htm.

When one examines the relationship between social characteristics and issue stands on traditional economic issues, one might expect to find dramatic differences among social groups. Figure 6-2 is based on a question in the 2008 American National Election Study (ANES) that offers respondents a choice between "cutting spending and decreasing services" and "increasing services and increasing spending." We look at responses to this question for several social categories, using race and ethnicity, education, and religion as variables. The pattern in the figure is not difficult to describe. The least economically secure—blacks, Hispanics, and less well-educated white evangelicals—support government services most strongly, as do the better educated who are religiously unaffiliated. The only group distinctively in favor of cutting spending and services is the better-educated Protestants. The other religious groups are either evenly balanced between the two positions, or they favor increasing spending and services. The modest relationship between attitudes and social status among whites—similar to 2004 but different from previous years—may result from the lowered spending on services during the George W. Bush administration.

Favoring services over spending cuts represents the type of choice in governmental policy that characterized the New Deal. Thus it would be reasonable to expect a dramatic difference between Democrats and Republicans on such an issue. Economic issues have divided Democrats and Republicans since the 1930s, whereas other issues have been

FIGURE 6-2   Attitudes toward Cutting Spending versus Increasing Government
Services, by Race, Ethnicity, Religion, and Education, 2008

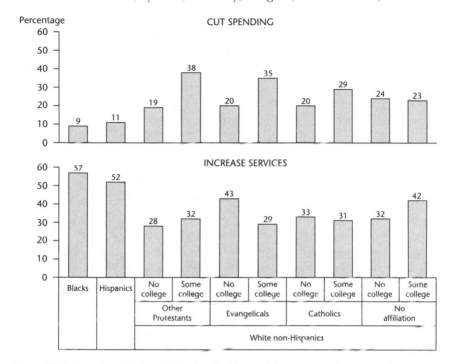

Source: 2008 American National Election Study, available at www.electionstudies.org.

of only temporary significance for the parties. As a consequence, the
relationship in Table 6-1 showing that Democrats disproportionately
favor increased government services and Republicans prefer cuts is no
surprise. Strong Democrats favor increased services over a reduction in
spending by a margin of 72 percent to 9 percent; strong Republicans
are just the opposite, favoring a reduction in spending over increased
services by a margin of 59 percent to 19 percent. This basic pattern has
existed for decades, but it is also important to observe that noticeable
proportions of Democrats and Republicans hold opinions opposed by
a majority of their fellow partisans.

Rising health care costs have been a concern for years and took
center stage in the first year of the Obama administration. Reforming
the health care system was first attempted early in the Clinton administration, when President Bill Clinton appointed First Lady Hillary Rodham Clinton to head a group to develop a proposal for a national health
care program. The managed competition program eventually proposed

TABLE 6-1   Attitudes toward Cutting Spending versus Increasing Government
Services, by Party Identification, 2008

	Strong Democrats	Weak Democrats	Independents	Weak Republicans	Strong Republicans
Favor cutting spending	9%	14%	23%	51%	59%
Neutral	20	24	26	20	21
Favor increasing government services	72	62	51	30	19
Total	101%	100%	100%	101%	99%
(*Weighted N*)	(182)	(132)	(397)	(133)	(133)

Source: 2008 American National Election Study, available at www.electionstudies.org.

was not the national health care program favored by the most liberal advocates, but the ensuing debate was cast in terms of governmentally mandated and regulated programs versus private insurance companies with individual choice in health care providers. Ultimately, the Clinton administration lost the battle in Congress and in the arena of public opinion. Initially in 1992 the public favored a governmental insurance plan, 44 percent to 24 percent, over private insurance plans.[4] After health insurance and pharmaceutical companies and the American Medical Association launched an extensive advertising campaign featuring a middle-American couple, "Harry and Louise," worrying about the government taking away their choice of doctor, the Clinton program went down in defeat. In 1996 public sentiment had reversed, with 40 percent of the ANES sample saying they thought medical expenses should be paid by private insurance plans and 34 percent opting for a governmental plan. In the 2008 campaign, health care was again an issue, and the public was again tilting in favor of a government program, with 48 percent in favor of a government plan and 34 percent preferring private health insurance.[5] As the debate in Congress geared up, Harry and Louise returned to the airwaves, sixteen years older, and this time supporting a health care reform package. Like most other issues of government involvement in social programs and regulation of the economy, clear differences between Democratic and Republican partisans appear on the issue of health care, as can be seen in Table 6-2.

Racial Issues

Race and attitudes associated with race hold a prominent place in American political history. For many years after Reconstruction, little

TABLE 6-2   Attitudes on Health Care, by Party Identification, 2008

	Strong Demo- crats	Weak Demo- crats	Indepen- dents	Weak Repub- licans	Strong Repub- licans
Favor governmental health insurance	65%	57%	52%	31%	13%
Neutral	19	22	22	11	15
Favor private health insurance	17	21	27	58	72
Total	101%	100%	101%	100%	100%
(*Weighted N*)	(202)	(149)	(436)	(127)	(135)

Source: 2008 American National Election Study, available at www.electionstudies.org.

overt public attention was paid to racial issues. The South was allowed to impose its system of segregation on its black population by law, while informal, de facto methods created much the same system of separate neighborhoods leading to segregated schools in the North. After integration became a major national and international focal point of attention in the 1940s and 1950s, a number of significant developments in the political attitudes of the public occurred. First, during the past fifty years southern blacks have become a concerned, involved, politically motivated group. As chronicled in chapter 2, removing the legal barriers to voting in the South has enabled the black population in southern states to command the attention of politicians at the ballot box and in state legislatures and governors' mansions.

Second, large numbers of southern whites have adjusted their opinions to accept the realities of the new legal and political position of blacks. The public, as a whole, has come to support the general principle of racial equality. Figure 6-3 shows the evolution of public opinion on support for school integration from the 1940s to 2008. The recent near-unanimity on this point means that Americans no longer support policies and practices that discriminate against racial groups, and making political appeals based on blatant racism is no longer consistent with the dominant political culture.

At the same time, the public has not moved significantly closer to supporting government programs designed to improve the economic and social position of racial groups. Northern, as well as southern, whites have consistently opposed busing for the purposes of integration. More than 80 percent of whites oppose affirmative action on behalf of racial minorities, and less than half support the federal government enforcing fair employment practices. The proportion of the public supporting various forms of governmental action to aid blacks is shown in Table 6-3.

FIGURE 6-3   Public Attitudes toward School Integration and Fair
Employment Practices, 1942–2008

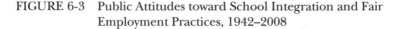

Percentage agreeing

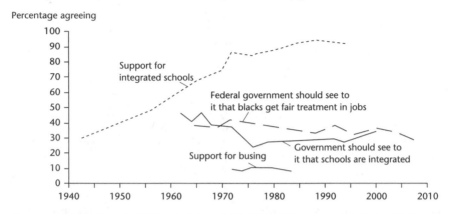

Sources: Hadley Cantril, *Public Opinion, 1935–1946* (Princeton: Princeton University Press, 1951), 508; National Opinion Research Center, 1956–1985; NBC News, 1989; Princeton Survey Research Associates, 1995, all available at the Roper Center for Public Opinion Research; and American National Election Studies, available at www.election studies.org.

In contrast to the near-unanimity of support for "letting black and white children go to school together," less than half the public supports positive actions on the part of government to improve the social and economic position of blacks.

The lack of connection between broad principle and policy implementation has been the focus of both political debate and scholarly disagreement. One side argues that opposition to programs to aid blacks is based on opposition to government activities in general and, in particular, programs that benefit a subgroup of society.[6] This position, often referred to as "racial conservatism," is seen as stemming from a general philosophical commitment to limited government and a belief in individualism. The attitudes, it is argued, are based on principles, not racism.

The other view argues that opposition to policy proposals to use governmental programs to aid the social and economic circumstances of blacks and other minorities stems from racial hostility, even though racial conservatives may have learned to cloak their racism in acceptable philosophical language. To complicate the matter further, scholars take different views of how racial hostility expresses itself in political attitudes. Scholars have used three dimensions of racial hostility to explain white support for or opposition to government policies regarding race:

TABLE 6-3   Public Attitudes on School Integration and Employment
           Practices

		Whites	
	Blacks	South	Non-South
Do you think the government in Washington should see to it that white and black children go to the same schools or stay out of this area as it is not the government's business? (2000)			
Government should see to it	78%	39%	50%
Not government's business	17	54	45
Other, don't know	5	7	5
Total	100%	100%	100%
(N)	(137)	(255)	(604)
There is much discussion about the best way to deal with racial problems. Some people think achieving racial integration of schools is so important that it justifies busing children to schools out of their own neighborhoods. Others think letting children go to their neighborhood schools is so important that they oppose busing. Where would you place yourself on this scale, or haven't you thought much about this? (1984)			
Bus to achieve integration	29%	4%	7%
Neutral	15	4	8
Keep children in neighborhood schools	56	92	85
Total	100%	100%	100%
(N)	(84)	(197)	(585)
Should the government in Washington see to it that black people get fair treatment in jobs or is this not the federal government's business? (2008)			
Government should see to it	89%	36%	50%
Not government's business	10	61	46
Other, don't know	2	4	5
Total	101%	101%	101%
(N)	(165)	(390)	(502)
Some people say that because of past discrimination, blacks should be given preference in hiring and promotion. Others say that such preference in hiring and promotion of blacks is wrong because it gives blacks advantages they haven't earned. What about your opinion—are you for or against preferential hiring and promotion of blacks? (2008)			
For preferential treatment of blacks	50%	8%	13%
Against preferential treatment	45	88	82
Other, don't know, refused to say	5	4	5
Total	100%	100%	100%
(N)	(241)	(699)	(948)

Source: American National Election Studies, available at www.electionstudies.org.

1. Racial resentment (the feeling that blacks are getting more than they deserve) or racial disapproval (the feeling that blacks do not live up to certain value expectations like working hard, etc.).[7] These contentions are often referred to as "symbolic racism."
2. Group conflict (zero-sum conflicts over scarce resources).[8]
3. Social dominance (protection of the status quo by a dominant group).[9]

Dimensions of this type can be interrelated and may reinforce one another. It is difficult to separate them or to be confident in measuring them or evaluating which dimension contributes the most to racial attitudes.[*]

To connect these dimensions with attitudes about policies designed to provide governmental aid to minorities, it seems reasonable to assume that people must view potential beneficiaries of government aid as deserving. How deserving blacks and other minorities are viewed by white Americans may depend on whether blacks are seen as individually responsible for their position or whether they are seen as victims of social and economic forces beyond their control. Presumably, whites who believe that blacks can improve their situation through their own efforts will not view them as deserving of special government programs on their behalf. This basis of opposition would fit the symbolic racism perspective. Whites who see social structures and conditions imposing special hardships on blacks regardless of their individual efforts will view blacks as deserving of special assistance.

Even if blacks are viewed as deserving, special programs may be opposed if whites see these programs as coming at the expense of whites. Another, similar basis for opposition to programs for blacks would be the expectation that the status quo, which favors whites, would be disrupted, which would be undesirable from the point of view of whites. These objections are examples of the group conflict and social dominance perspectives.

A racial conservative might make the argument that there once was a time when all the relevant democratic principles were on the side of helping blacks but that more recently such principles work both ways. Blacks should have an equal chance to get an education, find a job, and so forth, but they should not be given advantages over other deserving people. However, great differences are found in the perceptions of blacks and whites about whether or not blacks have an equal chance in American society.

---

[*]Although these dimensions are often labeled as if they were positive or negative in content, they have both pro-black and anti-black extremes. In other words, if a black person believes strongly that black people are not getting what they deserve, racial resentment may be involved just as much as when a white person believes that blacks are getting more than they deserve.

Racial attitudes have had a profound effect on the American political landscape. In their book *Issue Evolution,* Carmines and Stimson argue that an evolution of the racial issue since the early 1960s has led increasingly to the Democratic Party being perceived as the liberal party on civil rights issues and the Republican Party being perceived as the conservative party.[10] They see this distinction as the dominant perception of the parties in the eyes of the public. If this is so, it would represent a fundamental redefinition of the issue alignment that has characterized the parties since the New Deal.

Before the 1960s, Republicans were seen as more progressive on civil rights than Democrats, particularly in light of the strongly segregationist cast to the southern wing of the Democratic Party. Carmines and Stimson show that a change occurred during the 1960s and 1970s, when the elites of the two parties—members of Congress, presidential candidates—as well as party activists became distinctive in their racial views. The Democratic Party became dominated by northern liberals advocating stronger governmental action to ensure equal rights. At the same time, the leadership of the Republican Party became racially conservative—that is, opposed to government intervention to ensure equal rights for minorities. As the elites and activists sorted themselves into distinct groups on the basis of their attitudes toward racial issues, the perceptions that the mass public held of the parties followed suit. Increasingly through the late 1960s and 1970s, Carmines and Stimson argue, the partisan choices of individual citizens fell in line with their attitudes on racial questions.

The role of race and racial issues in American politics is not always easy to trace, however. Because certain issues that are not explicitly stated in terms of race are nevertheless symbols of race in the minds of some people, candidates can make appeals based on racist attitudes without using racial language. For example, "law and order" may mean "keeping blacks in their place" to some, "welfare" may carry racial overtones, and so on.

Furthermore, the lack of support among whites for policies that target assistance to blacks gives both parties an incentive to avoid embracing such policies, according to Donald R. Kinder and Lynn M. Sanders.[11] Republican leaders can oppose these policies and win support from their overwhelmingly white constituency, particularly southern whites. But Democratic leaders also have an incentive to avoid endorsing policies that would help blacks, so as not to alienate white support.

If race is not an issue to be openly discussed in political campaigns, then uncovering the political significance of race in people's attitudes and perceptions of the political parties becomes difficult. On the whole, straightforward efforts to capture distinctive party images along racial lines do not succeed. Although more than half of the public believed there were differences in what the parties stand for, typically only a small percentage characterized the differences in racial terms. Overwhelmingly, when people articulate differences between the parties it is in terms of symbols and issues associated with the New Deal realignment. This in all likelihood reflects the lack of overt discussion of racial issues by the political leadership of either party.

In 2008, with the first black candidate nominated by a major party, race was an issue whether anyone talked about it or not. From Bill Clinton's remarks downplaying a black candidate's win in the South Carolina primary, to Rev. Jeremiah Wright's videotaped sermons, to Obama's March 18 speech on race, to the increased black turnout and overwhelming support for Obama on election day, race was an often unspoken but constant presence throughout the campaign. In retrospect, it needs to be remembered that Obama did not have the unanimous support of black Democratic activists in the primaries. Former president Clinton was highly popular among blacks during and after his presidency, and Hillary Clinton benefited from that association. And early on, Obama was seen in some circles as "not black enough," given his mixed racial heritage and his upbringing by his white mother and grandparents. Once nominated, any Democratic presidential candidate can count on around 90 percent of the black vote in the November election. After Obama's nomination, he received not only virtually unanimous support from black voters, but high enthusiasm and turnout as well.

Social Issues

One of the more emotional aspects of the polarization of the two political parties over the past two decades has been conflict over so-called "traditional values." Issues such as abortion, gay rights including gay marriage, pornography, and sex education and prayer in the public schools have risen in prominence in recent years. Common wisdom positions Democrats on the liberal side and Republicans on the conservative side of these "culture wars," as they are often called, but significant numbers of leaders and followers in both parties are not so easily placed. Like the process of sorting out that occurred over racial issues in the 1960s and 1970s, a similar sorting out over traditional values has been occurring more recently. The Republican Party, especially, has had a difficult time portraying itself as a "big tent" that welcomes a wide range of people with varying beliefs, but people who are pro-life or opposed to gay marriage have also come to feel uncomfortable in the Democratic Party.

Certainly, one of the most potent of these social issues is abortion. The 1973 Supreme Court decision in *Roe v. Wade* immediately generated a polarized response, turning election races in some areas into one-issue campaigns. Thirty-five years later, so-called "partial birth" abortion is a hot-button issue, and both sides in the abortion debate gird for battle over any anticipated retirement from the U.S. Supreme Court.

One of the difficulties in examining public opinion on abortion lies in the responses that different question wording elicits. Although responses to the same question are similar over time, different phrasing of questions produces differing proportions of "pro-choice" or "pro-life" answers. In the following analysis we use data from the ANES, which has used the same question in each biennial survey since 1980.

The public's views on abortion are associated with several personal characteristics, most notably age, education, and religion. No matter what combination of characteristics is examined in the general public, invariably more than half of the people in the ANES surveys support the right to abortion under at least some circumstances.** In simple terms, older people are generally more likely to be pro-life than younger people, and the less educated are less supportive of legal abortion than are the better educated. Given the frequent labeling of abortion as a "women's" issue, it is worth noting that there is relatively little difference in the views of women and men, although women are more likely than men to take the extreme positions on both the pro-choice and pro-life sides.

Perhaps surprisingly, given the Roman Catholic Church's clear position in opposition to abortion, little difference is found between Catholics and Protestants in their positions on abortion. This is true even when the frequency of church attendance is taken into account. Figure 6-4 shows the percentages taking the most extreme pro-life position and the most extreme pro-choice position for Catholics and Protestants with different frequencies of church attendance. Among both Catholics and Protestants, opposition to abortion declines as church

----

**These figures undoubtedly underestimate the proportion taking the pro-life position. The two response choices at the pro-life end of the continuum are that abortion should never be permitted and that abortion should be permitted only in cases of rape or incest or to save the life of the mother. The first is a more extreme position than many pro-life advocates would take; the second includes circumstances that have been explicitly rejected by pro-life advocates in and out of Congress. Thus neither category is an entirely satisfactory indicator of pro-life sentiment. The most extreme pro-choice alternative offered is that by law a woman should always be able to obtain an abortion as a matter of personal choice. We have used the most extreme category at either end of the continuum to indicate pro-life and pro-choice positions.

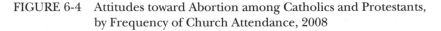

FIGURE 6-4   Attitudes toward Abortion among Catholics and Protestants,
by Frequency of Church Attendance, 2008

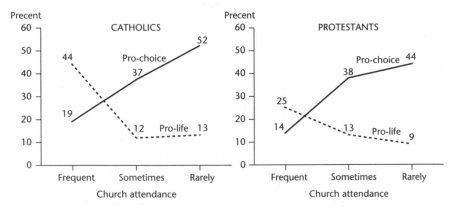

Source: 2008 American National Election Study, available at www.electionstudies.org.

attendance declines, but the percentages expressing pro-choice and pro-life sentiments are quite similar for the Catholic and Protestant groups. Regular churchgoers among Catholics are noticeably more pro-life than Protestants, but this is a change from recent years and results from both an increase in pro-life sentiment among churchgoing Catholics and a decline among their Protestant counterparts. Underlying this change is another trend—a smaller proportion of all Catholics claim to be regular churchgoers. Those who remain faithful in church attendance are also more pro-life. On the Protestant side, the proportion of regular churchgoers increased, along with an apparent dilution of pro-life sentiment.

The data in Figure 6-4 mask the different attitudes on abortion among Protestant groups, especially among whites. Table 6-4 divides white mainline Protestants from evangelicals and compares them with white Catholics and those with no religious affiliation, again controlling for frequency of church attendance. The evangelical Protestants who regularly attend church are about as pro-life as the Catholics who regularly attend. However, the mainline Protestants who regularly attend church are considerably more pro-choice than the frequent attenders of other faiths. Because most mainline Protestant churches take a position of individual moral responsibility on the question of abortion, the pro-choice stance of many of their adherents is not unexpected.

Position on abortion has become a litmus test for presidential candidates in both parties ever since the 1970s. Not surprisingly, then, a fairly strong relationship exists between partisanship and views on abortion, as can be seen in Table 6-5. Perhaps more unexpected is that the relationship is not stronger. Sizable minorities of both Republicans and

TABLE 6-4 Whites' Views on Abortion, by Religion and Frequency of Church Attendance, 2008

	Evangelical Protestants			Other Protestants			Catholics			No affiliation
	Frequent	Sometimes	Rarely	Frequent	Sometimes	Rarely	Frequent	Sometimes	Rarely	
Pro-life	26%	22%	14%	18%	10%	5%	37%	6%	14%	2%
Pro-life, with exceptions	50	43	32	29	6	27	33	18	15	22
Pro-choice, with limitations	19	18	17	19	37	22	9	25	32	13
Pro-choice	6	17	37	33	40	47	22	51	39	63
Other, don't know	0	0	0	1	7	0	0	0	0	0
Total	101%	100%	100%	100%	100%	101%	101%	100%	100%	100%
(Weighted N)	(99)	(23)	(90)	(71)	(30)	(79)	(56)	(23)	(84)	(160)

Source: 2008 American National Election Study, available at www.electionstudies.org.

TABLE 6-5   Attitudes on Abortion, by Party Identification, 2008

	Strong Demo- crats	Weak Demo- crats	Indepen- dents	Weak Repub- licans	Strong Repub- licans
Never permit abortion	9%	13%	14%	9%	29%
Permit only in special cases	19	29	27	30	37
Permit for other reasons	14	19	18	27	15
Always permit as woman's right	59	40	40	33	19
Total	101%	101%	99%	99%	100%
(*N*)	(195)	(148)	(431)	(139)	(128)

Source: 2008 American National Election Study, available at www.electionstudies.org.

Note: The full text of choices is:
1. By law, abortion should never be permitted.
2. The law should permit abortion only in case of rape, incest, or when the woman's life is in danger.
3. The law should permit abortion for reasons other than rape, incest, or danger to the woman's life, but only after the need for the abortion has been clearly established.
4. By law, a woman should always be able to obtain an abortion as a matter of personal choice.

Democrats take positions contrary to the stand of their party. This is one of several ways in which the polarization of the political activists and elites of the parties is not reflected in the rank and file.

The issue of gay marriage has become very contentious in recent years, with some states banning gay marriage through legislative actions or referenda, and others moving toward legalizing it. In 2004 the issue was suddenly injected into the presidential campaign when the Supreme Court of Massachusetts ruled that denying gays and lesbians the right to marry was unconstitutional in that state, and when the mayor of San Francisco began issuing marriage licenses to gay couples. This was a no-win situation for the Democrats and their presidential candidate, given that the American public opposed gay marriage by a two-to-one margin. Because proposed bans on gay marriage were on the ballot in several states that year, the issue also served to energize conservative voters in safe Republican states, thus raising George W. Bush's popular vote margin.

Over time, the American public has become more tolerant of the idea of gay marriage, or at least civil unions for gay couples. This is another social issue that has a fairly strong relationship with partisanship, as can be seen in Table 6-6. Democratic partisans are more accepting of the idea than Republicans, although a substantial minority of Democrats oppose it.

TABLE 6-6   Attitudes toward Gay Marriage, by Party Identification, 2008

	Strong Demo- crats	Weak Demo- crats	Indepen- dents	Weak Repub- licans	Strong Repub- licans
Allow gay marriage	46%	48%	46%	27%	9%
Not allow but permit civil union (volunteered answer)	20	23	24	33	36
Should not allow gay marriage	33	28	30	40	54
Total	99%	99%	100%	100%	99%
(*Weighted N*)	(416)	(343)	(896)	(282)	(299)

Source: 2008 American National Election Study, available at www.electionstudies.org.

Homeland Security and Terrorism

Since September 11, 2001, the eight-hundred-pound gorilla of American public opinion has been terrorism. Not only have the events of that day been seared into people's memories, but the fear of future terrorist attacks remains pervasive—although concern has ebbed a little as time passes without another attack. In the fall of 2004, a CBS News poll found that 71 percent of the public believed that the threat of terrorism will always exist.[12] In a 2009 survey by the Pew Research Center, 62 percent agreed that "occasional acts of terrorism in the United States will be part of life in the future."[13]

A wide-ranging survey in 2004 on Americans' perceptions of the threat of terrorism showed that concerns about a terrorist attack focus on chemical and biological weapons as the most worrisome.[14] Terrorism is seen as multifaceted, taking many possible forms with a wide array of possible targets. Even without another attack, many years will pass before substantial numbers of the public have no personal memory of September 11, so the feelings and issues surrounding terrorism will be around for a long time.

Terrorism is a "valence" issue—that is, one in which virtually every citizen of the United States agrees that it is bad—as opposed to a "position" issue, which some support and others oppose. At one level, terrorism is also an "easy" issue, in the sense that Carmines and Stimson use the term. It is easy, on a gut level, to understand what happened on September 11 and to find it abhorrent. Beyond this, however, the terrorist threat becomes more complicated—a "hard" issue—as one tries to imagine who might be terrorists, what motivates them, and what array of possible weapons they might use. Even more difficult is assessing the steps proposed and taken to thwart terrorists. Do they work? Are they cost-effective? How would one know?

More than most other international issues, the threat of terrorism involves domestic policies aimed at preventing terrorist attacks, such as security searches at airports and on mass transit systems. Most survey research in this area has focused on the public's reaction to the USA PATRIOT Act. Among the roughly 80 percent of the public who had heard of the act, opinion was fairly evenly divided between those who saw it as a necessary tool for finding terrorists and those who thought it went too far and threatened civil liberties.[15] These responses were strongly influenced by partisanship. Only 15 percent of Republicans thought it went too far, while 53 percent of Democrats held that view.

Up to some unknown point, Americans are willing to see their civil liberties compromised if they believe doing so will help prevent terrorism, even though three-fourths of the public has little confidence that the government will use personal information, gained through antiterror measures, appropriately.[16] Respondents are more willing to sacrifice the civil liberties of others than their own. For example, a CBS News poll in the spring of 2005 found that 56 percent of the public was willing to have government agencies monitor the telephone calls and e-mails of Americans the government finds suspicious; only 29 percent favored allowing this monitoring of "ordinary Americans."[17]

Typically, important valence issues such as terrorism have components that can be treated as position issues when segments of the public and their leaders hold differing views. So while everyone is opposed to terrorism, dissimilar views can be held about how well President George W. Bush handled the war on terrorism or whether the Iraq war made the United States more or less safe from terrorism. As might be expected, the positions people take on these matters are related to partisanship.

Using data from the 2008 ANES, Figure 6-5 shows the relationship between party identification and three attitudes toward terrorism. In 2008 Democrats were likely to believe that the war in Iraq increased the terrorist threat; Republicans did not. Republicans were likely to approve of the government's handling of the war on terrorism; Democrats did not. Even views on spending money on the war on terrorism were related to partisanship, with Democrats and independents more likely to support increased spending than Republicans.

International Affairs

During the cold war years, foreign policy—and the study of public opinion about foreign policy—focused on relations between the United States and the Soviet Union. Questions centered on the relative strength of the two countries, the likelihood of nuclear conflict between them,

FIGURE 6-5   Attitudes toward the War on Terrorism according to Party
Identification, 2008

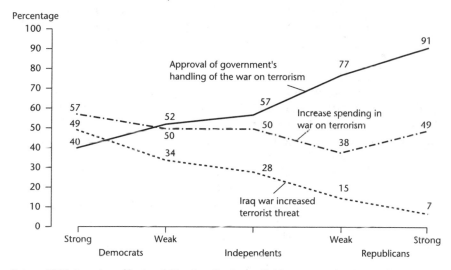

Source: 2008 American National Election Study, available at www.electionstudies.org.

and the preference for negotiation or military strength as a strategy for keeping the peace. With the breakup of the Soviet Union, the focus of foreign policy has shifted away from superpower military relations toward involvement, or noninvolvement, in trouble spots around the world, such as the Persian Gulf in 1991 and Afghanistan and Iraq since 2001 and 2003, respectively.

Issues of foreign affairs vary greatly in salience, particularly in response to involvement of the nation in a military conflict. In analyzing the public's attitudes toward international events, a distinction needs to be made between brief conflicts and longer-lasting wars. A truism now in American politics says the American public will support—usually enthusiastically—brief military involvement in a foreign conflict that seems to be successful (and they will quickly forget if it is not successful). If, however, combat drags on, support will diminish, especially if there are significant U.S. casualties. In the case of Vietnam, opposition to the war developed at a sluggish pace over a considerable period of time, as did recognition of the seriousness of U.S. involvement. In the early years, opposition to the war (as measured by support for a prompt withdrawal) was low—less than 10 percent. By 1968, it had grown to 20 percent; by 1970, it was more than 30 percent; and by 1972, more than 40 percent. Clearly, as the war dragged on, support for military involvement declined dramatically. The Korean War nearly sixty years ago offers similar evidence of the failure of public support for prolonged conflicts.

In contrast, military episodes that develop rapidly command great public attention and almost always garner public support. In the Persian Gulf War, deployment of American military forces to Saudi Arabia began in the late summer of 1990, in response to Iraq's invasion of Kuwait. In the late fall, as deployment of U.S. troops continued, the public was somewhat divided in its support of this policy. Fifty-nine percent of the public polled said they believed it was the correct policy to pursue, and 39 percent said they believed it was not. These views shifted fairly dramatically after the brief and well-televised war with Iraq in early 1991. When the same people were interviewed again in June 1991 following the war, 81 percent felt the war had been the right thing to do and only 18 percent thought the United States should have stayed out.

In the beginning, support for the second war in Iraq was high among the American public. In March 2003, immediately after the invasion, 69 percent of the public thought the United States had done the right thing in taking military action against Iraq. Only a quarter of the public thought the United States should have stayed out.[18] A little over a year later, on the anniversary of the declared end of formal hostilities, the public was evenly divided on whether or not the United States had done the right thing—47 percent thought so, 46 percent did not.[19] Small bursts of support appeared after the patriotic displays at both parties' national nominating conventions in the summer of 2004 and right before the presidential election in November 2004, but, generally, the trend of support was downward. By the fall of 2008, 70 percent of the public disapproved of President Bush's handling of the war in Iraq.[20]

Political analysts have long noted a "rally 'round the flag" phenomenon that occurs at times of international crisis.[21] Presidents invariably get a boost in popularity ratings in the polls in the midst of an international incident, even when the actions of the administration are not particularly successful. John F. Kennedy got such a boost after the disastrous Bay of Pigs invasion of Cuba in 1961, as did Jimmy Carter—temporarily—after a militant student group seized the American Embassy in Iran in 1979. And public approval of President George H. W. Bush's handling of the Gulf War was extremely high during and immediately following the conflict, representing a substantial increase over his earlier ratings. Similarly, George W. Bush saw an immediate gain in presidential job approval after the attacks on the World Trade Center and Pentagon on September 11, 2001. ABC News and the *Washington Post* completed a national survey the weekend before the attacks in which Bush's job approval was at 55 percent, about average for modern presidents in the first year of their first term. Immediately after the disaster, his job approval climbed to 86 percent. The change in "strong" approval was from 26 to 63 percent.[22] This enthusiasm did not survive the passage of time.

As with domestic issues, partisan differences are apparent, with partisans of the president in office more supportive of whatever actions are taken than are partisans of the party out of power. This was seen most clearly during the war in Vietnam. Republicans were more likely to think getting involved in Vietnam was a mistake before 1969, when Democratic president Lyndon B. Johnson was in charge; thereafter, with Republican Richard M. Nixon in the White House, Democrats were more likely to view the war as a mistake.

Similarly, in 2004, 61 percent of Republicans said that Iraq was an immediate threat that required military action, whereas only 14 percent of Democrats and 26 percent of independents held that view. The partisan differences extend to many attitudes toward the Iraq war. Republicans, for example, are much more likely than Democrats or independents to believe that the war in Iraq is a major part of the war on terrorism. Republican support for the war in Iraq has remained strong, whereas the support of Democrats and independents has fallen faster. In March 2003, 87 percent of Republicans said that attacking Iraq was the right thing to do. A year later, their support was still at 80 percent. Democratic support, meanwhile, dropped from 50 percent to 24 percent over the same time period, and independent support declined a comparable amount, from 70 percent to 45 percent.[23] As can be seen in Table 6-7, what question was asked about Iraq did not matter much. Republicans, Democrats, and independents responded consistently. Republicans continued to support the Republican president while Democrats did not. Independents were somewhere in between but became increasingly negative as time went on. Passing the baton of commander in chief to Democrat Barack Obama raises the question of whether the war in Iraq will lead to a shift in attitudes among partisans similar to the shift that occurred in the Vietnam era.

The public makes a distinction between the war in Iraq and the war in Afghanistan, although they share the characteristic of dragging on inconclusively. By the fall of 2008, 56 percent of the public thought sending military forces to Iraq had been a mistake, but only 28 percent thought it had been a mistake to send troops to Afghanistan.[24] Similarly, a little over 60 percent of the public thought the United States should keep troops in Afghanistan, while only 45 percent thought troops should be kept in Iraq. Republicans overwhelmingly thought troops should be kept in both countries, but Democrats were less sure. Fifty-three percent of all Democrats thought troops should be kept in Afghanistan, but only 25 percent felt that way about Iraq.[25] Because the war in Afghanistan has lasted longer, simple duration of a conflict does not determine the level of support. Most important, the connection between terrorism and the war in Afghanistan has not been questioned. But the cost in American lives and dollars also has been less in Afghanistan than Iraq, and news

TABLE 6-7   Attitudes toward the War in Iraq according to Party
Identification, 2004 and 2008 (in percentages)

	Democrat	Independent	Republican
Think the United States did the right thing in taking military action against Iraq (2004)	24	45	80
Think the war with Iraq has been worth the cost (2008)	8	19	56
Think Iraq was a threat to the United States that required immediate military action (2004)	14	26	61
Think the Bush administration tried hard enough to reach a diplomatic solution in Iraq (2004)	12	31	64
Think the war with Iraq has decreased the threat of terrorism against the United States (2008)	12	23	49
Approve of the way President Bush is handling the war in Iraq (2008)	7	25	69
Oppose setting a deadline for the withdrawal of troops from Iraq (2008)	17	28	60

Sources: CBS News Poll, April 6–8, 2004, data provided by Inter-university Consortium for Political and Social Research; 2008 American National Election Study, available at www.electionstudies.org.

coverage of successes and failures has been more extensive in Iraq. With the Obama administration's new emphasis on Afghanistan as the right place to fight terrorism, this may change.

Up until Vietnam, bipartisanship was touted as the hallmark of American foreign policy—that "politics stops at the water's edge." While strictly speaking this was never true, the division between internationalist and isolationist views on the United States' role in the world tended not to follow party lines. Today, the partisan polarization extends also to international issues, especially as they concern one or the other party's handling of them. As Table 6-8 demonstrates, although there is widespread bipartisan agreement on general principles, like keeping the country safe from various threats, partisan differences appear over humanitarian goals and the role of the United Nations.

TABLE 6–8   Attitudes toward Possible Foreign Policy Goals according to
Party Identification, 2008

	Percentage agreeing		
	Democrats	Independents	Republicans
Preventing the spread of nuclear weapons should be a very important U.S. foreign policy goal.	83	80	87
Promoting and defending human rights in other countries should be a very important U.S. foreign policy goal.	43	35	26
Strengthening the United Nations should be a very important U.S. foreign policy goal.	55	39	29
Combating world hunger should be a very important U.S. foreign policy goal.	70	59	45
Helping to bring a democratic form of government to other nations should be a very important U.S. foreign policy goal.	23	13	18
Promoting market economies abroad should be a very important U.S. foreign policy goal.	27	25	27
Combating international terrorism should be a very important U.S. foreign policy goal.	75	73	86

Source: 2008 American National Election Study, available at www.electionstudies.org.

Issues and Partisanship

As noted in previous sections, fairly strong and consistent relationships exist between partisanship and domestic and some foreign policy
issues. A leading assumption is that partisan identification provides
guidance for the public on policy matters—that is, most Americans
adopt opinions consistent with their partisanship. It also is likely that
policy positions developed independently of one's partisanship but

consistent with it will reinforce feelings of party loyalty or that attitudes on issues will lead to a preference for the party most in agreement with them. Furthermore, issue preferences inconsistent with party loyalty can erode or change it. For any particular individual it would be extremely difficult to untangle the effects of partisanship and policy preferences over a long period of time.

Even though on many issues most partisans of one party will hold a position different from that held by the majority of the other party, considerable numbers of people with issue positions "inconsistent" with their party identification remain loyal to that party. To account for this, it is variously suggested that: (1) issues are unimportant to many voters; (2) only the issues most important to individuals need to be congruent with their partisanship; (3) individuals regularly misperceive the positions of the parties to remain comfortable with both their party loyalty and their policy preferences; or (4) the positions of each party are ambiguous or dissimilar enough in different areas of the country that no clear distinction exists between the parties. Undoubtedly, all these explanations have some degree of truth, and no one should expect to find extremely strong relationships between partisanship and positions on particular issues. Nevertheless, as an indication of the recent increased polarization of the parties, racial issues and so-called "moral" issues have joined traditional domestic economic issues to clearly differentiate Democrats from Republicans.

Political Ideology

A political ideology is a set of interrelated attitudes that fit together into some coherent and consistent view of or orientation toward the political world. Americans have opinions on a wide range of issues, and political analysts and commentators characterize these positions as "liberal" or "conservative." Does this mean, then, that the typical American voter has an ideology that serves as a guide to political thought and action, much the same way partisanship does?

When Americans are asked to identify themselves as liberal or conservative, most are able to do so. The categories have some meaning for most Americans, although the identifications are not of overriding importance. Table 6-9 presents the ideological identification of Americans over the past four decades. A consistently larger proportion of respondents call themselves conservative as opposed to liberal. At the same time, about a quarter of the population regards itself as middle-of-the-road ideologically. The question wording provides respondents with the opportunity to say they "haven't thought much about this," and fully a quarter to a third typically respond this way. The series of liberal and

TABLE 6-9   Distribution of Ideological Identification, 1972–2008

	1972	1974	1976	1978	1980	1982	1984	1986	1988	1990	1992	1994	1996	2000	2004	2008
Liberal	9%	13%	8%	10%	8%	7%	9%	7%	7%	9%	10%	8%	9%	11%	11%	13%
Somewhat liberal	10	8	8	10	9	8	9	11	9	8	10	8	11	9	8	9
Middle-of-the-road	27	26	25	27	20	22	23	28	22	25	23	27	24	25	25	22
Somewhat conservative	15	12	12	14	14	13	14	15	15	14	15	14	16	13	12	12
Conservative	12	14	13	14	15	14	15	15	17	12	15	21	19	16	19	20
Haven't thought about it	28	27	33	27	36	36	30	25	30	33	27	22	21	27	25	25
Total	101%	100%	99%	102%	102%	100%	100%	101%	100%	101%	100%	100%	100%	101%	100%	101%
(N)	(2,155)	(2,478)	(2,839)	(2,284)	(1,565)	(1,400)	(2,229)	(2,170)	(2,035)	(1,987)	(2,481)	(1,795)	(1,714)	(838)	(1,212)	(2,306)

Source: 2008 American National Election Studies, available at www.electionstudies.org.

TABLE 6-10   Relationship between Ideological Self-Identification and Party
Identification, 2008

	Democrats	Independents	Republicans	Total
Liberal	17%	10	1	28%
Middle-of-the-road	9	15	4	28
Conservative	8	14	22	44
Total[a]	34%	39	27	100%

Source: 2008 American National Election Study, available at www.electionstudies.org.

[a]$N = 901$. "No opinion" and "haven't thought about it" responses are omitted.

conservative responses has been remarkably stable over the years. Ideological identification, in the aggregate, is even more stable than party identification. The slight drop in the percentages saying they "haven't thought about" themselves in these terms, and the corresponding increase in the proportion of those calling themselves conservatives in 1994 and beyond, may be a response to the heightened ideological rhetoric of the 1994 campaign and the increased polarization of the political parties. The overall stability of these numbers, however, should make one cautious of commentary that finds big shifts in liberalism or conservatism in the American electorate.

Table 6-10 shows the relationship between ideological self-identification and party identification. Democrats are more liberal than conservative, Republicans are disproportionately conservative, and independents are fairly evenly balanced. But conservatives are three times as likely to be Republicans as Democrats, and liberals are far more likely to be Democrats. The relationship between ideology and partisanship is shown in the low coincidence of liberal Republicans and conservative Democrats. Also, the electorate tends to perceive the Democratic Party as liberal and the Republican Party as conservative. Those who see an ideological difference between the parties believe the Republicans are more conservative than Democrats by a ratio of more than four to one.

Figure 6-6 presents the relationship between social characteristics and ideological self-identification. Self-identified liberals are most frequent among better-educated whites who claim no religious affiliation. Self-identified conservatives are most common among white evangelicals, but they are also found in substantial numbers among other Protestants and more educated Catholics. The major impact of education is to reduce the proportion of respondents who opt for the middle category. The better educated are more likely to call themselves either liberal or conservative than the high school educated. This tendency would be even greater if those who offered no self-identification were included.

FIGURE 6-6   Ideological Identification, by Race, Ethnicity, Religion, and
Education, 2008

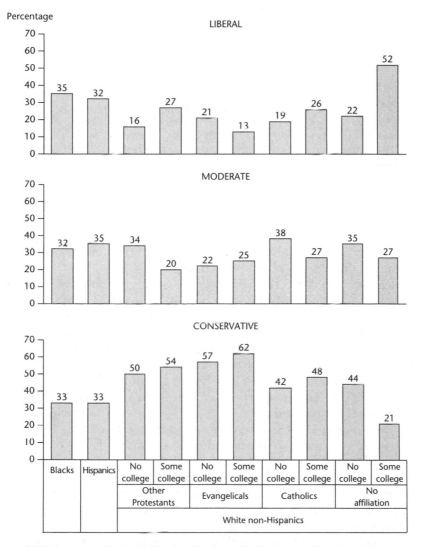

Source: 2008 American National Election Study, available at www.electionstudies.org.

Approximately half the public identifies itself as liberal or conservative. Do these individuals use ideological orientation to organize political information and attitudes? Does political ideology play a role for
Americans similar to the role of partisanship as a basic determinant of
specific political views? Analysis has usually centered on two kinds of

TABLE 6-11   Distribution of the Levels of Conceptualization, 1956–2000

Levels of conceptualization	1956	1960	1964	1968	1972	1976	1980	1984	1988	2000
Ideologues	12%	19%	27%	26%	22%	21%	21%	19%	18%	20%
Group benefit	42	31	27	24	27	26	31	26	36	28
Nature of the times	24	26	20	29	34	30	30	35	25	28
No issue content	22	23	26	21	17	24	19	19	21	24
Total	100%	99%	100%	100%	100%	101%	101%	99%	100%	100%
(N)	(1,740)	(1,741)	(1,431)	(1,319)	(1,372)	(2,870)	(1,612)	(2,257)	(2,040)	(1,807)

Sources: Richard G. Niemi and Herbert F. Weisberg, eds., *Controversies in Voting Behavior*, 3rd ed. (Washington, D.C.: CQ Press, 1993), 89; Michael S. Lewis-Beck, William G. Jacoby, Helmut Norpoth, and Herbert F. Weisberg, *The American Voter Revisited* (Ann Arbor: University of Michigan Press, 2008), 279.

evidence to assess the extent of ideological thinking in the American electorate: the use of ideological concepts in discussing politics and the consistency of attitudes on related issues, suggesting an underlying perspective in the individual's approach to politics.

Data reported in *The American Voter*, by Angus Campbell, Philip E. Converse, Warren E. Miller, and Donald E. Stokes, showed that few members of the electorate discussed their evaluations of the parties and the candidates in ideological language; only 12 percent did so in 1956.[26] Other scholars have contributed similar analysis of subsequent years.[27] As shown in Table 6-11, a change occurred in 1964, during and after the Barry Goldwater/Lyndon B. Johnson election, with its highly ideological rhetoric. The proportions of ideologues doubled in 1964 over 1956 but still constituted only about one-quarter of the electorate. This does not mean that most voters have no notions about what the parties stand for or what they are likely to do when in office. Large proportions of the electorate evaluate the parties with group symbols: "The Democrats help the working man," and "Republicans are good for business." Still, much of the public lacks a commitment to some set of abstract principles about the role of government in society from which they can evaluate the parties.

It is possible that individuals may simply be unsophisticated in the verbal descriptions of their feelings about politics and political parties. Their ideology may guide their political decisions, but they may be unable to articulate it. In that case, the individuals' attitudes toward public issues might be expected to show a degree of coherence and consistency; they would arrive at those positions by applying a common underlying set of political ideals. If individuals are liberal on one issue, one would expect them to be liberal on other related issues; if they are conservative on one, they would be conservative on others. The most sophisticated analysis of ideological perspectives and consistency in issue positions, usually called *issue constraint*, was carried out by Philip E. Converse using data from 1956, 1958, and 1960.[28] He found that the strength of the relationship among domestic issues and among foreign policy issues was about twice as strong as that between domestic and foreign issues. By normal standards even the strongest relationship among domestic issues did not suggest particularly impressive issue consistency. Norman H. Nie and Kristi Andersen later augmented this analysis with an additional decade of coverage.[29] As with several other patterns, a change occurred during the campaign of 1964. The degree of issue constraint on various policy matters increased in 1964 and remains at this higher level to the present.

As might be expected, the degree of consistency among attitudes on different issues varies with the level of education of the individual; the more educated are substantially more consistent in their views than the less educated. However, increasing levels of education do not appear to account for the increase in issue constraint. The work of Nie and Andersen shows convincingly that interest in politics is more critical. In other words, as members of the public become more concerned with issues and more attentive to political leaders, they perceive, and reflect, a higher degree of issue coherence. Almost certainly, the electorate has the capacity for greater issue constraint than it has shown. However, the exercise of the capacity depends much more on political leaders and events than on the characteristics of the electorate. When political leaders use ideological terms to describe themselves and the clusters of issues that they support, the electorate is capable of following suit.

The degree of issue constraint will depend on the range of issues considered. *The American Voter* documented a coherent set of attitudes on welfare policies and governmental activity, even in the 1950s. When the analysis moves to more disparate issues, such as support for welfare policies and civil liberties, the relationship weakens substantially. It can be argued that little relationship should be expected between positions in these different issue areas because they tap different ideological dimensions with no logical or necessary connections among them. For example, there is nothing logically inconsistent in a person's opposing government regulation of business and believing in racial equality. In the first half of the twentieth century, internationalist views in foreign policy were considered the liberal position and isolationist attitudes conservative. However, the cold war and Vietnam did much to rearrange these notions as liberals argued against American involvement and conservatives became more aggressive internationalists. In considering the question of issue constraint, two points should be kept in mind: (1) the meaning of the terms *liberal* and *conservative* change with time, as do the connections between these ideologies and specific historical events; and (2) analysts, in studying issue constraint, invariably impose on the analysis their own version of ideological consistency, which, in light of the ambiguities surrounding the terms, is likely to be somewhat artificial.

A less strenuous criterion than issue constraint for assessing the impact of ideology on political attitudes is simply to look at the relationship between individuals' ideological identification and their positions on various issues taken one at a time. Here, substantial relationships are found. The relationship between ideological identification and liberal views on various policy matters over the past thirty-six years is shown in Table 6-12. Between one-fourth and one-third of the people sampled did not have an ideological position or did not profess attitudes on these issues and are, therefore, missing in the analysis. Nevertheless, the data in Table 6-12 document strong, consistent relationships between ideological identification and many issue positions. The data do not, however, demonstrate that ideology determines issue positions.[30]

If everyone had a strong ideology, attitudes would be determined by that ideology. To a considerable extent, this appears to happen to the most politically alert and concerned in the society, but this group is only a small minority of the total adult population. To the extent that the major American political parties are ideologically oriented, then, by following the parties or political leaders in these parties, Americans have their opinions determined indirectly by ideology. American political parties are often characterized as nonideological, and the country has passed through substantial historical periods when the parties have seemed bent on obscuring the differences between them. At other times, such as 1964 and since the early 1990s, political leaders were more intent on drawing distinctions between themselves and the opposing party in ideological terms. At these times, the public responds by appearing more ideological as well.

Public Opinion and Political Leadership

The study of public opinion is of obvious relevance to public officials and political journalists who wish to assess the mood of the people on various topics, but the extent to which decision makers are influenced by public opinion on any particular policy is almost impossible to determine. Although policy makers must have some sense of the public mood, no one supposes that they measure precisely the attitudes of the public or are influenced by public opinion alone.

Political analysts and public officials both have difficulty assessing the likely impact of public opinion as measured by public opinion polls because the intensity of feelings will influence the willingness of the

TABLE 6-12   Relationship between Ideological Identification and Liberal Positions on Issues, 1972–2008

	Liberal	Somewhat liberal	Middle-of-the-road	Somewhat conservative	Conservative
Increase government services (2008)	81	55	54	29	28
Favor government health insurance (2008)	72	62	50	45	19
Pro-choice on abortion (2008)	79	50	43	34	16
Should allow gay marriage (2008)	72	53	43	28	12
Iraq war increased terrorist threat (2008)	46	45	30	22	12
Government help for blacks (2004)	48	26	20	14	11
Protect the environment (2004)	63	55	40	37	27
Oppose school vouchers (2000)	44	48	52	46	28
Protect homosexuals from job discrimination (1996)	87	79	68	63	39
Not worth it to fight in Persian Gulf (1992)	66	45	41	30	24
Support for the Equal Rights Amendment (1980)	91	78	64	48	38
Legalize marijuana (1976)	60	49	24	24	10
Oppose the Vietnam War (1972)	76	61	39	33	27

Source: 2008 American National Election Study, available at www.electionstudies.org.

Note: The numbers in the table are the percentages taking the liberal position on each issue.

public to act on their views. Public officials who value their careers must be conscious of the issues that raise feelings strong enough to cause people to contribute money, to campaign, and to cast their ballots solely on the basis of that issue. As a result, public officials may be more responsive to the desires of small, intense groups than to larger, but basically indifferent, segments of the public.

In American society public attitudes toward policies usually can be described in one of two ways: as permissive opinion, whereby a wide range of possible government activities are acceptable to the public; or, in contrast, as directive opinion, either supportive or negative, whereby specific alternatives are definitely demanded or opposed. Ordinarily, policy alternatives advocated by both political parties are within the range of permissive opinion, a situation that does not create highly salient issues or sharp cleavages in the public, even though political leaders may present their positions dramatically. Only when many people hold directive opinions will the level of issue salience rise or issue clashes appear among the public. For example, widespread directive support exists for public education in the United States. Most individuals demand a system of public education or would demand it were it threatened. At the same time, permissive support is evident for a wide range of policies and programs in public education. Governments at several levels may engage in a variety of programs without arousing the public to opposition or support. Within this permissive range the public is indifferent.

Occasionally, the public may out-and-out oppose some programs and form directive opinions that impose limits on how far government can go. For example, the widespread opposition to busing children out of their neighborhoods for purposes of integration has perhaps become a directive, negative opinion. Political analysts or politicians cannot easily discover the boundaries between permissive and directive opinions. Political leaders are likely to argue that there are supportive, directive opinions for their own positions and negative, directive opinions for their opponents' views. One should be skeptical of these claims because it is much more likely that there are permissive opinions and casual indifference toward the alternative views. Indifference is widespread and, of course, does not create political pressure. It frees political leaders of restrictions on issue positions but, on balance, is probably more frustrating than welcome.

Notes

1. Philip E. Converse, "The Nature of Belief Systems in Mass Publics," in *Ideology and Discontent*, ed. David Apter (New York: Free Press, 1964), 206–261.

2. Edward G. Carmines and James A. Stimson, "The Two Faces of Issue Voting," *American Political Science Review* 74 (1980): 78–91.
3. In the 2006 General Social Survey, for example, 38 percent said "too much" was being spent on "welfare"; however, 70 percent said "too little" was being spent on "assistance to the poor."
4. 1992 American National Election Study.
5. 2008 American National Election Study.
6. This view is most prominently associated with Paul M. Sniderman and Edward G. Carmines, *Reaching Beyond Race* (Cambridge, Mass.: Harvard University Press, 1997). See also Paul M. Sniderman, Philip E. Tetlock, and Edward G. Carmines, *Prejudice, Politics, and the American Dilemma* (Stanford: Stanford University Press, 1993).
7. A strong statement of the symbolic racism position is in Donald R. Kinder and Lynn M. Sanders, *Divided by Color* (Chicago: University of Chicago Press, 1996).
8. This position is most commonly associated with Lawrence Bobo. See his "Race and Beliefs about Affirmative Action," in *Racialized Politics*, ed. David Sears, Jim Sidanius, and Lawrence Bobo (Chicago: University of Chicago Press, 2000), chap. 5.
9. This position is represented by Jim Sidanius in *Social Dominance: An Intergroup Theory of Social Dominance and Oppression* (Cambridge, England: Cambridge University Press, 1999).
10. Edward G. Carmines and James A. Stimson, *Issue Evolution: Race and the Transformation of American Politics* (Princeton: Princeton University Press, 1989).
11. Kinder and Sanders, *Divided by Color*.
12. CBS News Poll, September 6–8, 2004, Roper Center for Public Opinion Research.
13. Pew Research Center for the People and the Press Values Survey, March 31–April 21, 2009, Roper Center for Public Opinion Research.
14. "America Speaks Out about Homeland Security Survey," conducted by Hart and Teeter Research Companies for the Council for Excellence in Government, February 5–8, 2004, Roper Center for Public Opinion Research.
15. Pew News Interest Index Poll, January 4–8, 2006, Roper Center for Public Opinion Research.
16. "America Speaks Out about Homeland Security Survey," Roper Center for Public Opinion Research.
17. CBS News Poll, April 2005, Roper Center for Public Opinion Research.
18. CBS News Monthly Poll 5, March 26–27, 2003.
19. CBS News/*New York Times* Poll, April 23–27, 2004.
20. 2008 American National Election Study.
21. John E. Mueller, *War, Presidents, and Public Opinion* (New York: Wiley, 1973), 208–213.
22. These data are available at www.pollingreport.com.
23. CBS News Monthly Poll 5; and CBS News/*New York Times* Poll, April 23–27, 2004. Data provided by the Inter-university Consortium for Political and Social Research.
24 Gallup/*USA Today* Poll, July 2008, Roper Center for Public Opinion Research.
25. Pew Research Center for the People and the Press, September 2008.
26. Angus Campbell, Philip E. Converse, Warren E. Miller, and Donald E. Stokes, *The American Voter* (New York: Wiley, 1960), 249.
27. John C. Pierce, "Ideology, Attitudes, and Voting Behavior of the American Electorate: 1956, 1960, 1964," Ph.D. dissertation, University of Minnesota, 1969, 63,

Table 3.1; Paul R. Hagner and John C. Pierce, "Conceptualization and Consistency in Political Beliefs: 1956–1976," paper presented at the annual meeting of the Midwest Political Science Association, Chicago, 1981; and Michael Lewis-Beck, William G. Jacoby, Helmut Norpoth, and Herbert F. Weisberg, *The American Voter Revisited* (Ann Arbor: University of Michigan Press, 2008, chap. 10. See also Norman H. Nie, Sidney Verba, and John R. Petrocik, *The Changing American Voter* (Cambridge, Mass.: Harvard University Press, 1976), chap. 7.

28. Converse, "The Nature of Belief Systems in Mass Publics," 206–261.
29. Norman H. Nie and Kristi Andersen, "Mass Belief Systems Revisited: Political Change and Attitude Structure," *Journal of Politics* 36 (September 1974): 541–591.
30. Nor do the data answer the question, "Where does ideology come from?" For an interesting possibility, see John R. Alford, Carolyn L. Funk, and John R. Hibbing, "Are Political Orientations Genetically Transmitted?" *American Political Science Review* 99 (May 2005): 153–167.

Suggested Readings

Carmines, Edward G., and James A. Stimson. *Issue Evolution: Race and the Transformation of American Politics.* Princeton: Princeton University Press, 1989. A fascinating account of the role of racial issues and policies in American politics in recent decades.

Converse, Philip E. "The Nature of Belief Systems in Mass Publics." In *Ideology and Discontent,* ed. David Apter. New York: Free Press, 1964. A classic analysis of the levels of sophistication in the American public.

Hochschild, Jennifer L. *What's Fair.* Cambridge, Mass.: Harvard University Press, 1981. An intensive, in-depth study of the beliefs and attitudes of a few people that deals with traditional topics from a different perspective.

Lewis-Beck, Michael S., William G. Jacoby, Helmut Norpoth, and Herbert F. Weisberg. *The American Voter Revisited.* Ann Arbor: University of Michigan Press, 2008. A rich reanalysis of the themes from the classic work, using mainly 2000 and 2004 data.

Mayer, William G. *The Changing American Mind.* Ann Arbor: University of Michigan Press, 1992. Analysis of changes in issue positions between 1960 and 1988.

Page, Benjamin J., and Robert Y. Shapiro. *The Rational Public.* Chicago: University of Chicago Press, 1992. Analysis of the American public's views on policy issues over the past fifty years.

Sniderman, Paul M., Richard A. Brody, and Philip E. Tetlock. *Reasoning and Choice.* Cambridge, England: Cambridge University Press, 1991. A political, psychological approach to the study of issues and ideology.

Stimson, James A. *The Tides of Consent: How Public Opinion Shapes American Politics.* Cambridge, England: Cambridge University Press, 2004. A complex analysis of changing policy views and their impact.

Internet Resources

The Web site of the American National Election Studies, www.electionstudies .org, has extensive data on the topics covered in this chapter. Click on "Ideological Self-Identification" for ideological items in a number of election years. Click on

"Public Opinion on Public Policy Issues" for a wide range of attitudes from 1952 to the present. Each political item is broken down by an extensive set of social characteristics.

The Roper Center for Public Opinion Research at the University of Connecticut has an enormous collection of survey data on American public opinion from the 1930s to the present.

The General Social Survey, www.norc.org/GSS+Website/, has been collecting public opinion data since 1972 on a wide range of topics. Some of these data can be analyzed online at http://sda.berkeley.edu.

Political Communication and the Mass Media

MUCH ATTENTION has been focused on the process of change in political opinions, both in terms of the conditions for such change and the possibilities of instigating widespread shifts in political beliefs through the mass media. At the extremes, the process of influencing political opinions is labeled *brainwashing* or *propaganda*. In reality, only a matter of degree separates these forms of influence from political persuasion, campaigning, or even education. All the efforts covered by these terms are directed toward changing individuals' political ideas, values, and opinions, or toward fostering some political action. Enormous amounts of time and money are expended in American society to change political views. The diversity of the efforts to influence the public mind, along with the diversity and complexity of the society itself, makes highly unlikely a quick or uniform public response to any one of these attempts. Only dramatic events or crises can quickly change the public's views. Although news of such events comes through the media, the impact results from the events themselves, not simply the media imagery.

Political persuasion probably is most effective in casual personal relationships. The impact of the mass media likely is important in shaping the contours of political discourse, but only gradually and over fairly long periods of time. At the same time, the role that the media have in making information widely available is significant in creating the conditions under which attitude change occurs. In this chapter we will consider the basic processes of opinion change and the impact of the mass media and election campaigns on individual political behavior.

Functions of Opinions for Individuals

Social psychology suggests that an individual's opinions can serve various purposes: cognitive, social, and psychological. Cognitive functions of opinions cover the efforts to give meaning to the social environment and to relate elements of belief and knowledge to one another. Opinions generally relate directly or indirectly to an individual's most significant goals or values. Somehow the policy supported by a political opinion is expected to be consistent with one's most important political values.

Opinions serve a social function if they aid the individual in adjusting to others or in becoming part of a group. In some cases individuals may use opinions to set themselves apart from others. Political and social issues may be too unimportant in general to serve social purposes for most people, and little evidence suggests that strong social conformity pressures affect their views on most political issues. Nevertheless, for highly salient issues an individual is apt to find that holding a socially unacceptable view is both uncomfortable and costly.

An opinion also may serve purposes for an individual that are not dependent on its social, economic, or political meaning but on its special psychological significance for the individual. For example, an individual might hold strongly prejudicial opinions against some group because it enhances self-esteem to feel superior to others, or an individual might project undesirable qualities onto a certain group and thereby disassociate him- or herself from those qualities. The problem with psychological attachments of this kind is that the opinions based this way are not responsive to ordinary influence because of their psychological importance to the individual. Most Americans do not appear to attach strong psychological meaning to their political opinions, although the small minority who do may become dangerous to the tolerant give-and-take that is necessary to the maintenance of a democracy. In general, in a modern, pluralistic society with its open political processes, opinions on significant political subjects are unlikely to remain privatized and solely of psychological relevance to the individual. Opinions also take on social and cognitive functions.

Most discussions of political opinions imply a more or less reasoned handling of opinions by individuals. They imply that individuals intelligently relate their opinions to one another and that a logical relationship exists between a goal and a preference for policies leading to that goal. The implication of this perspective is that opinions can be changed if the cognitive content of the attitude is changed—that is, if new information is brought to the attention of the individual. However, if individuals hold their opinions for the social or psychological purposes they serve, instead of for the cognitive, providing these individuals with more information or altering the policy implications of the opinion will not necessarily lead to opinion change.

Opinion Consistency and Dissonance

The analysis of inconsistency in opinions has much in common with the cross-pressure hypothesis (considered in chapter 5). In psychology this analysis of opinions has taken the form of identifying elements of several opinions as consistent with one another or as being in conflict (dissonant). Because dissonance is assumed to be disturbing, an individual presumably will try to avoid or reduce it. An example of dissonance should clarify these concepts.[1]

Suppose a Republican believes that all Democratic administrations are corrupt and that Republicans stand for honest government, and the individual's party loyalty is justified on this basis. If the individual hears that a Republican governor is taking bribes, the information conflicts with the person's earlier views and may create dissonance among them. The dissonance could be reduced by justifying his or her loyalty on a new basis, or by denying or discrediting the new information. A denial might take the form of deciding that the governor is being framed by opponents.

Individuals have many psychological defenses against the potential dissonance represented by new information that conflicts with their existing attitudes: *selective exposure,* not paying attention to conflicting information; *selective perception,* misinterpreting such information or rejecting the sources of the information as lacking credibility; *compartmentalization,* not making the connections between dissonant attitudes; and *rationalization,* developing an unwarranted interpretation of a situation to avoid confronting the real one. Should the meaning of the information be unavoidable, attitude change to restore harmony may result. Typically, individuals will change dissonant patterns in the easiest way. The opinions or beliefs that are least important to the individual will be changed, not important ideas or values.

Political opinions are probably most often changed simply by providing individuals with more information. The additional information may be no more than some new facts about the environment or indications that many political leaders whom an individual respects hold a particular view. The low salience of most political issues, plus the widespread emphasis on debate and discussion, leads to circumstances that improve the opportunities for changing opinions with information.

Political Communication and Attitude Change

Individuals in the public receive ideas and information intended to alter their political opinions from a variety of sources. Some sources are political leaders and commentators whose views arrive impersonally through the mass media; others are friends, coworkers, and family members who influence opinions through personal contact. Much remains to be learned about political persuasion and communication, but at least occasionally many Americans engage in attempts to influence others, and almost everyone is regularly the recipient of large quantities of political communication.

A somewhat oversimplified view of the transmission of political information would have the media beaming a uniform message to a mass audience made up of isolated individuals. The audience would receive all or most of its information from the media. Thus public opinion would be a direct product of the information and perspective provided through the media. A more complex view suggests that information is transmitted in a "two-step flow of communication."[2] Information is transmitted from "opinion elites" (leaders in society, such as politicians, organizational heads, and news commentators) to a minority of the public—the "opinion leaders"—and from them to the remainder of the public:

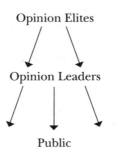

The information from opinion elites usually is sent through the mass media, but this view implies that only a portion of the audience—the opinion leaders—is attentive to any particular type of information such as political news. The opinion leaders, as intermediaries, then interpret, modify, and explain facts and events to those friends and neighbors who are less interested in or concerned with these happenings. In the process, the original message conveyed through the media becomes many somewhat different messages as it reaches the public.

The two-step flow model may not be strictly true in most cases, and public opinion research has generally failed to turn up many people who recognize themselves as opinion leaders. Even so, most members of the public probably do receive information from the mass media in the context of their social groups. Thus they filter the information and interpretations of the media through not only their own perceptions, experiences, and existing attitudes, but also those of people around them. Only when the media have the attention of most members of the audience and a virtual monopoly over the kinds of information received by a public that has few existing attitudes about the subject can the media produce anything like a uniform change in public attitudes.

A somewhat different argument, also based on the role of social influences on the development of public opinion, has been made by Elisabeth Noelle-Neumann in *The Spiral of Silence*.[3] She argues that members of society sense that some views are increasing in popularity, even if these ascending viewpoints are held only by a minority. Under such circumstances people become reluctant to express opinions contrary to the presumed ascending view, whereas individuals holding that view are emboldened and express themselves more freely. This furthers the illusion that one viewpoint is widely shared. People then adopt the viewpoint because of this largely imaginary public pressure. Although intriguing, the attractiveness of this argument is diminished somewhat by the almost total lack of evidence in support of it.

In the remainder of this chapter we will consider the impact of the mass media on political attitudes in the context of political campaigns. Because the media can be influential only if people are paying attention, we will look at the question of the overall attentiveness of the public to political news. Because the impact of the media varies depending on the existing attitudes and information of the audience, we will examine the impact of the media on different kinds of people and in different campaign contexts.

To begin, however, we need to draw some distinctions among the various types of media. First, the impact of information may be different depending on the type of media through which it is received. Precisely the same information received through television, radio, or a newspaper may impress the recipient differently. For example, viewing a speech on television may be more dramatic than hearing it on the radio or reading the text in a newspaper. Something like this occurred in 1960 when television viewers of the first of three presidential debates between John F. Kennedy and Richard M. Nixon had a less favorable impression of Nixon than did radio listeners.[4] A difficult topic, however, may be more easily absorbed by reading and rereading an article in the newspaper than by watching a story flash by once on television.

Second, the media differ in what they offer. Simple elements of information are more quickly and dramatically presented to a large audience on television than they can be through the print media. Television, however, may systematically under-inform its audience by rarely offering more than a "headline service" of a minute or two on any one story. The more the public wants information and is motivated to seek it, the more important newspapers, magazines, and the Internet become. It is easy to search for information on the Internet, more difficult but possible in the print media, and much more difficult with radio and television. The characteristics of the media give them different roles in the formation of public opinion. In general, television alerts the public to a variety of topics and newspapers inform a smaller segment of the public in greater depth. The Internet does some of both.

Third, an increasing diversity of news sources is available through television, especially over the past twenty years. CNN, MSNBC, and Fox News are genuine alternatives to the broadcast networks, especially when it comes to fast-breaking stories and to news and commentary with a political slant. Surveys done by the Pew Research Center for the People and the Press in 2008 estimated that more than half the public watched CNN at least "sometimes" and 24 percent did so "regularly."[5] The Fox News cable audience was just as large. The C-SPAN channels provide extensive coverage of both the U.S. House of Representatives and the Senate, as well as other political events, without the intermediary of network editing and commentary. Over 20 percent of the public reports watching C-SPAN at least occasionally.[6] Call-in television and radio provide lengthy discussions of public issues and, since 1992, offer a mechanism whereby candidates can bypass the normal news channels and receive unmediated coverage.

The Internet as a news source is a more recent development, with intriguing characteristics. Providing almost unlimited access to information, it requires the consumer to seek out that information actively. It also offers opportunities to "talk back" or comment on the news, and to be put in touch with other like-minded people. Few "gatekeepers" operate on the Internet, and the issues of the reliability and credibility of information are largely left to the user to determine. Opportunities abound for whispering campaigns of rumor and misinformation.

Fourth, the impact of editorial endorsements by newspapers (television and radio stations rarely make endorsements) should be assessed independently of news coverage, although editorial preferences may bias news stories. Newspaper endorsements seemingly have a minimal impact in presidential elections, given that many other sources of influence exist.[7] In less visible, local races, a newspaper editorial may influence many voters.[8] Some concern exists that major newspaper chains could wield significant power nationally by lining up their papers behind one candidate. In recent years, however, the large chains have generally left their papers free to make decisions locally.

Fifth, throughout our discussion we need to make the distinction between the impact of news coverage by the media and political advertising carried by the media. This is not an easy task, especially because the news media often cover political advertising as if it were news and consciously or unconsciously pick up themes from political ads and weave them into their own coverage.[9] Placing political advertising in news programs makes it harder to separate news from ads. Even the "ad watches" that news organizations use to critique candidates' advertising may contribute to the confusion over what is news and what is paid advertising.

Attention to the Media

For the media to have an impact on an individual's political attitudes and behavior, the individual must give some degree of attention to the media when political information is being conveyed. Almost all Americans have access to television and watch political news at least some of the time. In 2008 a majority of Americans (54 percent) reported reading a daily newspaper regularly, often online.[10] Somewhat fewer reported reading a newspaper for political news. This represents a decline in daily newspaper readership from more than 70 percent early in the 1990s. Occasional newspaper reading is higher. Television remains the main source of news for most Americans, but the Internet has passed newspapers and radio as the second most commonly used source.[11]

Much discussion has ensued in the scholarly literature on mass media about the capacity to bring matters to the attention of the public or to conceal them.[12] This is usually referred to as *agenda setting*. The literature suggests that the media have great influence over what the public is aware of and concerned with. Television news and front-page stories in newspapers focus the public's attention on a few major stories each day. This function, sometimes called headline service, tells the public: Here are important developments you should be aware of. Major events, such as the September 11, 2001, terrorist attacks; or scandals, such as President Bill Clinton's sexual liaison with White House intern Monica Lewinsky; or celebrity milestones, such as the death of Michael Jackson, push other stories off the agenda. The media make it almost impossible for an ordinary American to be unaware of these events. That is agenda setting.

Television often plays a critical role in bringing events and issues to the public's attention, presenting certain types of information in an exceptionally dramatic or impressive way. The Persian Gulf War and the start of the Iraq war were televised to an unprecedented extent. The American public watched a real-life video arcade of modern warfare. In January 1991, 67 percent of a national sample reported following the Persian Gulf War "very closely."[13] Attention was not as high in 2003, but over half the public followed the invasion of Iraq very closely.[14] In the short run, the coverage created the impression of an overwhelming military victory and great satisfaction with the performance of each president. In each instance, the president's job approval ratings soared and support for the war increased dramatically.[15] With the passage of time, evaluations became more mixed.

Perhaps nothing in television history compares with the coverage of the attacks on the World Trade Center and the Pentagon on September 11. The major news channels abandoned regular programming and focused on the attacks and their aftermath for days. Virtually everyone in the country was attentive to this coverage, and most people had strong emotional reactions to what they saw.

The news media, particularly television, can rivet public attention on certain issues and, in doing so, limit the policy-making options of political leaders. The range of subjects on which this can be done is narrow, however. Death, destruction, intrigue, or pathos are generally essential ingredients. More abstract or mundane political issues are easily ignored by most of the public.

However, many potential news items are never reported, either in the print media or on television. This is the result of a process often referred to as *gatekeeping*.[16] The media are more selective than a phrase such as "all the news that's fit to print" suggests. Bias in gatekeeping and agenda setting can occur when items are kept from the public that would have been of considerable interest, or when items the public otherwise would have ignored are made to seem important. Neither of these effects is easily demonstrated with political information and opinions. It is fairly easy to show that a particular newspaper or a given television station may ignore certain topics or exaggerate others, but it is difficult to find evidence of any impact of selective coverage on the public.

Although the media may focus on certain news items, the public has an enormous capacity for ignoring the coverage and being highly selective about what to take an interest in. First the *Los Angeles Times Mirror* and later the Pew Research Center for the People and the Press have engaged in an extensive project to explore the public's awareness of and interest in news stories.[17] Some news stories, such as the explosion of the space shuttle *Challenger* and the 1989 San Francisco earthquake, were followed with great interest by most of the public. As shown in Table 7-1, almost all the news stories from January 1986 to August 2009 that were followed "very closely" by large percentages of the public were military operations or disasters of one sort or another. In contrast, less than

TABLE 7-1   Most Closely Followed News Stories and Other Selected News
Items, 1986–2009

News stories	Percentage following very closely
Ten most closely followed news stories	
Explosion of the space shuttle *Challenger* (January 1986)	80
Terrorism attacks on the United States (September/October 2001)	74
San Francisco earthquake (November 1989)	73
High price of gasoline (September 2005)	71
Condition of U.S. economy (September 2008)	70
Hurricane Katrina (September 2005)	70
Verdict in Rodney King case and subsequent violence (May 1992)	70
TWA 800 crash (July 1996)	69
Rescue of little girl in Texas who fell into a well (October 1987)	69
Columbine High School shooting (April 1999)	68
Other news stories	
End of Persian Gulf War (January 1991)	67
Increases in the price of gasoline (June 2008)	66
Hurricane Andrew (September 1992)	66
Sniper shootings near Washington, D.C. (October 2002)	65
News about situation in Iraq (May 2003)	63
Debate about war in Iraq (February 2003)	62
Debate over Wall Street bailout (October 2008)	62
Increases in the price of gasoline (October 1990)	62
Increases in the price of gasoline (June 2000)	61
News about presidential election (October 2008)	61
Increases in the price of gasoline (June 2004)	58
War with Iraq (March 2003)	57
Condition of U.S. economy (February/March 2009)	56
News about situation in Iraq (May 2004)	54
Death of Princess Diana (September 1997)	54
U.S. military effort in Afghanistan (April 2009)	52
U.S. military effort in Afghanistan (January 2002)	51
Health care reform debate (August 2009)	49
Terrorist bombings in London (July 2005)	48
Bill Clinton's health care reform proposals (December 1993)	45
Breakup of the Soviet Union (October 1991)	47
Outcome of the presidential election (November 2000)	38
George W. Bush's proposal to deal with Social Security (March 2005)	38
Charges that Newt Gingrich violated House ethics rules (January 1997)	23
Mapping the human genetic code (July 2000)	16
U.S. Supreme Court decision on campaign finance (December 2003)	8

Source: Pew Research Center for the People and the Press, available at www.people-press.org.

25 percent of the public paid close attention to news stories about the mapping of the human genetic code, charges that Speaker Newt Gingrich violated House ethics rules, or the U.S. Supreme Court decision on campaign finance.

As would be expected, a large percentage of the public followed news about the terrorist attacks on September 11 very closely. Some of the people who did not follow the story said they were so distraught they avoided the news. Public attention to the military activities in Afghanistan following the attacks, shown in Table 7-1 at 51 percent, is noticeably below the level of attention to the Persian Gulf War in 1991, at 67 percent. Public attention to the debate about going to war in Iraq during several months in the spring of 2003 (around 62 percent) was greater than the attention to the onset of the war itself in March of that year (57 percent).

Large numbers of Americans (70 percent) followed the news of Hurricane Katrina in the late summer of 2005.[18] Most (89 percent) relied on television coverage, especially that of cable news channels, for their news about Katrina and its aftermath. Interestingly, equally large numbers (71 percent) paid close attention to the news about high gasoline prices in the wake of the storm; Table 7-1 reflects concern about gas prices at other times as well.

Not surprisingly, in the fall of 2008 a large percentage of the public paid close attention to news about the economy, and these high levels of attention continued through early 2009. More unusual was the relatively high level of interest in the presidential campaign throughout the fall of 2008. At its high point in October, 61 percent reported following the campaign very closely, an all-time high for interest in presidential elections during the time covered by Pew's News Interest Index.[19] In contrast, the disputed outcome of the 2000 presidential election was followed closely by only 38 percent.

The combination of television, Internet, radio, newspapers, and magazines represents an extraordinary capacity to inform the public rapidly and in considerable depth about major political news items. Add to this the informal communication about the news of the day that most people engage in, and it is easy to see that the American public is in a position to be well informed. The fact that as many people persist in *not* informing themselves about most political news is not evidence of a failure of the mass media to make the news available in a variety of forms.

A number of scholars have pointed out that it may be rational for voters to ignore much of the political information around them. Rational choice theorists, following the lead of economist Anthony Downs, argue that the benefits derived from reaching a "correct" decision on a candidate or policy may not be worth the costs the voter incurs in finding out the information.[20] It is rational, therefore, for the voter to take a number of information shortcuts, such as relying on someone else's judgment or voting according to one's established party identification. Samuel L. Popkin uses the analogy of "fire alarms" versus "police patrols" to explain how most people view political information.[21] Instead of patrolling the political "neighborhood" constantly to make sure nothing there requires their attention, most citizens rely on others to raise the alarm when something important happens. Television news and newspaper headlines may be enough to tell average citizens whether they need to delve deeper into a particular story.

A minority of people are motivated to follow political news and inform themselves broadly about public affairs. Some people need to be informed about government and politics—or some aspects of it—to do their jobs. Others are simply interested in politics, so searching out information is less burdensome to them. Not surprisingly, scholars studying media behavior have consistently found a strong relationship between interest in politics and attention to political news. In his study of the media behavior of voters in Erie, Pennsylvania, and Los Angeles, California, during the 1976 presidential election, Thomas E. Patterson found that the most interested voters not only paid the most attention to the media but could recall political news they had heard on television or read in the newspaper better than the less interested.[22] Interested individuals are better equipped than the uninterested and inattentive to retain and use new elements of information that come their way.

Because the most interested voters are also the most partisan, a relationship also exists between attention to the media and partisanship. The fact that strong partisans and politically interested people are most attentive to the media accounts for the somewhat paradoxical finding that those with the most exposure to the media are among the least affected by it. Philip E. Converse, in his study of the impact of mass media exposure on voting behavior in elections in the 1950s, drew several conclusions based on findings similar to those represented in Figure 7-1.[23] The voters most stable in their preferences (whether stability is measured during a campaign or between elections) would be those who are highly attentive to mass media but firmly committed to their party or candidate. Those who pay no attention to media communication remain stable in their vote choices because no new information is introduced to change their votes. The shifting, unstable voters are more likely to be those with moderate exposure to mass media. Unfortunately, efforts at replicating Converse's findings for other election years have failed to uncover similar patterns. One difficulty may be that in recent years there have been hardly any voters with no exposure to the mass media. Nevertheless, the reasoning behind this expected relationship is compelling: The impact of the media is likely to be greatest when the recipients of the message have little information and few existing attitudes.

FIGURE 7-1   Hypothetical Relationship between Mass Media Attention and
Stability of Voting Behavior

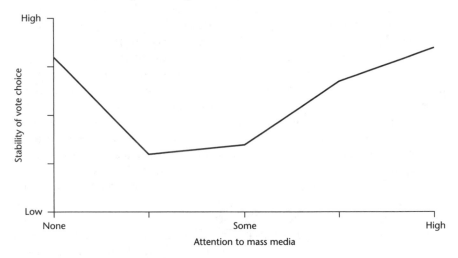

Did Iraq Have Weapons of Mass Destruction?

Attitudes may be surprisingly resistant to new information. After President George W. Bush declared the end of "formal hostilities" in Iraq in May 2003, many surveys documented a pattern of beliefs among partisans about the factual evidence for the existence of weapons of mass destruction (WMDs) in Iraq, Iraqi nuclear arms development, and Iraqi dictator Saddam Hussein's involvement in the attacks on September 11.

A year later, Bush supporters disproportionately believed that Iraq had WMDs and, to a lesser degree, that they had actually been found in Iraq. People not sympathetic to the president believed the opposite. In a CBS/*New York Times* Monthly Poll in April 2004, views on the existence of WMDs were strongly associated with vote intention, partisanship, and ideological self-identification. The belief that Saddam Hussein was involved in September 11 showed a similar, if weaker, pattern.

Misinformation or ignorance usually is considered a result of apathy or inattention, but that is not always the case. Given what has been said so far, the expectation is that the better educated and those more interested in politics would be less likely to believe that Iraq had WMDs. For the whole 2004 sample this is true to a moderate degree, but it is solely a function of the supporters of Democratic presidential nominee John Kerry. Among Bush supporters, those who were highly attentive and least attentive to the election campaign were equally likely to believe

FIGURE 7-2   Percentages Believing Iraq Has Weapons of Mass Destruction
by Attention to the Campaign and Vote Intention, 2004

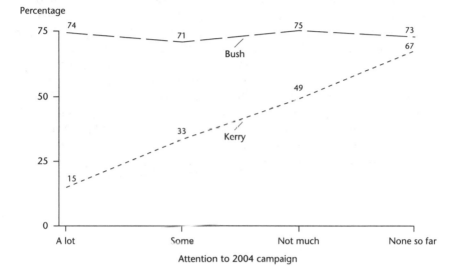

Source: CBS News/*New York Times* Monthly Poll, April 2004.

there were WMDs in Iraq. In Figure 7-2, the flat line at the top of the graph represents this lack of relationship. The Kerry supporters, represented by the sloping line, had different views depending on their level of interest in the campaign. The least attentive Kerry supporters had about the same views as the Bush supporters.

A study by the Program on International Policy Attitudes (PIPA) shows some evidence of a relationship between viewing Fox News and believing that WMDs had been found in Iraq.[24] A simple argument would be that Fox News's content led its audience to this belief. But that argument is too simple. Almost all of the Fox News audience also paid attention to media sources that offered a different perspective than Fox.[25] Why did these people appear to believe Fox News and not their other news sources? Even Fox News stories were not consistent in their bias.[26] Why did their viewers believe some stories but not others?

A more plausible explanation is that people who believe that WMDs had been found in Iraq have characteristics that make them more likely to view Fox News. They may have watched Fox News because they hoped to view stories that would support their beliefs about WMDs, but probably more general orientations, such as support for President Bush and the Republican Party, led them to seek out Fox News as a conservative voice.

This pattern of behavior can be referred to as "dissonance reduction." Because these individuals supported Bush, who used the presence of WMDs as a reason for going to war, accepting the idea that these weapons did not exist might create negative feelings toward Bush. To avoid the cognitive dissonance that would result, the individuals persisted in believing that Iraq had such weapons.

Over time, it doubtless becomes more difficult to believe that Iraq had WMDs, and another dissonance reduction step might appear. One possibility would be changing the belief that the existence of WMDs was a significant reason for going to war. Eventually President Bush and others offered the view that the reason for going to war was not WMDs but the removal of Saddam Hussein and the establishment of democracy in Iraq. This might be considered an example of reducing dissonance through rationalization.

The Media and Presidential Approval Ratings

Presidential approval ratings, regularly measured by public opinion polling organizations, reflect both the effect media coverage can have on political attitudes and its limitations. Media polls regularly ask about and report on the public's views on how the president is handling his job.

The various polling organizations ask the question in different ways, but what they generally report—and what we report here—is the percentage of the public that approves of the way the president is doing his job, not the degree of enthusiasm they feel. The approval measure sometimes behaves oddly. For example, President Ronald Reagan's approval rating jumped 10 percent after he was shot, presumably an expression of sympathy and not an assessment of the job he was doing.

In one sense, the ratings are a function of media content, because media coverage is the only source of information about the president for most people. The most precipitous changes in approval ratings, though, result from dramatic and important events. Although media coverage colors the recipient's perception of events, the media are usually not free to ignore them; the events themselves, not just the coverage, make them compelling.

Most presidents begin a term with high ratings, a phenomenon referred to as a "honeymoon effect." Presidents usually suffer a decline in approval ratings the longer they are in office. Not only are the ratings expected to decline over time, but, as the public becomes more knowledgeable about a president, the approval ratings also should become more stable and more retrospective. In other words, the more people know about the president, the less impact some new element of information has and the more their approval or disapproval represents a summary judgment. As this happens, the day-to-day events covered by the media, and the coverage itself, have less impact in shaping the attitudes of the public.

Extraordinary events can boost a president's popularity while in office. International crises usually produce an increase in approval ratings as the public rallies 'round the flag and its representative, the president. Winning a second term (or even campaigning for one), with the accompanying election fanfare, also lifts presidential approval scores. These boosts usually prove to be temporary, and popularity ratings tend to drift downward again as time in office passes.

The approval ratings of both George H. W. Bush and George W. Bush illustrate the transitory nature of the increase in popularity associated with international crises. Both presidents' approval ratings improved dramatically during their respective wars in Iraq, both of which started far into their first terms as president. Poll results varied, but generally the senior Bush received approval ratings as high as any president had ever received, approaching 90 percent. His son did not do as well, but his ratings went over 70 percent in early April 2003.

In both cases their approval ratings began to fall immediately after the declared end of hostilities, for much the same reason initially. The public shifted its attention and concern away from the war and to the economy. For the senior Bush the sagging economy drove his approval ratings down for the remainder of his presidency as the Persian Gulf War became irrelevant. By the fall of 1992, he was receiving ratings about as low as any past president.[27]

President George W. Bush found his approval ratings dropping because of the economy and because of the continuing insurgency in Iraq. His ratings dropped even further (to new lows) after Hurricane Katrina in the late summer of 2005. The approval ratings of both presidents followed a remarkably similar path over the course of their respective crises, as shown in Figure 7-3.

What happened to the ratings of the two Bushes illustrates the public's shifting focus on what matters in assessing the president. Throughout 1990, 1991, and 1992, President George H. W. Bush received low ratings for his handling of the economy, so when the economy mattered most to people, his overall approval ratings were low. During the Persian Gulf War, attention shifted to foreign affairs—an area in which Bush had always enjoyed high ratings—and this translated, for a while, into high overall approval ratings.

President George W. Bush had enjoyed very high approval ratings after September 11—almost as high as his father's after the Persian Gulf War. But by early 2003, his approval ratings had dropped thirty percentage points, back to their level before the terrorist attacks. Public attention on the military action in Iraq raised his job approval ratings about

FIGURE 7-3   Approval Ratings of Presidents George H. W. Bush and George
W. Bush before and after Middle Eastern Wars, August 1990–
January 1992 and October 2002–March 2004

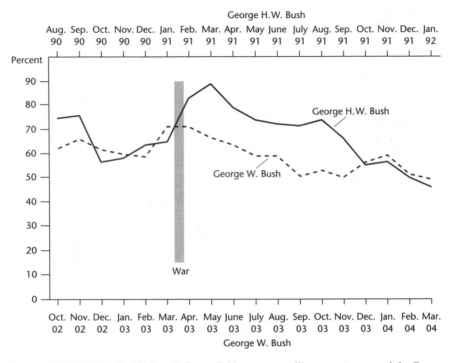

Sources: CNN/ *USA Today*/Gallup Polls, available at www.pollingreport.com and the Roper
Center for Public Opinion Research.

twenty percentage points. During the next year his ratings dropped to
the point that more people disapproved of the job he was doing than
approved. Figure 7-4 shows George W. Bush's approval ratings from the
start of his term until December 2008. His ratings differ considerably
depending upon whether the question focused on his overall job performance, his handling of the situation in Iraq, or the war on terrorism.

The trend of President Clinton's approval is somewhat unusual in
that he reversed a precipitous decline in popularity on the basis of a con-
frontation with Congress over domestic politics, rather than his handling of
an international crisis. Clinton ended his term in office in January 2001 with
approval ratings of 61 percent, unprecedented for a modern president at
the end of his second term. Commentators and politicians have asked
repeatedly how Clinton could maintain such high approval ratings when
the public was thoroughly aware of his personal misbehavior and disapproved of it. An overwhelming majority of Americans thought Clinton

FIGURE 7-4 Approval Ratings of President George W. Bush in Handling His Job as President, the Economy, the War in Iraq, and Terrorism, 2001–2008

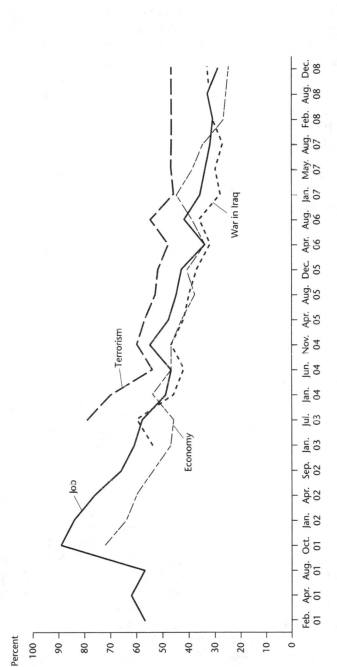

Sources: CNN/*USA Today*/Gallup Poll, available at www.pollingreport.com, with these exceptions: the May 2003 and the December 2008 data on "terrorism" came from CBS News Polls; the December 2008 "Iraq" data came from an NBC News/*Wall Street Journal* Poll; and the December 2008 "economy" data came from an ABC News/*Washington Post* Poll, all from the Roper Center for Public Opinion Research.

Note: The October 2001 poll was conducted immediately after 9/11. The spike in three lines in the spring of 2003 corresponded with the military phase of the war in Iraq. The spike in January 2004 followed the capture of Saddam Hussein.

lacked the ability to provide moral leadership for the country, and that providing moral leadership was important for a president to do. The explanation, to the extent that one exists, appears to be another dissonance reduction device—compartmentalization. Republicans made the connection between personal misbehavior and the job Clinton was doing as president and reported their disapproval. Democrats and, to a lesser extent, independents did not link the two views. In July 1998 a CBS News poll asked people whether they thought of "this whole situation [with Monica Lewinsky] more as a private matter having to do with Bill Clinton's personal life, or more as a public matter having to do with Bill Clinton's job as president."[28] Eighty percent of the Democrats and 68 percent of the independents—but only 37 percent of the Republicans—said they regarded this as a "personal matter."

In the early months of his presidency, Barack Obama's approval rating reached 68 percent, high even by "honeymoon" standards. Given his full plate of financial and economic crises, two wars, and moves to reform health care, his approval rating slipped somewhat in his first six months in office, but was still a respectable 56 percent in September 2009.[29]

Campaigns

Political campaigns are efforts to present candidates or issues to voters with information, rationales, characterizations, and images to convince them that one candidate or position is better than the alternatives and to get them to act on that preference. Massive amounts of money are spent in modern campaigns to saturate the airwaves in an effort to influence voters. A perennial question for politicians, political commentators, and scholars is: "How much difference does a campaign make?"

Although most professional politicians take for granted the efficacy of political campaigns, scholarly analysis has often questioned their impact. In most elections the majority of voters decide how they will vote, based on partisanship or ideological leanings, before the general election campaign begins. Beyond this, the generally low level of political information among the less politically interested throws doubt on the ability of undecided voters to absorb ideas during a campaign. Andrew Gelman and Gary King have offered an especially interesting form of this argument.[30] They contend that a voter's eventual choice can be predicted satisfactorily at the start of a campaign, well before the candidates are even known. Furthermore, because a voter may move away from this ultimate choice during the course of a campaign, intermediate predictions—so popular in media coverage and campaign organizations—are misleading.

Other analysts, using economic forecasting models, argue that the outcome of the election—and the margin of victory—can be predicted long before the election campaign from such variables as the rates of economic growth, inflation, and unemployment.[31] It may be difficult to believe that an individual voter's choice is made before the start of a campaign or is determined by economic forces; yet evidence indicates that in most years the vote choices of most voters are not affected by the general election campaigns. The ANES regularly asks voters when, during the presidential campaign, they made their voting decisions.[32] In most years about two-thirds of the electorate reports deciding before or during the conventions, with the final one-third deciding during the campaign. Over the years, fewer people report deciding during the conventions— presumably because, in recent decades, the candidates have essentially been chosen by the end of the presidential primaries in the late spring.

The decision times of partisans and independents are different because the loyal party votes line up early behind the party's candidate. In all recent presidential elections, the strong partisans made their decisions by the end of the conventions, whereas many of the less committed partisans and independents were typically still undecided at the start of the general election campaign. In fairly close elections, this relatively uncommitted group can swing the election either way, with 10 to 15 percent of the voters making a decision in the last days of the election campaign.

The possibility clearly exists that campaigning can influence a small but crucial proportion of the electorate, and many elections are close enough that the winning margin could well be a result of campaigning. Professional politicians drive themselves and their organizations toward influencing undecided voters in the expectation that they are the key to providing, or maintaining, the winning margin. One can easily think of examples of elections in which the only explanation for the outcome was the aggressive campaign of one of the candidates. Multimillionaire publisher Steve Forbes could never have won the 1996 Republican presidential primaries in Arizona and Delaware without the expensive media advertising campaign he waged in those states. One can, however, just as easily think of examples of well-financed campaigns that failed. In early 1996 Sen. Phil Gramm of Texas raised more money and won fewer delegates than any other Republican presidential candidate. The simple, if unsatisfying, answer to the question "do campaigns work?" seems to be "sometimes."

In this section we will explore the conditions under which campaigns, and the information they seek to convey, are likely to have the most impact. In general, the effect of information provided in a campaign will depend on: (1) the amount already known about the candidate, or issue; (2) the extent to which the information is countered by competing claims; and (3) the extent to which the information is in a form that resonates with the concerns and life experiences of the voter.

New information has the greatest impact in situations in which little is known about the candidate or issue, and in which the voters have few existing attitudes. The application of this generalization can be seen in many areas. For example, the candidate who is less well known has the most to gain (or lose) from joint appearances, such as debates. The 1960 debates between Kennedy and Nixon, the first-ever series of televised presidential debates, appear to have had a substantial impact on the election outcome, in large part because at the time Kennedy was not well known to the public. According to several different public opinion polls in 1960, about half of the voters reported that they were influenced by the debates, with Kennedy holding an advantage of three to one over Nixon.[33] Although Nixon's poor showing is often blamed on his five o'clock shadow, it is unlikely that his appearance caused many to turn against him, because he had been in the public eye as vice president for eight years. Instead, Kennedy's advantage came from undecided Democrats who had little information about Kennedy (but were favorably disposed toward him because he was the Democratic candidate) and who were influenced by his attractive appearance and good performance. The immediate effect of the 1960 experience was the abandonment of presidential debates until 1976. Incumbent presidents or campaign front-runners were unwilling to offer such opportunities to their lesser-known challengers.

The 2008 debates presented a similar situation for Barack Obama. As the younger, less experienced, and less familiar candidate, he had the chance and the challenge to shape the impressions that voters had about him to a greater extent than the more familiar candidate, John McCain. Although public opinion polls generally showed that Obama "won" all the debates,[34] his greater victory was probably in reassuring those already leaning in his direction that he had the right characteristics to be president, as Kennedy had done in 1960.

Because new information has the greatest impact when little is known, voter preferences or opinions will be more volatile when candidates or public figures are not well known. When McCain plucked Sarah Palin from Alaska to be his running mate, she was viewed favorably by 22 percent of the public, with 66 percent not knowing enough about her to render an opinion. A week later, after her well-received introduction at the Republican National Convention, her "favorability" rating had doubled, to 44 percent. After her widely panned and satirized interview with Katie Couric, her rating slid to 32 percent, then bounced back to 40 percent after her debate with Joe Biden. It sunk to 31 percent thereafter, before recovering to 37 percent by election day.[35] In the brief two months of the general election campaign, each piece of new information had a disproportionate impact on evaluations of her as a candidate, and her ratings by the public bounced up and down as a result.

Similarly, public opinion "trial heats" that are intended to gauge the preferences of the electorate during the course of an election

FIGURE 7-5   Trial Heat Results from the Democratic Presidential Primary
and the General Election, 2008

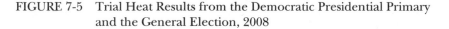

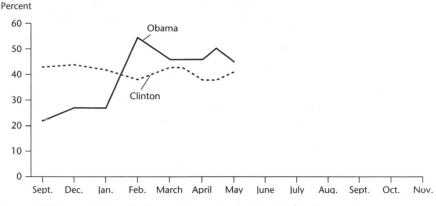

Source: CBS News Polls at the Roper Center for Public Opinion Research.

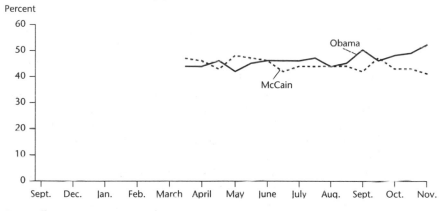

Source: Gallup Polls, available at www.pollingreport.com.

campaign can be highly unstable when one or all of the candidates are
not well known. In the contest for the Democratic presidential nomination in 2007–2008, Hillary Clinton began as a well-known figure, after
eight years as first lady and six and a half years as senator from New York.
Obama, on the other hand, was largely unknown as a first-term senator,
despite his splash as keynote speaker at the 2004 Democratic National
Convention. The trial heats, from September 2007 to May 2008, presented
in the top half of Figure 7-5, show a steady base of support for the well-
known Clinton, but much greater volatility in preferences for Obama as
he introduced himself to the public during the primary campaign. In
contrast, the trial heats for Obama and McCain, found in the bottom

half of Figure 7-5, show less volatility over the course of the campaign after both had clinched their respective nominations.

The second condition under which campaigns and the information they provide are most effective in influencing attitudes is when counter-information is not available. The obvious example is when one candidate has substantial resources for campaigning and the opponents do not. The well-financed candidate can present a favorable image of him- or herself—or an unflattering image of the opponent—without having those images contradicted. This situation is more likely to occur in primaries, when candidates must rely on their own funds and whatever they can raise from others, than in general elections, when both candidates can tap party resources. However, strategic decisions may also lead to a failure to counter information. In 2004 John Kerry delayed responding to the Swift Boat Veterans for Truth ads attacking his war record. The swift boat veterans had been following him with similar accusations for years. He may have underestimated their potential harm to him when these allegations were played on a national stage, with higher stakes and an audience less knowledgeable about him than were his constituents in Massachusetts. Most major campaigns now have a "rapid response team" as part of their campaign staff in order to fire back when hit with unexpected and potentially damaging attacks. Obama reportedly beefed up his team after his campaign was slow to respond when allegations about his connections to 1960s radical William Ayers and indicted Chicago developer Tony Rezko surfaced in the spring of 2008. Even with the capability to respond quickly, candidates and their advisers still must make the strategic decision whether a response will be effective or will only serve to keep the story alive.

In presidential elections, the national nominating conventions offer each party the opportunity, at least temporarily, to get its message to the public without the annoyance of sharing the stage with the other party. The televised acceptance speech of the nominee, the ability to showcase rising stars and celebrate past heroes—all before a prime-time audience—offer unique opportunities for the political parties to present themselves and their campaign themes as they wish the public to see them. Although the news media interject commentary and analysis, the media's view of what is interesting generally leads them to emphasize strategy and motives instead of outright contradiction of a party's claims. The result of this nationwide opportunity for favorable publicity is the convention "bounce" that presidential nominees typically receive in their approval ratings and trial heat results immediately after their party's convention.[36] In Figure 7-5, one can see Obama's convention bounce of about 5 percent at the end of August, and McCain's bounce of the same amount after the Republican convention a week later.

The political parties have not always been able to use the nominating convention to their advantage. The battle-marred Democratic National Convention in 1968 and George McGovern's acceptance speech long after midnight in 1972 represent dramatic failures to use this opportunity to benefit the party's nominee. Opponents within one's party may present the case against a nominee as effectively as the opposing party could. In recent years, when the nomination has been a foregone conclusion well before the nominating convention, both parties have tried to control their conventions as tightly as possible, keeping controversial issues and personalities under wraps. However, as the conventions become more staged in an effort to promote the most favorable image of the candidate, the audience and the news coverage for them have shrunk, making it less likely that those images would be conveyed to the public. In 2008 the Obama campaign sought to increase the audience appeal of the Democratic convention by showcasing the nominee's acceptance speech in a stadium filled with over eighty thousand enthusiastic supporters. Although the speech was well received, the effect was short-lived, as McCain countered by announcing his running mate the following morning.

Another, less obvious, situation in which unchallenged information has an impact is when all parties agree on the characterizations of a candidate or issue. If, for example, both candidates agree on which of them is liberal and which is conservative (although not on which position is "good" and which is "bad"), this information will be effectively conveyed to voters during the course of a campaign. Thomas E. Patterson and Robert D. McClure suggest that a major impact of television advertising may be on increasing voters' awareness of the issue stands of the candidates.[37] They conclude that television advertisements, more than television news stories, contain the most explicit information about the candidates' stands on issues, and that they have a correspondingly greater impact on voters' awareness of the candidates' issue positions. Television news stories are too brief and focus too much on campaign action to convey much issue information to the viewer.

A third factor affecting whether information in a campaign will have an impact on voter attitudes is the extent to which the voters accept it as being relevant to their own concerns. In *The Reasoning Voter*, Samuel L. Popkin offers "Gresham's law of information," which states that small amounts of personal information drive out large amounts of impersonal information.[38] In other words, because personal information has more meaning to average voters—they use similar kinds of data every day in assessing friends and colleagues—they use such information about a candidate to make inferences about the kind of person that candidate is and how he or she will perform in office. In the short run, Palin's biography as "hockey mom" and mother to a special-needs child trumped her lack of knowledge about foreign policy in appealing to some voters.

Information will also be more or less effective depending on the context in which the recipient receives or understands it. Cognitive psychologists use the concept of "framing" to study how people's preferences or decisions depend on the context or frame in which the alternatives are presented. For example, in the summer of 1979, in public opinion polls, Democrats preferred Sen. Edward M. Kennedy over President Jimmy Carter by a margin of three to one as their party's nominee for president.[39] By March 1980 Carter was ahead of Kennedy by two to one among Democrats.[40] Although a number of things had intervened between these times, an important element seems to have been reminding the voters of Senator Kennedy's involvement in the accidental death of Mary Jo Kopechne a decade earlier. When the voters' frame of reference was an unpopular president viewed as responsible for high inflation, Kennedy was an attractive alternative. Later, when Kennedy was framed as a fatally irresponsible playboy, Carter was preferred. A similar situation happened to George H. W. Bush in 1992 and John McCain in 2008. When the election was framed in terms of national security, they did well; when the frame changed to the economy, their opponents prevailed.

The fact that voters respond differently to information depending on its presentation offers campaign managers opportunities to use sophisticated techniques to create favorable images of their candidates. Highly paid political consultants use an arsenal of social science knowledge and techniques in an attempt to do just that. Although some of these attempts have been notably successful, serious limitations also exist.

To successfully "sell" a candidate with advertising techniques, image makers must be able to control the information available about their candidate, thereby controlling the perceptions the voters hold about him or her. Reagan was more successfully handled in this way than most other presidential candidates. Perhaps his training as an actor made him more amenable to management by his advisers. However, to a considerable degree, maintaining his public image depended more on protecting him from the press and public exposure than on manipulating the content of publicity about him. This approach was especially effective in the 1980 campaign, when the focus of attention and public dissatisfaction rested on President Carter and not the challenger, Reagan.

For most candidates, however, manipulating a public image by controlling information is either impossible or self-defeating. For a relatively unknown challenger, such as Bill Clinton in 1992 or Obama in 2008, this type of strategy would appear self-defeating because few candidates have had the resources to become well known nationwide through advertising and staged appearances alone. (Billionaire Ross Perot in 1992 was an exception.) Instead, unknowns scramble for exposure in any forum they can find, and this prevents the careful manipulation of an image. Conversely, well-known candidates or incumbents, who can afford to sit back and let the public relations people campaign for them, probably already have images that are impossible to improve in any significant way over the relatively short period of time available in an election campaign. The most famous alleged attempt to repackage a candidate was the effort of the Nixon campaign staff in the 1968 presidential election.[41] However, the evidence suggests that more voters decided to vote for other candidates during the course of the campaign than decided to vote for Nixon. After about twenty years of nationwide public exposure, a "new Nixon" reinforced existing images, both negative and positive. He simply could not create a new, more attractive image.

Campaign organizations also attempt to affect the public image of their candidates by supplying the news media with favorable information. If successful, this strategy can be particularly effective, because the information arrives through the more credible medium of news coverage, instead of paid advertising. Media events can be staged that provide the media—particularly television—with an attention-grabbing headline, sound bite, or photo opportunity. The campaigns of Nixon in 1968 and George H. W. Bush in 1988 were particularly successful in manipulating news coverage favorable to their candidates by staging media events and otherwise limiting access to the candidates. In 2004 the campaign of George W. Bush went to great lengths to handpick the audiences at appearances of the president or vice president, thereby ensuring an enthusiastically supportive crowd.

Limiting exposure of the candidate to staged media events works better for well-known incumbents than for challengers. Attempts by the McCain campaign to keep Sarah Palin under wraps were ultimately unsuccessful because the press and public demanded to know more about a person who might be a heartbeat away from the presidency. Furthermore, recent advances in technology make carefully controlling the image of a candidate even more daunting. A casual remark at a reception of supporters, captured by cell phone video and uploaded to YouTube, can become an overnight sensation on the Internet with catastrophic consequences for the candidate.

In recent years campaign organizations have had difficulty getting news stories aired or printed about their issue positions and policy stands, but they have had more success with negative stories and attacks on other candidates. Another tactic is to seduce the media into covering paid political advertising as if it were news. In her book *Dirty Politics,* Kathleen Hall Jamieson details how, in 1988, the news media continually reinforced the premise behind the infamous Willie Horton ads that attacked Democratic candidate Michael Dukakis's position on crime.[42] For some years afterwards, television and newspapers regularly featured ad watches that attempted to dissect the claims made in candidates' paid advertising; ironically, in the course of doing so they provided the ads with a wider audience.

Although selling a candidate by manipulating an image in a positive way may be difficult, a far greater opportunity exists to hurt an opponent's image through negative campaigning and advertising. In recent years candidates' campaigns and independent organizations have attacked the images of candidates in personal and political terms. The volume of this particular form of negative advertising, sometimes called attack ads, has increased greatly. Many of these ads are paid for by committees, interest groups, and organizations not connected directly to a candidate or a campaign. The Supreme Court has ruled that such attack ads are issue advocacy and therefore cannot be limited because of the First Amendment.[43] As a result, a candidate can be hit with a massive campaign for which the opposing candidate need take no responsibility, and that is basically outside the regulations and agreements governing the candidates and their campaign organizations. Two generalizations about negative campaigning can be made: (1) the public disapproves of negative campaigning; and (2) even so, it sometimes works. Because the public disapproves of negative advertising, some candidates have managed to be positive in their own ads while allowing independent organizations to trash their opponents for them.

If negative campaigning illustrates the capacity to use the mass media to accomplish political purposes, the difficulty candidates have in using the media to respond to these attacks reveals its limitations. Victims of negative campaigning have tried to ignore the attacks, attempted to answer the charges, or counterattacked with their own negative campaign. None of these responses appears to be notably successful—a fact that encourages the continued use of negative campaigning. Attacks in the form of ridicule or humor may be particularly difficult to answer. Some strategists have urged the victims of negative campaigning to respond immediately and defend themselves aggressively. This may be good advice, but following it requires much from the victim. To respond promptly with advertising requires a great deal of money (perhaps near the end of a campaign, when resources are limited) and a skilled staff. Moreover, victims of negative campaigning need to have a strong, effective answer to such attacks.

In their study of the 1992 presidential campaign, Marion R. Just, Ann N. Crigler, Dean E. Alger, Timothy E. Cook, Montague Kern, and

Darrell M. West offer a useful way to look at the "construction" of a candidate's persona over the course of an election campaign.[44] Instead of the candidate's image being the creation of a campaign staff or the product of straight news coverage, it will evolve through the three-way interaction of the candidate's campaign, the news media, and the public. The candidates' initial attempts at establishing themselves face a range of reactions from the press and public—encouragement, incredulity, boredom—and the candidates adjust accordingly. Likewise, the news reporters assess and react to the response of colleagues and the public to their coverage of candidates. Finally, the public's judgments in public opinion polls, radio call-in programs, live interviews, and e-mail indicate displeasure or support of the behavior of both candidates and news media. The final picture may not be a faithful reflection of the candidate's inner being, but neither is it an artificial creation of campaign technicians, nor the distortion of an overbearing press.

Presidential Primary Campaigns

Because the impact of new information is greatest when there are few existing attitudes, the impact of campaigns should be greatest in primary elections, especially with little-known candidates. In primaries, when all the candidates are of the same party, the voter does not even have partisanship to help in the evaluation of candidates. In such situations, whenever new information is provided it can have a substantial impact.

After 1968, reforms in the presidential nominating process led to an increased use of presidential primaries as a means of selecting delegates to the Democratic and Republican nominating conventions. The purpose of the reforms was to make the choice of the presidential candidates more reflective of the preferences of the party's supporters in the electorate. In fact, the increased use of presidential primaries opened the door, at least initially, to the nomination of candidates little known to the general public. Political newcomers, such as Carter in 1976, Gary Hart in 1984, Steve Forbes in 1996, and Howard Dean in 2004, had an opportunity to focus their energy and campaign resources on a few early primaries or caucuses, gain national media attention by winning or doing surprisingly well in those early contests, and generate momentum to allow them to challenge more established and well-known potential nominees. Such candidates often do not have long-term viability. Their early appeal, based on little information, dissipates as more, often less flattering, information becomes available. Nevertheless, by the time this happens, the candidate may already have secured the nomination (Carter in 1976) or severely damaged the front-runner, as Hart damaged Walter F. Mondale in 1984. Primaries can do considerable harm to candidates' images under some circumstances. Well-known front-runners such as George H. W. Bush in 1992 and Bob Dole in 1996 suffered a loss of popularity that they never recovered under the campaign attacks of fellow Republicans. Intraparty fighting is typically destructive for established candidates. Ever since 1972, segments of the Democratic Party expressed concern that the new reliance on presidential primaries was preventing the party from nominating its best or most electable candidates.

Before the 1988 election season, southern Democratic leaders decided that concentrating their states' primaries early in the election year would focus media and candidates' attention on the southern states as well as give a head start to more conservative candidates who could pick up a large bloc of delegate votes from these states. Although this strategy did not work in the short run—the Democrats nominated the liberal northeastern governor Dukakis in 1988—the creation of Super Tuesday considerably shortened the primary season by allowing candidates to amass enough delegates to secure the nomination months before the summer convention.

Every four years since 1988, additional states have moved their primaries forward, hoping to capture some media attention or, at least, to have a say before the nominations had been decided. By 2008 this process had gone so far that half the states had their primaries or caucuses on February 5, far supplanting the old Super Tuesday in early March. This "front-loading" of primaries originally had the effect of favoring the front-runner and decreasing the opportunity for lesser-known candidates. Because the primaries are so close together in time, candidates cannot concentrate their resources in a few states and use victories there to generate favorable coverage in other states. Instead, after the early states of Iowa and New Hampshire, which now have their caucuses and primary in early January, candidates must campaign all across the country in many states. Unknown candidates have almost no time to capitalize on early success in Iowa or New Hampshire by raising money and creating state campaign organizations. The established, well-known candidates again seem to have the advantage.

Although the Obama phenomenon in 2008 seems to contradict the conventional wisdom about the front-loading of primaries advantaging the front-runner, we should be careful about jumping to conclusions. Obama was unusual among lesser-known candidates because he was able to raise an enormous amount of money and create a substantial grassroots organization across many states before the primary season began in January 2008. None of the other non-front-runners (except Dean in 2004) were able to come close to that. Whether other lesser-known candidates of the future will have those fund-raising and organizational skills—and the staying power that Obama had and Dean did not—is unclear. In any event, if the Democrats had held a national primary on February 5 (a national primary being the logical outcome of the current process of moving more and more primaries to the beginning of the season), it is quite likely that Hillary Clinton, the established front-runner, would have won, according to the nationwide trial heat results of the time (see Figure 7-5).

The role of the news media in influencing presidential primaries with their coverage has changed as the format of the primaries has changed. In the 1970s and 1980s, the media had considerable potential to enhance one candidate's campaign momentum and to consign others to obscurity. Thomas E. Patterson's study of the role of the media in 1976 shows that, during the primaries, Carter benefited from the tendency of the press to cover only the winner of a primary, regardless of the narrowness of the victory or the number of convention delegates won.[45] Even the accident of winning primaries in the eastern time zone gave Carter disproportionately large, prime-time coverage on evenings when other candidates enjoyed bigger victories farther west.[46] This was possible because few voters were well informed about or committed to any of the many Democratic candidates. During the same period the media exaggerated the significance of President Gerald R. Ford's early primary victories without noticeably influencing the public's feelings about him or his challenger, then-governor of California Reagan.[47] It is much more difficult to influence voters who have well-informed preferences.

The "winner-take-all" commentary on the presidential primaries has been replaced in recent years by talk of "unexpected" winners and losers. The most favorable coverage may be given to a second- or third-place finisher, and the real winner in terms of numbers of votes or delegates may be treated as a loser if he or she has not had a big enough win. Attention focuses on who does better or worse than expected, regardless of the number of votes they receive. This was the case with Hillary Clinton's third-place finish in Iowa (which led to the media writing her candidacy off), as well as her "surprise" win in New Hampshire, where she won more votes—but ultimately fewer delegates—than Obama. The irony of this type of commentary is that it essentially converts the errors in the media's preelection coverage into newsworthy political change. With the front-loading of the primaries, however, media coverage becomes less relevant after the first few primaries.

Inequality in the resources available to candidates in presidential primary campaigns is likely to have a greater effect than in the presidential general election, in which public financing is available to both major-party candidates. In the 2000 election campaign, George W. Bush raised more than $100 million, more money by far than any of the other candidates and more than twice as much as any previous candidates for president. He also raised his money early. Six months before the first primary, he had raised more than half his eventual total. This enormous war chest served both to discourage other potential candidates and to defeat his most serious rival for the nomination, John McCain. In 2008 Hillary Clinton followed a similar strategy of raising and spending so much money that it would create an aura of invincibility and scare off would-be rivals for the nomination. Unfortunately for the strategy, her fund-raising was more than matched by Obama's, and Clinton's campaign was chronically short of funds later in the season. Indeed, Obama's fund-raising prowess was so formidable that it enabled him to forego public financing in the general election, giving him a considerable financial advantage over Republican John McCain, who had accepted public financing.

Campaign Strategy

Those attempting to communicate with the American public on political matters face an awkward dilemma. The attentive members of the public, the individuals most likely to receive political messages, are least likely to be influenced by one or a few items of information. Meanwhile, the individuals who are open to persuasion are uninterested in politics and not likely to pay attention to politics in the media.

By way of conclusion, we can use material from this chapter as a basis for generalizing about political communication and campaign effects from the perspective of a candidate. In political campaigns, candidates stand little chance of altering the electorate's issue preferences on policies that are sufficiently prominent to affect their vote choices. In the short run, to change individuals' preferences on issues that they care about is difficult by any means, and it is particularly difficult through the impersonal content of mass media. To change an individual's preferences or pattern of behavior, personal contact is more effective than the media. Therefore, if vote choice or turnout is to be influenced at all, it is likely to be by an acquaintance of the individual.

To a limited degree, candidates can alter the prominence of a few issues for some segments of the public, but their capacity to increase or decrease the importance of issues is slight compared with what will happen in the ordinary course of events. For example, a candidate cannot make corruption in government a salient issue solely through his or her campaign, but a major scandal can make it an issue whether the candidates want it to be or not. Nevertheless, it is worth some effort to increase the visibility of issues that are expected to benefit the candidate, even though that effort will probably fail. It is also worth some effort to attempt to reduce the salience of issues that hurt a candidate, though again, this strategy is not likely to succeed.

The public's perceptions of candidates' positions on issues are much more susceptible to change. News and advertising through the mass media can convey a considerable amount of information on issue stands and dramatize the differences between candidates. The more factual the information and the more the candidates agree on the respective characterizations, the more fully the information is absorbed by the public. This is the area of attitude change and public awareness in which candidates can accomplish the most.

In the final analysis, candidates are most interested in winning votes, regardless of how strong a preference each vote represents. But there are grounds for wanting large numbers of supporters with very strong preferences. Individuals with an overwhelming preference, holding no significant conflicting views, form the base of support for a candidate that yields campaign contributions and workers. These are the individuals all through society who casually influence the people around them to hold views favorable to a candidate. These are the opinion leaders who interpret and misinterpret the news on behalf of their candidate.

The more obviously partisan or one-sided the content of either media message or personal contact, the less likely it is to influence the uncommitted, not to mention the hostile. This poses a problem for the campaigner. Even though extreme messages are most likely to attract the attention of the relatively apathetic, uncommitted voter, those same messages are least likely to get results. For this reason, in part, events dramatizing an issue can be valuable or damaging to a candidate. Events that affect a candidate's personal image are especially important because these perceptions are the most difficult to change through direct appeals in campaign advertising.

There are several overall implications of this discussion. A long time and probably noncampaign periods of low intensity are needed to switch individual issue stands or party loyalties. The media presentation and personal discussion of political and social conditions or events have a greater impact on attitudes than advertising or party contacts.

To a considerable degree, these generalizations about political influence and communication imply that, by the time a candidate wins nomination, he or she faces a constituency whose basic values and preferences can be changed only by events over which the candidate probably has little or no control. The only impact the candidate can have through campaigning is to make his or her issue positions known as dramatically as possible and to contrast those positions with the opponent's. No candidate will know in advance what the net effect of these efforts will be, and most will never know. But most elections are contested under conditions that give one candidate a great initial advantage in the partisan loyalty and issue preferences of the constituency. The best chance for candidates is to exploit what they believe are their advantages, but in most cases the stable party loyalties and unchanging issue preferences of a constituency impose significant constraints on how much difference campaign strategies can make.

Speculation on the nature of political communication has ranged from alarm over the mass public's vulnerability to manipulation through the media to annoyance at the difficulty of reaching the public. The American people make use of the mass media to inform themselves on matters of interest, but this does not mean that they pay attention to everything in the media. Individuals have a remarkable ability to ignore information—one as fully developed as the ability to absorb information. Influencing individuals on a subject about which they feel strongly is extremely difficult because they reject the media content, and influencing individuals on a subject about which they are indifferent offers problems because they ignore the media content.

Also, the media are difficult to use for manipulation because so many different points of view are found within them. An extremely wide range of political perspectives is available to some degree in the mass media, although some perspectives are much more frequently available and more persuasively presented than others. The media in American society allow all views to enjoy some expression, although media coverage of many topics may be expressed in a manner favorable to some viewpoints and unfavorable to others. Disentangling the bias associated with the news and commentary in the media from the distortion found in the individual's reception of political information would be difficult. Either of these conditions would be adequate to account for considerable discrepancy between political reality and the public image of that reality.

Notes

1. The classic statement on cognitive dissonance was Leon Festinger, *A Theory of Cognitive Dissonance* (Evanston, Ill.: Row, Peterson, 1957). For some of the most interesting experimental work in this field, see Milton J. Rosenberg, Carl I. Hovland, William J. McQuire, Robert P. Abelson, and Jack W. Brehm, *Attitude Organization and Change* (New Haven: Yale University Press, 1960).
2. Elihu Katz and Paul F. Lazarsfeld, *Personal Influence: The Part Played by People in the Flow of Mass Communications* (New York: Free Press, 1964).
3. Elisabeth Noelle-Neumann, *The Spiral of Silence* (Chicago: University of Chicago Press, 1984).
4. This well-known example is supported by remarkably little evidence. Seemingly the only data on the separate television and radio audiences are in an

obscure report on surveys by Sindlinger and Co. of Philadelphia in *Broadcasting*, November 7, 1960, 28–30.

5. Pew Research Center for the People and the Press, "2008 Biennial Media Consumption Survey," April 30–June 1, 2008, available at www.people-press.org.
6. Ibid.
7. Everette E. Dennis, *The Media Society* (Dubuque, Iowa: Wm. C. Brown, 1978), 37–41.
8. Michael B. MacKuen and Steven L. Coombs, *More Than News* (Beverly Hills, Calif.: Sage Publications, 1981).
9. Kathleen Hall Jamieson, *Dirty Politics: Deception, Distraction, and Democracy* (New York: Oxford University Press, 1992).
10. Between 15 and 20 percent report reading a newspaper online. Pew Research Center for the People and the Press, "2008 Biennial Media Consumption Survey."
11. Pew Research Center for the People and the Press, News Interest Index, "Internet Overtakes Newspapers as News Outlet," December 23, 2008.
12. For an early statement of this point, see Bernard C. Cohen, *The Press and Foreign Policy* (Princeton: Princeton University Press, 1963).
13. Times Mirror Center for the People and the Press, "The People, the Press, and the War in the Gulf," January 31, 1991.
14. Pew Research Center for the People and the Press, early April 2003 War Tracking Poll, available at www.people-press.org/reports/print.php3?PagesssID=699.
15. CBS News/*New York Times* Poll, press release, January 17, 1991, and CNN/*USA Today*/Gallup Poll, March–April 2003, available at www.pollingreport.com.
16. See Dennis, *The Media Society*, chaps. 5, 7.
17. A variety of publications, including monthly reports, is available on the Web site of the Pew Research Center for the People and the Press at www.people-press .org.
18. These data on attention to news stories can be found in the "Hurricane Katrina Survey," September 6–7, 2005, available at www.people-press.org.
19. Pew Research Center for the People and the Press, News Interest Index, December 23, 2008.
20. Anthony Downs, *An Economic Theory of Democracy* (New York: Harper and Brothers, 1957).
21. Samuel L. Popkin, *The Reasoning Voter* (Chicago: University of Chicago Press, 1991), 47–49.
22. Thomas E. Patterson, *The Mass Media Election* (New York: Praeger, 1980), 14–15.
23. Philip E. Converse, "Information Flow and the Stability of Partisan Attitudes," *Public Opinion Quarterly* 26 (winter 1962): 578–599.
24. Steven Kull, "Misperception, the Media, and the Iraq War," Program on International Policy Attitudes and Knowledge Networks, October 2, 2003, available at www.pipa.org.
25. Pew Research Center for the People and the Press, "2004 Biennial Media Consumption Survey."
26. "The State of the News Media 2005," Project for Excellence in Journalism, available at www.stateofthemedia.org.
27. Pew Research Center for the People and the Press, "Modest Bush Approval Rating Boost at War's End, Economy Now Top National Issue," April 18, 2003, available at www.people-press.org.
28. CBS News Poll, July 30, 1998. Data provided by the Inter-university Consortium for Political and Social Research.

29. CBS News/*New York Times* surveys, available at www.pollingreport.com.
30. Andrew Gelman and Gary King, *Why Do Presidential Election Campaign Polls Vary So Much When the Vote Is So Predictable?* (Cambridge, Mass.: Littauer Center, 1992).
31. Michael S. Lewis-Beck and Tom W. Rice, *Forecasting Elections* (Washington, D.C.: CQ Press, 1992). These economic forecasts limit themselves to two-party races and cannot accommodate third-party candidates such as Ross Perot.
32. American National Election Studies, 1948–2004.
33. Recomputed from Elihu Katz and Jacob J. Feldman, "The Debates in the Light of Research: A Survey of Surveys," in *The Great Debates: Background, Perspective, Effects,* ed. Sidney Kraus (Bloomington: Indiana University Press, 1962), 212.
34. Post-debate polls by *USA Today*/Gallup and CNN/Opinion Research Corporation, available at www.pollingreport.com.
35. CBS News Surveys, August 29–November 2, 2008, available from the Roper Center for Public Opinion Research.
36. James E. Campbell, Lynna L. Cherry, and Kenneth A. Wink, "The Convention Bump," *American Politics Quarterly* 20 (July 1992): 287–307.
37. Thomas E. Patterson and Robert D. McClure, "Television News and Televised Political Advertising: Their Impact on the Voter," paper presented at the National Conference on Money and Politics, Washington, D.C., 1974; and Thomas E. Patterson and Robert D. McClure, *Political Advertising: Voter Reaction to Televised Political Commercials* (Princeton: Citizens' Research Foundation, 1973).
38. Popkin, *The Reasoning Voter,* 73.
39. *Gallup Opinion Index* 183 (December 1980): 51.
40. "Opinion Roundup," *Public Opinion* 3 (April/May 1980): 38.
41. Joe McGinniss, *The Selling of the President* (New York: Trident Press, 1969).
42. Jamieson, *Dirty Politics,* chap. 1.
43. Federal legislative attempts to curb negative ads, such as the McCain-Feingold Act, have generally been thwarted by the courts. In 2007 the Supreme Court ruled in *FEC v. Wisconsin Right to Life, Inc.* (551 U.S. 449) that issue ads may not be banned.
44. Marion R. Just, Ann N. Crigler, Dean E. Alger, Timothy E. Cook, Montague Kern, and Darrell M. West, *Crosstalk: Citizens, Candidates, and the Media in a Presidential Campaign* (Chicago: University of Chicago Press, 1996).
45. Thomas E. Patterson, "Press Coverage and Candidate Success in Presidential Primaries: The 1976 Democratic Race," paper presented at the annual meeting of the American Political Science Association, Washington, D.C., 1977.
46. James D. Barber, ed., *Race for the Presidency* (Englewood Cliffs, N.J.: Prentice-Hall, 1978), chap. 2.
47. Patterson, *The Mass Media Election,* 130–132.

Suggested Readings

Graber, Doris. *Processing the News.* New York: Longman, 1988. An in-depth study of a few respondents on the handling of political information from the media.
Jamieson, Kathleen Hall. *Dirty Politics: Deception, Distraction, and Democracy.* New York: Oxford University Press, 1992. A blistering commentary on political advertising strategies and the interaction between advertising and news coverage.
Just, Marion R., Ann N. Crigler, Dean E. Alger, Timothy E. Cook, Montague Kern, and Darrell M. West. *Crosstalk: Citizens, Candidates, and the Media in a Presidential*

Campaign. Chicago: University of Chicago Press, 1996. A multimethod study of the 1992 presidential election campaign.

Neuman, W. Russell, Marion R. Just, and Ann N. Crigler. *Common Knowledge*. Chicago: University of Chicago Press, 1992. An interesting analysis of mass media and political attitudes.

Pew Research Center for the People and the Press. *Audience Segments in a Changing News Environment: Key News Audiences Now Blend Online and Traditional Sources*, 2008. A rich analysis of media behavior that continues Pew's biennial survey. Available at www.people-press.org/reports/pdf/444.pdf.

Popkin, Samuel L. *The Reasoning Voter*. Chicago: University of Chicago Press, 1991. A wide-ranging discussion of campaigning and presidential vote choice.

West, Darrell M. *Air Wars: Television Advertising in Election Campaigns, 1952–2008*. Washington, D.C.: CQ Press, 2009. The fifth edition of a study of many aspects of television advertising in presidential elections.

Internet Resources

The Pew Research Center for the People and the Press conducts numerous political surveys throughout the year as well as the best study of American media behavior done in the spring of even-numbered years. The center not only makes the data available freely, at www.people-press.org, but the Web site also offers extensive analysis of many political and media topics. For information, click on "Commentary," "Survey Reports," and "News Interest Index."

During election years most major news organizations have Web sites with survey data on many political items.

Vote Choice and
Electoral Decisions

A CENTRAL FOCUS of research on American political behavior is vote choice, especially presidential vote choice. No other single form of mass political activity has the popular interest or analytic significance that surrounds the selection of a president every four years. Most Americans follow presidential campaigns with greater attention than they give other elections, and eventually over 50 percent of the electorate expresses a preference by voting. The results of presidential balloting are reported and analyzed far more extensively than any others. This chapter will explore the main determinants of vote choice and the interpretation of election outcomes in light of these determinants. We will attempt to generalize the discussion beyond presidential choice, but inevitably most of the illustrations are drawn from recent presidential election studies.

In their pioneering work *The American Voter,* Angus Campbell, Philip E. Converse, Warren E. Miller, and Donald E. Stokes introduced the metaphor of the "funnel of causality" to depict the way multiple factors impact an individual's vote choice.[1] As they envision it, at the narrow end of the funnel is the dependent variable, vote choice. At the wide end of the funnel are social characteristics, like race, gender, social class, and level of education—factors that shape many facets of an individual's life and that are related to political attitudes and, ultimately, vote choice. These relationships, however, are not especially strong. Next in the funnel are long-term predispositions, like partisanship and ideology, that orient and predispose an individual to view the world and act in particular ways. These predispositions are more strongly related to vote choice than are the social characteristics, but by no means do they determine it. They are themselves related to the social characteristics, but again, are not wholly determined by them. Moving further toward the narrow end of the funnel, we find attitudes toward issues that are important to the individual, as well as evaluations of the current parties and of particular candidates. Again, these attitudes are related to the long-term predispositions of party and ideology and, to a lesser extent, to the individual's social characteristics. They are also more closely linked to, and more predictive of, how the individual will vote. We can think of the funnel of causality as a diagram of factors of varying proximity to final vote choice, with more distant factors influencing those that are more proximate, but having a weaker overall relationship to vote choice itself. As we get closer to the narrow end of the funnel, the connection to vote choice becomes stronger.

The funnel of causality is not offered as a statistical model or a predictive theory of vote choice. However, it is a convenient way to conceptualize the factors that influence vote choice, and we will use it to organize the material in this chapter.

Social Characteristics and Presidential Vote Choice

Social characteristics like an individual's race, religion, social class, or education are unlikely to change over the course of a campaign. They are, rather, a set of long-term factors that both analysts and politicians link to vote choice. Social analysis of the 2008 presidential election reveals striking patterns of behavior, shown in Figure 8-1 that uses the same social characteristics as introduced in chapters 5 and 6.

In 2008 black voters were nearly unanimous in their support of Democratic candidate Barack Obama. It must be remembered that black voters have overwhelmingly supported the Democratic candidate—usually by 90 percent or more—for decades. The impact that a black candidate had on black voting behavior was seen more in heightened turnout and enthusiasm than in actual vote choice.

The effect of having a person of color on a major-party ticket is also seen in the vote choices of other minority groups. In recent years, Republicans have had hopes of making inroads among Hispanic voters, but in 2008 Hispanics voted 76 percent for Obama, an increase over Democrat John Kerry's share of 61 percent in 2004. In data not shown in Figure 8-1, Asian Americans, a traditionally less-Democratic minority group, voted 62 percent for Obama and 35 percent for John McCain.[2]

White Protestants were McCain's strongest supporters, with better-educated evangelicals giving him 80 percent of their vote. He also gained majority support from mainline Protestants and less-educated evangelicals. Catholics split along educational lines, with 61 percent of better-educated Catholics voting for McCain and 66 percent of less-educated

FIGURE 8-1 Vote for President, by Race, Ethnicity, Religion, and
Education, 2008

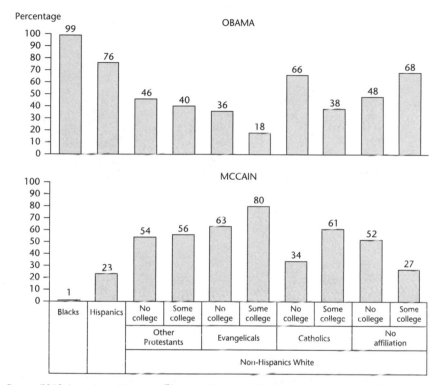

Source: 2008 American National Election Study, available at www.electionstudies.org.

Catholics voting for Obama. Among the better educated with no religious affiliation, support was high for Obama.

In the nation as a whole, Obama received 44 percent of the white vote, but this overall figure hides a deep regional divide. In the South, Obama had just 32 percent of the white vote; in the rest of the country he won a majority of white votes at 53 percent. There was a small gender gap among white voters, with 41 percent of men and 47 percent of women supporting Obama. A bigger marriage gap appeared, with 37 percent of married white men and women voting for Obama, in comparison with 54 percent of unmarried whites.

We can also look at the ways various social groups contributed to the vote totals of the two candidates. Shown in Figure 8-2, this analysis of the "composition" of Obama's and McCain's votes—in contrast to how the social groups voted—is similar to our analysis of partisanship in chapter 5. Blacks made up 25 percent of Obama's vote (and less than

FIGURE 8-2   Social Composition of the Vote for President, by Race,
Ethnicity, Religion, and Education, 2008

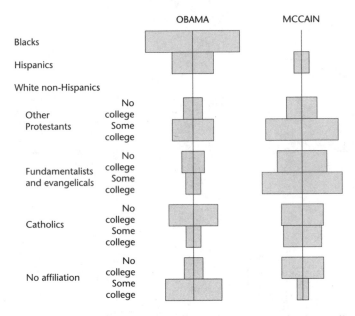

Source: 2008 American National Election Study, available at www.electionstudies.org.

0.5 percent of McCain's); Hispanics contributed another 11 percent to Obama's vote; and white Protestants contributed rather similar shares, with even evangelicals representing 10 percent. McCain's vote was overwhelmingly white non-Hispanics, with evangelicals contributing one-third of his total support.

Partisanship and Ideology

As seen in earlier chapters, party loyalty is a basic characteristic that influences many aspects of an individual's political behavior, including vote choice, and is itself influenced by an individual's social characteristics. In Table 8-1 we see the relationship between partisanship and vote choice in 2008. As strength of partisanship increases, so does the likelihood of voting for one's party, so that strong Democrats and strong Republicans are nearly unanimous in supporting their respective party's nominee. As strength of partisanship declines, so does the impact on vote choice.

Ideology works in much the same way as partisanship as a long-term predisposition that shapes attitudes and behavior. When voters have a

TABLE 8-1 Presidential Vote, by Party Identification, 2008

	Strong Democrat	Weak Democrat	Independent Democrat	Indpendent	Independent Republican	Weak Republican	Strong Republican
Barack Obama	94%	84%	90%	51%	17%	12%	4%
John McCain	5	14	9	41	78	88	96
Other	1	3	1	8	5	1	*
Total	100%	101%	100%	100%	100%	101%	100%
(N)	(345)	(242)	(225)	(110)	(185)	(232)	(255)

Source: 2008 American National Election Study, available at www.electionstudies.org.

* Less than 0.5 percent.

clear ideological view, it is highly related to vote choice, as can be seen in Table 8-2. Among those who call themselves "moderate," or who disclaim any ideology, it offers no guide to how they might vote.

As we have seen in chapter 6, partisanship and ideology are related to each other—although perhaps not as closely as one might have thought—and it would be very difficult to untangle the causal connections between the two. No doubt some individuals adopt a party because it fits their ideological world view; others may call themselves liberals or conservatives because their admired party leaders are so labeled; and others may have both party and ideology from childhood socialization. Partisanship—or party identification—has taken a more central role than ideology in explaining voting behavior, in part because more Americans think of themselves as partisans or independents than as ideologues. Also important analytically, candidates are more clearly connected to their party than to their ideology because the candidate usually has chosen a party label under which to run (while possibly avoiding or obfuscating an ideological label). Nonetheless, as we think about the factors that influence a person's vote, we can think of ideology as holding a similar place in the chain of factors—or funnel of causality—that leads to the final voting decision.

Short-Term Forces

In seeking to understand vote choice, an individual's partisanship can be construed as a long-term predisposition to vote for one party or another, other things being equal. In other words, in the absence of any information about candidates and issues or other short-term forces in an election, individuals can be expected to vote according to their partisanship. However, to the extent that such short-term forces have an impact on them, they may be deflected away from their usual party loyalty toward some other action. The more short-term forces there are in an election—or the more a voter is aware of them—the less will be the impact of partisanship. This idea is crucial for understanding the relative impact of partisanship in different types of elections. In highly visible presidential elections, when information about candidates and at least some issues is widely available, partisanship will typically be less important to the voter's decision than in less visible races down the ticket. Furthermore, more potent short-term forces would be required to cause a very strong partisan to vote for another party than would be necessary to prompt a weak partisan to defect. An individual's vote in an election can be viewed as the product of the strength of partisanship and the impact of short-term forces on the individual.

TABLE 8-2 Presidential Vote, by Ideological Identification, 2008

	Strong liberal	Liberal	Slightly liberal	Moderate	Slightly conservative	Conservative	Strong conservative
Barack Obama	99%	93%	80%	59%	30%	11%	10%
John McCain	1	5	19	37	68	89	86
Other	*	2	*	3	2	1	4
Total	100%	100%	99%	99%	100%	101%	100%
(N)	(57)	(180)	(148)	(342)	(198)	(310)	(53)

Source: 2008 American National Election Study, available at www.electionstudies.org.

* Less than 0.5 percent.

In most elections, both candidates and political commentators give their attention to short-term forces, such as the candidates' personalities, the issues, and the parties' records, because these elements might be modified by the actions of candidates and campaign strategies. Although in many respects partisanship is the most important element, it is taken as a constant because, in the short run, it is not likely to change. This section will consider the impact of the short-term forces of candidate image, current party images, and issues within a setting of stable party loyalties.

Candidate Image

The appeal of candidates has been given more attention in recent elections than any other short-term influence. During the past sixty years national samples have been extensively questioned about likes and dislikes concerning the presidential candidates. During this period several very popular candidates, such as Republican Dwight Eisenhower and Democrat Lyndon Johnson, had extremely favorable images, and several others, such as Republican Barry Goldwater and Democrat George McGovern, were rejected by the electorate largely on the basis of their personal attributes.

Figure 8-3 displays the mean ratings of presidential candidates since 1968 on the American National Election Studies' (ANES) "feeling thermometer," which asks respondents to rate how "warmly" or favorably they feel toward a candidate on a scale of 0 to 100, with 100 being very warm and 0 being very cold. Perhaps the most prominent feature

FIGURE 8-3   Democratic and Republican Presidential Candidate Evaluations, 1968–2008

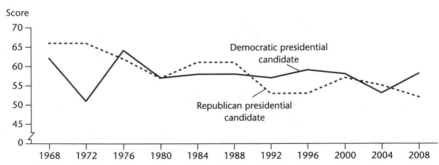

Source: 2008 American National Election Studies, available at www.electionstudies.org.

Note: The values in the figure represent "thermometer scores," in which respondents are asked to rate the candidates on a scale of 0 to 100, where 0 is a very negative view and 100 is very positive.

of this series is its downward trend. Presidential candidates of both parties are viewed less favorably now than in the past. Other indicators of candidate image show that this trend would be even steeper if elections in the 1950s and early 1960s were included. The disenchantment with government and politics, catalogued in chapter 1, clearly extends to the personal images of the presidential candidates.

In light of subsequent events, it may be surprising how favorably Richard Nixon was viewed in 1968 and 1972 and how relatively unfavorably Ronald Reagan was seen in his initial election of 1980. In recent elections, Democratic presidential candidates have been rated slightly more positively than Republican candidates. Obama's mean rating was typical of Democratic candidates over the past three decades; McCain's rating was on the low end of the evaluations of past Republican candidates.

Throughout its long history, the ANES has asked respondents open-ended questions to ascertain their likes and dislikes about the candidates, giving an idea of the specific content of the candidates' images. These opinions range widely in seriousness—from "he's too old" to "he's dishonest"—but they often give a clear indication of how the candidates are viewed. For example, President George H. W. Bush's reneging on his 1988 campaign promise of "read my lips, no new taxes" showed up as a damaging contributor to his image problem in 1992.

Respondents' comments also illustrate a complication in thinking about the concept of candidate image. For some candidates, the "likes" mentioned often have to do with issues—"I like what he's saying about health care"; "I hate that he got us into Iraq"—feelings quite far removed from the candidate's personality. This was especially true about Bill Clinton's image in both 1992 and 1996. He was not viewed so favorably in personality terms (for example, on his honesty or for his avoidance of military service during Vietnam), but this perception was more than offset by positive comments about his vigorous discussion of issues. Similarly, in 2000 Al Gore drew both unfavorable reactions to his personal style and many favorable comments about his positions on a wide range of issues. In 2004 the most frequent reason given for liking John Kerry was that he wasn't George W. Bush. Clearly, the voter sees more than the personal traits of the candidate when asked for an evaluation, and this complicates the idea of candidate image.

A good deal of nonsense has been written in recent years about winning elections by manipulating the images of the candidates, mainly through the mass media. The implication has been that the images of candidates are easily created and altered; but, as discussed in chapter 7, to do either is difficult, particularly with well-established candidates about whom voters are reasonably well informed. Campaigns do have some choices about raising particular issues; for example, in 1960

John F. Kennedy's campaign had to decide whether to raise or avoid the issue of his Catholicism—a factor that would generate both positive and negative reactions. But once such a decision is made, less leeway exists in controlling the impact of the issue. In most other cases, candidates have little control in deciding whether to raise certain topics, for often the opponent or the media will do so anyway. Obama may have preferred not to raise the issue of race in 2008, but once the tapes of Rev. Jeremiah Wright's sermons began to circulate, he had no choice but to confront it.

An incumbent candidate or a former vice president benefits from a perception of being experienced, which is not purely a result of campaign advertising. Also, negative reactions aroused by being involved in an unpopular administration cannot be avoided. The public's impressions of candidates for major office seem to be realistic, gained primarily through ordinary news coverage. This is not to say that these images are accurate, fair, or sophisticated, but they are not fictitious pictures created by public relations personnel. In 2008 McCain was perceived positively as experienced and patriotic, an image gained through his long tenure in the Senate and years as a prisoner of war. There was little his opponent could have done to change that. McCain was also viewed as old, and there was little he could do about that.

Unlike incumbents and established candidates, presidential candidates who are less well known have a greater opportunity to create a favorable image during the relatively brief period of the campaign. Conversely, such candidates are also more vulnerable to an attempt by an opponent to pin an unattractive image on them. The 2008 campaign offers examples of both these possibilities. Obama was not well known entering the campaign. Although his image eventually emerged in good shape by the general election, the primary season had provided some challenges because of his inexperience and his connection to the controversial Reverend Wright. His address on race, his long contest with Hillary Clinton, and his financial resources gave him the national exposure and the time to solidify a generally positive image for the campaign in the fall. In contrast, Sarah Palin's recent entrance onto the national stage led the McCain campaign organization to protect her from media exposure while giving her a crash course on public affairs. This made her appear even more unprepared for the presidency and led to even more intense scrutiny when she was eventually allowed to meet the media. Ironically, Palin's candidacy benefited Obama. Her lack of national experience made it difficult for the Republicans to criticize Obama's.

Few candidates for other offices are as well known or as well publicized as candidates for the presidency. Most candidates in most elections are unknown quantities for the average voter. Typically, voters will be aware of the candidate's party affiliation and whether he or she is an incumbent, but not much more. In fact, these pieces of information may come to the voter's attention only if they are indicated on the ballot.

Normally, the impact of candidate image on vote choice declines as one goes farther down the ticket to less visible and less well-known offices. This does not mean that the candidate's personal qualities are unimportant in winning election to these offices. They may be of paramount importance in obtaining the nomination or endorsement of the party organization, in raising financial support, in putting together a campaign staff, and in gaining backing from the leadership of influential organizations. But these personal attributes are unlikely to influence the decisions of the average voter simply because the voter is unlikely to be aware of them.

Party Image

The images of the parties are another short-term factor that can influence the voting decisions of the electorate. Even though party images are strongly colored by long-standing party loyalties, the focus of this analysis is a set of potentially variable attitudes toward the parties that can be viewed as short-run forces at work in an election. These attitudes usually have to do with the ability of the parties to manage government, to keep the economy healthy, and to keep the country out of war. Party images also affect and are affected by the images of the candidates running under the party label and by the attitudes toward issues espoused by the candidates or the party platforms. These factors can be kept distinct conceptually, though disentangling the effects may be impossible in any actual situation.

Traditionally, the Republican Party has been viewed as the party best able to keep the country out of war; the Democratic Party held a similar advantage as the party of prosperity. Figure 8-4 shows the trends in these party images in recent years. The Democrats briefly lost their traditional advantage as the party best able to handle the economy in 1994, and the Republicans lost their foreign affairs advantage in 2000 and beyond. The post–September 11 atmosphere has created a paradox. The Republican Party is seen as best able to handle the threat of terrorism, even as it is seen as less able to keep the country out of war. However, about one-third of the electorate does not perceive a difference between the parties on these items.

The role of party images in vote choice has been labeled "retrospective voting" by Morris P. Fiorina, who argued that voters continuously evaluate the performance of the political parties, especially the president's party.[3] Voters use the evaluation of past performance as an indicator of future performance, and they take this retrospective

FIGURE 8-4   Party Better Able to Handle the Nation's Economy and Keep
the Country Out of War, 1988–2008

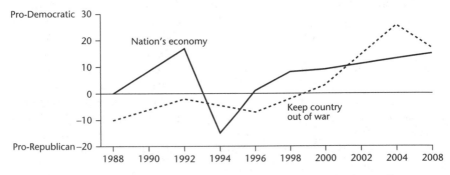

Source: 2008 American National Election Study, available at www.electionstudies.org.

Note: The data points in the figure represent the percentage of respondents answering
"Democrats" minus the percentage answering "Republicans."

assessment into account when making their vote choices. Because
these assessments are likely to involve the performance of the current
administration, questions about the incumbent president's handling
of certain policy areas have been used as indicators of the extent of
retrospective voting. In a sophisticated analysis of presidential voting
in 1988, J. Merrill Shanks and Warren E. Miller demonstrated that voters' approval or disapproval of Reagan's performance as president had
a noticeable impact on the choice between Vice President George
H.W. Bush and Michael Dukakis.[4] In 1992 Bush, as the incumbent
president, had very low evaluations, and this had a disastrous impact
on his reelection prospects. It was just the opposite in 1996 for President Clinton, who came into the race with fairly positive evaluations of
his performance in office. In 2004 George W. Bush's approval ratings
offered a mixed bag. His negative ratings on handling the economy
and the war in Iraq were offset by positive evaluations of his handling
of the threat of terrorism. As will be seen in Table 8-8, in 2008 the
negative evaluations of the Bush administration had a strong impact
on the fortunes of his would-be successor.

Party images and presidential evaluations are strongly related to
partisanship, with partisans more likely to embrace positive images of
their party and to reject negative ones than independents or partisans
of the opposition. Partisanship and party image are not synonymous,
however, because individuals often hold unfavorable perceptions of
their party without changing party identification. Yet, at some point,
negative images of one's own party or positive perceptions of the other
party undoubtedly lead to partisan change. One of the difficulties for

the Republican Party in 2008 (as well as a complicating factor for the analysis of voting in that year) was that the unpopularity of the Republicans over the last two years of the Bush administration carried with it a slight but noticeable shift along the party identification continuum in the direction of the Democrats—slightly higher numbers of Democrats, including strong Democrats, and slightly fewer Republicans. It is hard to separate the short-term impact of Republican misfortunes from a longer-term shift in underlying partisanship.

The images of local or state parties may be considerably different from and independent of those of their national counterpart. A state or local party organization may be perceived in different terms from the national party, and many a local or state party has gained a reputation for ineptitude or corruption that did not influence voting decisions for national offices. At the same time, such local images may become increasingly important in voting for offices at lower levels because party labels become a more important identifying characteristic in those races.

Issue Impact

Candidate images and party images may be closely related to issues, and under some circumstances they are indistinguishable. The perception of the stands of candidates and parties on issues is a basis for making vote choices, a basis usually distinct from either personality characteristics or long-standing symbolism. Most significant, candidates can establish issue positions or alter their appeals through their presentation of issues in ways that are not applicable to personal images or party characteristics. In the short run, candidates cannot change their job experience, religion, or party, but they can take new stands on issues or attempt to change the salience of issues. Therefore, candidates can attempt to appeal for votes on the basis of issues.

Over the years, considerable commentary has focused on the rise of single-issue voting. Collections of voters, caring intensely about a particular issue, vote for whichever candidate is closest to their views on that issue, regardless of the candidate's party, personal characteristics, or positions on other issues. There is nothing new about this phenomenon. The classic example of single-issue voting in American politics was abolition, an issue so intense that it destroyed the Whig Party, launched several new parties including the Republican Party, and was a major contributing factor to the Civil War. Abortion is currently an issue that determines the way many people will vote.

Although organizational sophistication and increased opportunities for dissemination of information make single-issue groups a potent force in American politics today, politically ambitious candidates have always searched for issues of this type to help them gain a following. At the same time, incumbent candidates and the broadly based political parties have seen advantages in avoiding or glossing over such issues. Intense concentration on a single issue is potentially divisive and damaging to parties that must appeal to a broad range of voters or to those in office who must cast votes on a wide range of issues. Nevertheless, the political opportunity for the candidate who can capture a group of voters willing to vote on the basis of a single issue or cluster of issues is so great that it is unlikely that any intense concern in the electorate will be long ignored.

Several characteristics of electoral behavior conflict with this description of the role of issues in influencing vote choice. For one thing, in most elections many voters are unaware of the stands candidates take on issues. Voters commonly believe that the candidates they support agree with them on issues. This suggests that voters may project their issue positions onto their favorite candidate more often than they decide to vote for candidates on the basis of their position on issues. Furthermore, when voters agree on issues with the candidate they support, they may have adopted this position merely to agree with their candidate. Candidates and other political leaders frequently perform this function for members of the electorate; they provide issue leadership for their following. Within the enormous range of possible issues at any given time, complete indifference to many is common. Most issues important to political leaders remain in this category for the general public.

The extent to which voters are concerned with issues in making vote choices is a subject of considerable debate. Several prominent scholarly efforts were designed to rescue the voter from an undeserved reputation for not being issue-oriented.[5] *The Changing American Voter*, by Norman H. Nie, Sidney Verba, and John R. Petrocik, documents a rise in issue voting associated with the election of 1964.[6] According to their data, the correlation between attitudes on issues and vote choice peaked in the ideological Johnson/Goldwater campaign but remained through 1972 at a considerably higher level than in the "issueless" 1950s. More recently, in a thorough assessment of the impact of issues in the elections of 1988 and 1992, J. Merrill Shanks and Warren E. Miller found relatively low levels of issue impact.[7]

In 2008, as in most years, a fairly strong relationship existed between a domestic issue such as increasing or decreasing government services and the vote for president. As Table 8-3 shows, those who favored increasing governmental services and spending voted overwhelmingly for Obama over McCain, and those who favored decreasing services and spending preferred McCain over Obama by an even greater margin.

TABLE 8-3   Presidential Vote and Attitude toward Government
Services, 2008

	Decrease government services		Neutral		Increase government services
Barack Obama	14%	27%	53%	64%	76%
John McCain	82	71	45	36	23
Other	4	3	2	*	1
Total	100%	101%	100%	100%	100%
Weighted (*N*)	(119)	(98)	(154)	(159)	(169)

Source: 2008 American National Election Study, available at www.election studies.org.

*Less than 0.5 percent.

TABLE 8-4   Presidential Vote and Attitude toward Government Help
for Blacks, 2008

	Government help for blacks		Neutral		Let blacks help themselves
Barack Obama	90%	80%	63%	49%	32%
John McCain	10	20	37	51	68
Total	100%	100%	100%	100%	100%
Weighted (*N*)	(172)	(129)	(299)	(187)	(568)

Source: 2008 American National Election Study, available at www.electionstudies.org.

On another domestic issue—whether the government should help blacks versus letting blacks help themselves, shown in Table 8-4—a similar liberal/conservative relationship exists. Those people who favor government programs to help blacks voted overwhelmingly for Obama over McCain, 90 percent to 10 percent. The voters who said blacks should help themselves favored McCain, 68 percent to 32 percent. If one looks at this relationship only among white voters, the relationship remains very strong.

Because both these issues deal with themes that have long divided the parties, it is not surprising that substantial relationships exist between holding a certain view and supporting a particular candidate. The issue of abortion has not always been so closely related to vote choice. The strong relationship found in 2008 and shown in Table 8-5, also true in 2000 and 2004, suggests increasing polarization between the major

TABLE 8-5   Presidential Vote and Attitude toward Abortion, 2008

	Pro-life ◄————————————————————► Pro-choice			
Barack Obama	26%	44%	45%	73%
John McCain	74	56	55	28
Total	100%	100%	100%	101%
Weighted (N)	(100)	(204)	(150)	(324)

Source: 2008 American National Election Study, available at www.electionstudies.org.

TABLE 8-6   Presidential Vote and Attitude toward War in Iraq, 2008

	War in Iraq increased threat of terrorism	Stayed the same	War in Iraq decreased threat of terrorism
Barack Obama	82%	58%	22%
John McCain	18	42	78
Total	100%	100%	100%
Weighted (N)	(420)	(417)	(724)

Source: 2008 American National Election Study, available at www.electionstudies.org.

parties on social issues. McCain's support was higher on the pro-life side of the issue; Obama drew more votes from the pro-choice side. Respondents taking the two moderate positions on the abortion issue divided slightly in McCain's favor.

One of the questions asked in the 2008 ANES was whether people thought the war in Iraq increased or decreased the threat of terrorism. Table 8-6 shows a strong relationship between people's perceptions of the Iraq war and their vote for president. Those who saw the war as increasing the risk of terrorism voted solidly for Obama; those who saw Iraq as decreasing the threat of terrorism voted strongly for McCain.

Figure 8-5 looks at vote choice in a somewhat different manner by illustrating the electorate's perceptions of the ideological positions of Obama and McCain, as well as the relationship between the voters' own ideological positions and their vote choices between the two candidates. In the 2008 ANES survey, voters were asked to locate each candidate on a seven-point scale ranging from "extremely liberal" to "extremely conservative." In Figure 8-5 the frequency distributions in the lower half of the chart illustrate the voters' perceptions of the two candidates' ideological positions. For example, 23 percent of the respondents labeled Obama as extremely liberal and only 3 percent labeled him as extremely conservative; 11 percent placed McCain in

FIGURE 8-5   Vote for President according to Voters' Ideological Identification
and Perceptions of the Candidates' Ideology, 2008

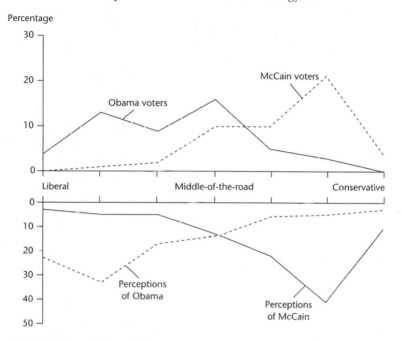

Source: 2008 American National Election Study, available at www.electionstudies.org.

the most extreme conservative position. Most voters placed Obama on
the liberal and McCain on the conservative ends of the scale.

Voters were also asked about their own ideological position using
the same seven-point scale. The distributions in the upper half of
Figure 8-5 indicate the self-placements of those who voted for Obama
and McCain. They show that McCain drew most of his support from
conservative voters, and Obama received most of his from liberals.
Obama also gained a greater share of the votes of those in the middle
of the ideological spectrum. Figure 8-5 also reinforces a point we made
earlier: The electorate sees itself as more middle-of-the-road than the
leaders of the respective parties. The parties may be polarized, but the
electorate is not.

A number of factors must be present for issues to have an impact
on vote choice. First, voters must be informed and concerned about an
issue; second, candidates must take distinguishable stands on an issue;
and third, voters must perceive the candidates' stands in relation to
their own. These conditions often are not achieved. Voters may be
unable to locate themselves or the candidates on one or more issues. In
2008, 15 percent of the electorate had no opinion on the issue of cutting

government services and spending versus increasing government spending and services. An additional 6 percent were unable to locate the position of either Obama or McCain on this issue. Similar proportions of the electorate could not locate themselves or the candidates on the issue of government help for blacks. Voters may misperceive the candidates' positions. For example, a few voters viewed Obama as an extreme conservative or McCain as an extreme liberal, although most perceptions appeared accurate.

A weak relationship between an individual's issue positions and vote choice may result from the fact that the analyst chooses the issues for analysis, and these might be issues that are not important to the individual. If the voter is allowed to define what he or she sees as the most important issue, a somewhat stronger relationship between his or her position on issues and voting decisions is found.[8] Others have argued that a rational and issue-oriented voter judges the past performance of the candidates instead of simply comparing the candidates' promises for the future.[9]

This analysis also does not reveal what causes these relationships. Position on issues may cause an individual's vote choice. Alternatively, a preference for a candidate on other grounds may lead individuals to adjust their positions on issues in support of their vote choice. Analysts have tried to resolve this question, but it has been impossible to do so conclusively. Regardless of the causal relationship, it is significant that, although many voters lack opinions on issues or on the candidates' positions, those who do have opinions show considerable consistency between issue positions and vote choice.

Determinants of Vote Choice

The preceding sections considered candidate images, party images, and issues as short-term forces that either reinforce or deflect voters from their long-term party loyalty. An interesting, but far more difficult, question is the relative impact of these factors on vote choice. Because all these factors are strongly interrelated and almost certainly all influence each other, disentangling their effects using the kinds of data available in nationwide surveys is virtually impossible. If one assumes that issues are all-important in determining vote choice, most voting behavior can be accounted for by issues alone, ignoring other factors. However, if one assumes that party identification and a few social characteristics are all-important, most voting behavior can be accounted for with these variables, ignoring issues. The conflicting conclusions that are reached are largely a matter of the theoretical assumptions with which one starts.

In light of these difficulties, some analysis of the impact of short-term forces has focused on the unique impact of each element in the presence of others. One of the best examples of this mode of analysis is Donald E. Stokes's effort to measure attitudinal forces influencing presidential vote choices.[10] Following Stokes's method, Arthur H. Miller and Martin P. Wattenberg analyzed the nine presidential elections from 1952 to 1984.[11] Recently, Michael S. Lewis-Beck et al. have added the analysis of 2000 and 2004 to the set.[12] The results of the analyses for these various years are shown in Table 8-7. Negative values indicate a factor that helped the Democratic candidate; positive values indicate a benefit to the Republican candidate. The perception of group benefits is a consistently large pro-Democratic element in all eleven elections. Foreign policy matters have almost always helped the Republican candidate, with the exceptions of Goldwater in 1964, Reagan in 1984, and Bush in 2004. The impact of foreign affairs and domestic policies was unusually strong and pro-Republican in 1980. This reflected the strongly unfavorable reactions to Jimmy Carter's handling of the economy and the Iranian hostage crisis. At the same time, the candidates' personalities had an unusually weak influence on vote choice in 1980. In 2000 and 2004, the candidate images of Bush and his opponents benefited Bush. A similar pattern has helped the Republicans in the past, especially in McGovern's disaster in 1972 and in Reagan's reelection in 1984.

Shanks and Miller published a much more complex analysis of the 1988 and 1992 presidential elections in *The New American Voter*. Their results cannot easily be compared with those of Stokes and others in Table 8-7, but overall they argue for the importance of long-standing predispositions and retrospective evaluations in contrast to issues and personality traits.

In Table 8-8 we offer an analysis of the determinants of the choice between Obama and McCain in 2008. For simplicity, we consider only seven possible factors influencing vote choice. The first column of the table shows the strength of the relationship between the variable and vote choice. The higher the coefficient is, the greater the impact on the individual's choice. The other columns are the net benefits of that variable to a candidate, similar to those given for earlier elections in Table 8-7.

As Table 8-8 shows, party identification was the factor most strongly related to the choice between Obama and McCain in 2008. At the same time, because party identification was so evenly balanced, it produced only a small net gain for Obama. In similar analyses in previous years, party has almost always benefited the Democratic candidate. An exception was 2004, when party identification gave a small benefit to the Republican, Bush.

TABLE 8-7   Net Impact of Six Attitudinal Components in Determining Vote Choice, 1952–1984 and 2000–2004

	1952	1956	1960	1964	1968	1972	1976	1980	1984	2000	2004
Domestic policy	-1.3	-0.9	-0.5	-2.4	1.1	1.4	-0.7	3.1	1.5	0	-0.7
Foreign policy	3.3	2.5	1.8	-0.3	1.0	3.2	0.4	2.8	-0.3	0.6	-1.3
Party management	5.4	1.2	1.2	-0.3	1.5	0.0	0.2	0.6	0.5	0.6	0.6
Group benefits	-4.3	-5.5	-4.0	-2.6	-3.6	-4.6	-4.5	-4.5	-5.6	-4.1	-3.2
Democratic candidate	-1.2	0.2	-2.0	-4.0	0.9	4.3	-0.1	-0.4	1.3	0.7	1.6
Republican candidate	4.4	7.6	5.7	-2.6	1.6	4.0	2.2	-0.5	1.5	0.4	1.4

Sources: For 1952–1980, Arthur H. Miller and Martin P. Wattenberg, "Policy and Performance Voting in the 1980 Election," cited in *Controversies in Voting Behavior,* 2nd ed., ed. Richard Niemi and Herbert Weisberg (Washington, D.C.: CQ Press, 1984), 91; for 1984, Martin P. Wattenberg (personal communication); for 2000 and 2004, Michael S. Lewis-Beck, William G. Jacoby, Helmut Norpoth, and Herbert F. Weisberg, *The American Voter Revisited* (Ann Arbor: University of Michigan Press, 2008), 396.

Note: Positive values are pro-Republican effects; negative values indicate a Democratic advantage. The values can be interpreted as the percentage of the vote moved in one partisan direction or the other.

TABLE 8-8   Determinants of Presidential Vote Choice, Barack Obama versus John McCain, 2008

	Strength of relationship	Net shift of votes	
		Pro-Obama	Pro-McCain
Party identification	0.41	1%	
Ideological identification	0.14		2%
Bush's handling of the job of the presidency	0.07	4	
Bush's handling of war in Iraq	0.14	4	
Policy positions			
Government services and spending	0.03		
Government seeing to fair treatment of blacks	0.08		4
Approve/disapprove starting of war in Iraq	0.14	2	

Source: 2008 American National Election Study, available at www.electionstudies.org.

Note: Standardized partial regression coefficients are used to represent the strength of relationship between each variable and presidential vote choice controlling for the other variables. Multiple R-squared is 0.68. These variables correctly predict 90 percent of the votes.

The two retrospective assessments of Bush as president—evaluation of his handling of his job as president and his handling of the war in Iraq—account for most of the impact on vote choice in 2008. These factors favored the Democratic candidate strongly. McCain benefited from the impact of ideological identification and from the white public's opposition, on balance, to the government's seeing to the fair treatment of blacks in hiring and promotion. In interpreting these assessments, it is important to bear in mind that they represent the contribution of each factor in explaining vote choice after the other factors are accounted for (or "controlled").

During the conventions and the brief period of the general election campaign, political parties cannot do much about the basic strength each party commands. Therefore, they concentrate on presenting candidate images and issue positions calculated to have greatest appeal to the uncommitted voters. Even if the outcome of an election is not substantially affected by party strategies, the content of the campaign and the meaning the election comes to have for leaders and the public are created by these strategies. The data in Tables 8-7 and 8-8 can be viewed as measures of the content of the campaign and its meaning for voters.

The Popular Vote and the Electoral College

In chapter 1 we pointed out that one of the requirements of a democracy is a reasonably faithful translation of popular votes into governmental control. In considering the presidential vote choices of Americans, we need also to consider the possibility that those votes will not determine the outcome of the election.

In 2000, for the first time in more than one hundred years, the electoral college chose a president who was not the winner of the popular vote. In 2004 the possibility loomed again, although it did not happen—in part because of Republican strategists' efforts to mobilize extra voters in safe Republican states to prevent a second popular vote loss for Bush. In a system that purports to be a democracy, it is a significant occurrence when the candidate with fewer votes is declared the winner. How did this happen in 2000? What, if anything, is likely to be done to change the system so that it does not happen in the future?

Under the constitutional system adopted in 1787 and amended in 1804, the president is selected by the electoral college, with each state having electoral votes equal to the combined seats that it has in the U.S. House of Representatives and Senate. Voters cast a ballot for one or the other party's presidential and vice presidential nominees. Legally, however, the voter is casting a ballot for that party's slate of electors, which was certified months before by the party's formal submission of the slate to a state official. The electors of the winning party in each state meet in their respective state capitals on the Monday following the second Wednesday in December and cast their votes for president and vice president. Almost without exception they respect their pledge and vote for their party's nominees. A majority of the electoral votes is required to elect a president—270 electoral votes at this time.

To understand how the electoral college could produce a winner who is not the popular vote winner, it is important to remember that all states (except Maine and Nebraska) use a winner-take-all procedure for deciding who wins the states' electoral votes. In other words, it does not matter whether a candidate wins the state narrowly or by a wide margin—all of the electoral votes go to the winner. If one candidate wins many states narrowly and the other candidate wins states by a wide margin, the first candidate can win in the electoral college while the second candidate can have more popular votes. Usually the second candidate is said to have wasted votes by winning by a larger margin than needed to carry the state.

In 2000 Gore won by large margins in a number of big states such as California and New York, accumulating a huge number of popular votes, while George W. Bush won some big states, such as Florida, narrowly. In 2000 another factor was at work to a degree. Bush won a large share of the small states, in which the two electoral votes assigned to every state to represent their seats in the U.S. Senate create something of a bonus. If turnout is comparable, each electoral vote in a small state represents fewer voters than in a large state. In 2000 each electoral vote in Wyoming represented seventy thousand popular votes, and in California each electoral vote represented more than two hundred thousand popular votes.

Although only rarely does the electoral college produce a winner who has not won the popular vote, the consequences of a winner-take-all system are well known to campaign strategists in presidential elections. The electoral college arrangement strongly influences presidential campaign strategy. The closer the expected margin in a state and the larger the number of electoral votes available, the more resources the campaigns will put in the state and the more aggressively the candidates will attempt to respond to the political interests in the state. These are the battleground states, where both candidates have a chance to win and much is at stake. In contrast, safe states are relatively unimportant to both candidates in a general election campaign—taken for granted by one and written off by the other—although they may be visited by one or both candidates to raise funds to spend in competitive states. The 2000 presidential election was deceptive in making every state appear crucial because the result was so close, but, in fact, a winning strategy in this and other presidential elections calls for slighting most states.

In retrospect, it may seem odd that the founders created such a peculiar scheme for selecting a president. Their main concern was to devise a method for selecting the president that would result in the selection of George Washington as the first president. The allocation of electoral votes simply combined the state representation in the Senate and the House of Representatives, an easy decision after the Great Compromise had been reached. In the context of the Constitutional Convention, the electoral college had another virtue: it treated the states as they viewed themselves—as sovereign entities. In the current climate, retaining the states as meaningful units in a federal system is one rationale for maintaining the electoral college.

The fact that the electoral college was extremely indirect democracy was not a concern for the founders; most of them were wary of too much democracy and approved the idea of state legislatures selecting the electors. The founders did not anticipate the emergence of political parties that quickly changed the process of selecting electors into intense partisan conflict. By 1824 most state legislatures had turned the selection process over to the public to avoid the political hassle.

Over the years, proposals have been put forth to change or abandon the electoral college.[13] Some proposals are modest, such as getting rid of the slate of electors (who occasionally do not vote the way they are pledged) and have the secretary of state simply certify each state's electoral votes. Proponents of greater change have resisted this proposal, though in itself noncontroversial, for fear that adopting it would reduce the incentive to make more substantial changes in the system.

The most sweeping proposal, and the one most commonly discussed by political commentators, would be the substitution of a nationwide popular election for the electoral college. This is an obvious alternative method of selecting the president, answering the main criticism of the electoral college—the potential (which was realized in 2000) that the popular vote winner is not the electoral college winner. A nationwide popular election, however, has problems of its own. It is generally believed that a national popular election would attract more and more candidates—third-party candidates, independent candidates, and major-party candidates who failed to get their party's nomination. Candidates with a small but crucial constituency could threaten to take votes away from the major-party nominees as a way to win concessions. But presumably more candidates would stay in the race to demonstrate their strength, so gradually the percentage of the vote needed to win would shrink. The popular vote winner could have 35 percent or 25 percent of the total vote, and arguably, this would undermine the legitimacy of the winner. As a consequence, most proposals for a national popular election have included provisions for a run-off election if the winner's percentage was below, say, 40 percent. The prospect of two presidential elections and the political maneuvering associated with run-off elections has reduced enthusiasm for making such a change.

The current interest in adopting "instant run-off" in some local elections offers a possible solution. Under instant run-off arrangements, if there are more than two candidates in a race, voters rank their preferences among them. When the votes are counted, the candidate with the fewest number of votes is eliminated and the second choices of the voters who voted for the eliminated candidate are then counted and added to those candidates' totals. This process is continued until one candidate has a majority (50 percent plus one) of all votes cast. Such a system would produce a majority winner without a run-off. There are a number of objections and potential problems with instant run-off, some of which may become apparent when it is adopted in local elections around the country. If it proves workable, however, it might answer some of the perennial concerns about a direct popular vote for president.

Two other proposals have been advanced that would not require a constitutional amendment, although a constitutional amendment would be required to adopt them uniformly across the country. The district method, now used in Maine and Nebraska, allows two electors to be selected statewide and the remainder to be selected within congressional districts. The proposal does not eliminate the winner-take-all characteristic, but it does reduce the magnitude of the distortions that can occur. The proportional method would allocate all of the electoral votes on a statewide basis, but through proportional representation instead of to the plurality winner. Given the typical margin of victory in the popular vote in a state, a winning candidate would be unlikely to gain more than a one-vote electoral margin from a state using proportional representation. No individual state is likely to adopt this method because, with only one electoral vote at stake, it would become the least attractive state in the nation for presidential candidates to campaign in.

For years, political scientists and some political commentators predicted that the electoral college would be immediately abandoned if, in the modern age, it produced a nonpopular vote winner. Why, then, has so little happened to jettison the electoral college since the 2000 election? There are probably a number of reasons that a movement to change the college has not materialized. One is that the 2000 election produced new, more pressing issues for reform—notably ballot type and vote-counting procedures. The nationwide popular vote alternative also appears less attractive after the Florida recount, as the possibility of a nationwide recount is contemplated. Most important, perhaps, is the realization on the part of Republicans that the presence of the electoral college produced a Republican president. When a substantial part of the political elite senses a benefit in current arrangements, little likelihood exists that the extraordinary majority needed to change the U.S. Constitution could be assembled. Much more likely is the possibility that some individual states will decide to follow the examples of Maine and Nebraska and adopt the district method of apportioning electors.

Vote Choice in Other Types of Elections

Vote choice can be thought of as the product of a voter's long-term partisanship and the impact of the campaign's short-term forces of candidate characteristics, issue positions, and evaluation of the party's performance. In presidential elections, in which information about the candidates and issues is widespread and easily available, short-term forces often overcome partisanship and cause substantial numbers of voters to defect from a party. In less prominent races, voters make choices with less information and fewer factors influencing their decisions.

In voting for members of Congress, most of the electorate has relatively little information about the candidates, especially candidates challenging incumbents. Party-line voting becomes stronger for less visible offices, including Congress, because issues and personal attributes of the candidates are less likely to have an impact on the voter in less publicized races.

Another significant factor in congressional elections is incumbency. Studies have shown that voters are about twice as likely to be able to identify the incumbent as the challenger in congressional races, and almost all the defections from partisanship are in favor of the more familiar incumbent.[14] Both Republicans and Democrats seem strongly susceptible to voting for incumbents, with more than one-third typically abandoning their usual party for an incumbent representative of the other party. Strong partisans of both parties frequently defect to incumbents of the other party but, on balance, support the challengers from their own party more often than not. Both Democratic and Republican weak partisans, in contrast, are more likely to defect for incumbents than to vote for challengers from their own party.

The advantage that incumbents have does not mean that congressional districts are invariably safe for one party, though many are. Instead, it suggests that even in those districts in which the outcome is virtually a toss-up when two nonincumbents face each other, the representatives who manage to survive a term or two find reelection almost ensured. This tendency becomes accentuated as the opposition party finds it increasingly difficult to field an attractive candidate to challenge a secure incumbent. Thus many incumbent representatives are elected again and again by safe margins from districts that may fall to the other party once the incumbent no longer seeks reelection. Put another way, the existence of a safe incumbent in a district may say little about the underlying partisan division in that district. It may simply reflect short-term forces that were at work in the last election in which two nonincumbents faced each other.

A Senate election has relatively high visibility and, unlike most congressional races, is amenable to a mass media campaign using television. The more information about the election that gets through to the voters, the less they rely on either partisanship or the familiarity of the incumbent's name. The visibility of a Senate race makes an incumbent senator vulnerable to a well-financed campaign by an attractive opponent. Incumbency may even become a disadvantage in such circumstances, because the incumbent has a voting record to defend.

Despite the advantages of incumbency, national electoral tides can make enough of a difference in enough districts to change the balance of power in one or both houses of Congress. The elections of 2006 and 2008 saw such nationwide tides in favor of the Democrats, significantly increasing the Democratic numbers in both the House and Senate. Especially noteworthy is that these Democratic tides occurred in successive elections. Usually, an electoral sweep brings into the House narrow winners in marginal districts who are vulnerable to defeat in the next election.

In the midterm election of 2006, the Democrats picked up 30 seats to take majority control of the House with 233 seats. No Democratic incumbents lost their seats, while the Republicans lost 21. The Democrats also won 9 open seats previously held by Republicans without losing any of their own open seats. In the Senate, the Democratic tide was equally pronounced, producing a gain of 6 seats and moving the Democrats from a minority of 45 to a majority of 51 (including two independents who caucused with the Democrats). Like the House, no Democratic incumbent in the Senate lost.

The congressional election in 2008 added to these gains. In the House, Democrats had a net gain of 21 seats, bringing their majority to 257 seats to 178 for the Republicans. Twenty-six Republican seats were won by Democrats, while 5 seats switched from Democratic to Republican. In the Senate, the Democrats picked up 8 seats, defeating five incumbent Republicans and taking 3 open seats. Like 2006, no Democratic incumbents lost. After the election, the Democrats picked up another seat when Republican senator Arlen Specter switched his allegiance to the Democrats. Some commentators had expected even larger Democratic gains in the House, but few had expected that the Democrats could win so many Senate seats from the Republicans. Among the losers were Elizabeth Dole of North Carolina and Ted Stevens of Alaska, senators in normally safe Republican states.

We need to keep these stunning changes in perspective. Despite the electoral tide favoring the Democrats, in both years 95 percent of the House incumbents who chose to run for reelection won. This was about the normal rate of incumbent reelection—although the balance between Democrats and Republicans favored the Democrats. In 2008 an additional 10 percent of the members of the House retired rather than defend their seats. Not surprisingly, most of the retirees were Republicans, perhaps seeing the handwriting on the wall or simply not enjoying life in the minority. The Democrats who did not run all retired to run for higher office. Nevertheless, the picture that emerges is one of considerable institutional stability, but with significant change occurring at the margins.

The Meaning of an Election

Politicians and news commentators spend much time and energy interpreting and explaining the outcome of an election. The difficulties in assigning meaning to election results are easy to exaggerate. The most important element is usually clear—the winner. Elections are primarily a mechanism for selecting certain governmental leaders and, just as important, for removing leaders from office and preventing others from gaining office. Nevertheless, an effort is often made to discover the policy implications of patterns of voting and to read meaning into the outcome of elections. This effort raises two problems for analysis: first, the policy implications of the winning and losing candidates' issue stands; and second, the issue content of the voters' decisions.

In both 1980 and 1984 Ronald Reagan articulated an unusually clear set of ideological and policy alternatives. Not all elections offer voters a clear choice between a conservative and a liberal candidate, but the 1980 and 1984 races between Reagan and his opponents—Jimmy Carter and Walter F. Mondale, respectively—were widely perceived as doing so. Because Reagan won both elections by wide margins, his administration understandably claimed a popular mandate for a wide range of policies. Similarly, the victory of the House Republicans in 1994 made it easy for them to claim a popular mandate for their Contract with America. In 2008 it was easy to see the presidential election results as a mandate for change. Exactly which changes the voters had in mind is more difficult to discern.

It is perfectly appropriate to attribute policy significance to an election on the basis of the policy preferences of the winning candidates, so long as it is not implied that the voters had these policy implications in mind when they voted. In other words, it is appropriate to observe, particularly in presidential elections, that the election outcome means lower taxes or expanded programs because the victor has pledged to implement lower taxes or to expand programs. But it is very difficult to establish that the voters' preferences have certain policy meanings or that the votes for a particular candidate provide a policy mandate. Several obstacles lie in the way of stating simply what policies are implied by the behavior of the voters. In many elections, the voters are unaware of the candidates' stands on issues, and sometimes the voters are mistaken in their perceptions.

Furthermore, many voters are not concerned with issues as such in a campaign but vote according to their party loyalty or a candidate's personality. Their votes have no particular policy significance but reflect a general preference for one candidate. Voters who supported Reagan in 1980 had an unfavorable view of Carter's performance as president, especially his handling of the Iranian hostage crisis. The dissatisfaction with Carter was clear enough. However, the expectations about Reagan were vague and perhaps limited to the hope that he would strengthen national defense and balance the budget. In 1992 many voters cast a ballot against the elder Bush because of dissatisfaction over the state of the economy, though not for any particular policies. This characteristic of the vote, added to Clinton's low percentage (well below 50 percent) of the overall vote, made it difficult for Clinton to claim any clear mandate. In 1996 the reelection of Clinton, simultaneously with the election of Republican majorities in both the House and Senate, was interpreted on both sides as a mandate for bipartisan cooperation. The 2000 election was so close and featured such conflicting signals that no serious claim of a mandate emerged. The policy significance is undeniable, however, as George W. Bush achieved his goal of cutting tax rates (and thereby, by design or inadvertently, eliminating the budget surplus he had inherited). After his victory in 2004, Bush's claim to have received affirmation of his policies in Iraq and in the war on terrorism needed to be taken seriously. However, little time passed before the administration discovered that a mandate to privatize Social Security was not what the voters had in mind when they reelected him. Obama may discover, as Clinton did before him, that his electoral victory did not involve a mandate to reform health care if it means a government-run option or cost containment.

Occasionally in a congressional election an incumbent's loss can be traced to a position or action at odds with majority sentiment among the district's constituents. More commonly, election victories say more about the incumbent's attention to constituent service and the advantages of incumbency than about the policy views of the candidates or voters.

A candidate has considerable freedom under most circumstances to interpret a victory with respect to the issues. President Reagan, for example, felt free to interpret his mandate as requiring a massive tax cut but not dictating a balanced budget. There was no more basis for this distinction in public opinion than a mandate to reduce social programs drastically. Conversely, Clinton chose to interpret his election in 1992 as a mandate for health care reform. As it turned out, the public was not as committed to the idea as he was.

Most election outcomes are just as vague and conflicting with respect to most issues, which partially explains the failure of the American political system to impose policy stands on elected officials. This situation illustrates as well the opportunities for leadership afforded to electoral victors. If they are perceived as successful in handling their job, political leaders can convert their following to support their policies, and subsequently it will appear as if the public had demanded the policies in the first place.

The supporters of a candidate usually do not intensely or widely oppose his or her stands. Voters will often vote for candidates who hold views they do not share, but these views are on matters of little interest to the voters. Presumably, voters seldom support candidates who hold views with which they disagree intensely. Although the electorate is capable on occasion of responding to issue appeals both positively and negatively, the electorate does not appear to be easily moved by most appeals. The electorate offers the parties modest opportunities to gain voters without offering extreme temptations to reckless appeals.

On the one hand, American elections are hardly a classic model of democracy with rational, well-informed voters making dispassionate decisions. On the other hand, American elections provide an acceptable opportunity for parties and candidates to attempt to win or hold public office. Despite the polarization of the political elite and political activists, a sizable portion of the electorate is moderate or unconcerned about ideology and lacking in firm partisan attachments. For the present at least, this segment of the electorate holds the key to electoral victory. The political parties, their officeholders, and their candidates ignore this situation at their peril.

Notes

1. Angus Campbell, Philip E. Converse, Warren E. Miller, and Donald E. Stokes, *The American Voter* (New York: Wiley, 1960), chap. 2.
2. 2008 exit poll, available at www.cnn.com/ELECTION/2008/results/polls/. The ANES sample had too few Asian Americans to analyze.
3. Morris P. Fiorina, *Retrospective Voting in American National Elections* (New Haven, Conn.: Yale University Press, 1981).
4. J. Merrill Shanks and Warren E. Miller, "Partisanship, Policy, and Performance: The Reagan Legacy in the 1988 Election," *British Journal of Political Science* 21 (1991): 129–197.
5. A good discussion of this topic in a single source is the collection of articles and commentary by Gerald Pomper, Richard Boyd, Richard Brody, Benjamin Page, and John Kessel in *American Political Science Review* 66 (June 1972): 415–470. See also Benjamin I. Page, *Choices and Echoes in Presidential Elections* (Chicago: University of Chicago Press, 1978).
6. Norman H. Nie, Sidney Verba, and John R. Petrocik, *The Changing American Voter* (Cambridge, Mass.: Harvard University Press, 1976), chap. 10.
7. J. Merrill Shanks and Warren E. Miller, *The New American Voter* (Cambridge, Mass.: Harvard University Press, 1996).
8. David RePass, "Issue Salience and Party Choice," *American Political Science Review* 65 (June 1971): 368–400.
9. Fiorina, *Retrospective Voting in American National Elections.*
10. Campbell, Converse, Miller, and Stokes, *The American Voter,* 524–531; and Donald E. Stokes, "Some Dynamic Elements of Contests for the Presidency," *American Political Science Review* 62 (1966): 19–28.
11. Arthur H. Miller and Martin P. Wattenberg, "Policy and Performance Voting in the 1980 Election," paper presented at the annual meeting of the American Political Science Association, New York, 1981, cited in *Controversies in Voting Behavior,* 2nd ed., ed. Richard Niemi and Herbert Weisberg (Washington, D.C.: CQ Press, 1984), 91.
12. Michael S. Lewis-Beck, William G. Jacoby, Helmut Norporth, and Herbert F. Weisberg, *The American Voter Revisited* (Ann Arbor: University of Michigan Press, 2008), 396.

13. See Lawrence D. Longley and Alan G. Braun, *The Politics of Electoral College Reform* (New Haven, Conn.: Yale University Press, 1972) for a survey of the proposals for electoral college reform.
14. Donald E. Stokes and Warren E. Miller, "Party Government and the Saliency of Congress," *Public Opinion Quarterly* 26 (winter 1962): 531–546.

Suggested Readings

Abramowitz, Alan I., and Jeffrey A. Segal. *Senate Elections*. Ann Arbor: University of Michigan Press, 1992. An extensive analysis of the factors contributing to election outcomes in Senate races.

Bartels, Larry M. *Presidential Primaries and the Dynamics of Public Choice*. Princeton, N.J.: Princeton University Press, 1988. The best available analysis of public opinion and vote choice during presidential primaries.

Fiorina, Morris P. *Retrospective Voting in American National Elections*. New Haven, Conn.: Yale University Press, 1981. An important conceptual argument for viewing vote choice as judgments about the past.

Jacobson, Gary C. *The Politics of Congressional Elections*, 6th ed. New York: Longman, 2006. An authoritative survey of a broad topic and the literature surrounding it.

Lewis-Beck, Michael S., William G. Jacoby, Helmut Norpoth, and Herbert F. Weisberg. *The American Voter Revisited*. Ann Arbor: University of Michigan Press, 2008. A rich reanalysis of the themes from the classic work, using mainly 2000 and 2004 data.

Mayer, William G., ed. *The Swing Voter in American Politics*. Washington, D.C.: Brookings Institution Press, 2008. A collection using several definitions of "swing voters" to analyze them currently and over time.

Niemi, Richard G., and Herbert F. Weisberg eds. *Classics in Voting Behavior*. Washington, D.C.: CQ Press, 1993. Niemi, Richard G., and Herbert F. Weisberg eds. *Controversies in Voting Behavior*, 4th ed. Washington, D.C.: CQ Press, 2001. These two collections offer the best readings from decades of research on public opinion and voting behavior.

Shanks, J. Merrill, and Warren E. Miller. *The New American Voter*. Cambridge, Mass.: Harvard University Press, 1996. A sophisticated analysis using an elaborate model of vote choice.

Internet Resources

The Web site of the American National Election Studies, www.electionstudies .org, has extensive data on topics covered in this chapter. Click on "Vote Choice," "Evaluation of the Presidential Candidates," and "Evaluation of Congressional Candidates" for a variety of political items from 1952 to the present. In addition, all of these political items are broken down by social characteristics.

Charles Franklin of the University of Wisconsin, Madison, has a blog, political arithmetik.blogspot.com, that touches on many political topics. He also produces commentary for a public opinion Web site, pollster.com.

Pollingreport.com and pollster.com have current political information on elections as well as public opinion data. Major news organizations like CNN and the *New York Times* post results of exit polls on their Web sites. Candidates for office, like the political parties, have Web sites that can be located with search engines.

Survey Research Methods

MANY OF THE DATA in this book have come from survey research, and most of the analysis cited has been based on findings from survey research. For more than forty years the data from the American National Election Studies (ANES), as well as from other major survey projects in political science, have been available through the Inter-university Consortium for Political and Social Research and have formed the basis for countless research projects in many fields by scholars, graduate students, and undergraduates. Given this widespread use of survey data, it is appropriate to give some description of the data collection methods that underlie them.

During the past seventy years, social scientists have developed an impressive array of techniques for discovering and measuring individual attitudes and behavior. Basically, survey research relies on giving a standard questionnaire to the individuals to be studied. In most major studies of the national electorate over the years, trained interviewers ask the questions and record the responses in a face-to-face interview with each respondent. A few studies depend on the respondents themselves filling out the questionnaires. Recently, the rising costs of survey research, the pressure for quick results, and the availability of random-digit telephone dialing have led both commercial and academic pollsters to rely increasingly on telephone interviewing. The ANES used both face-to-face and telephone interviewing in 2000 but returned to using face-to-face interviews exclusively in 2004 and 2008.

The development of the Internet has allowed a different form of survey research, with respondents filling out questionnaires on a survey organization's Web site. Also, for several decades news organizations have conducted exit polls on election day to give an early estimate of the outcome and gather additional information about voters that election statistics do not provide.

Survey Data Collection

We will describe four data-collection phases in the survey research process, noting the ways these steps vary depending on whether the surveys are face to face, telephone, Internet, or an exit poll. The four phases are sampling, questionnaire constructing, interviewing, and coding.

Sampling

The key to survey research is probability sampling. It may seem inappropriate to analyze the entire American electorate using studies composed of fewer than two thousand individuals, which is about the average number of respondents in the studies used in this book. But it would be prohibitively expensive to interview the entire electorate, and the only way to study public opinion nationally is by interviewing relatively few individuals who accurately represent the entire electorate. Probability sampling is the method used to ensure that the individuals selected for interviewing will be representative of the total population. Probability sampling attempts to select respondents in such a way that every individual in the population has an equal chance of being selected for interviewing. If the respondents are selected in this way, the analyst can be confident that the characteristics of the sample are approximately the same as those of the whole population.

It would be impossible to make a list of every adult in the United States and then draw names from the list randomly. All survey organizations depart from such strict random procedures in some way. The ANES surveys, the General Social Survey, and other high-quality surveys using face-to-face interviews employ stratified cluster samples, based on households.

Stratification means that random selection occurs within subpopulations. In the United States the sample is customarily selected within regions to guarantee that all sections are represented and within communities of different sizes as well. *Clustering* means that relatively small geographical areas, called primary sampling units, are randomly selected within the stratified categories so that many interviews are concentrated within a small area to reduce the costs and inconvenience for interviewers. Finally, the ANES samples *households* instead of individuals (although within households individuals are randomly selected and interviewed), which means that within sampling areas households are enumerated and selected at random. (This sampling procedure means that no respondents are selected in military bases, hospitals, hotels, prisons, or other places where people do not live in households. However, after the enfranchisement of eighteen-year-olds the ANES and General Social Survey began to include college dormitories as residences to be sampled.)

Increasingly, the commercial polling organizations have turned to telephone interviewing as a faster and cheaper alternative to field interviewing. Random-digit dialing is typically used by these polling operations to select both listed and unlisted numbers and to give each residential number the same chance of being called. Telephone sampling has an advantage over field surveys because it does not require clustering.

Telephone sampling only recently added cell phone–only households and still ignores individuals without telephones. Otherwise, no major obstacles prevent drawing an excellent sample of telephone numbers. The problems begin at that point. Success in finding someone at home and completing a telephone interview is uneven, and failures may run as high as 50 percent. Some polling organizations make repeated callbacks, as the chances of getting an answer increase with the number of callbacks. Repeated callbacks, however, slow the data collection and increase the costs. Because an important reason for using the telephone is speed and low costs, most polling organizations do not call back.

Once the telephone is answered, or the household is contacted for a face-to-face interview, a respondent from the household must be selected. Some randomizing procedure is typically used to select the respondent. There are two methods for selecting respondents, and they have different consequences. The best sampling procedure, but a costly and time-consuming one, is to identify all the eligible members of the household and select one at random. If the respondent selected is not at home, an appointment is arranged for a callback. In a high-quality survey such as the ANES, many attempts are made to interview the individual randomly selected, but no substitutions are made. Telephone surveys typically allow a huge proportion of their respondents to be substitutes for the respondents who should have been interviewed. The alternative, and more common, method of selection identifies the respondent among those eligible who are at home, and the interview is conducted immediately. This further compromises the sample, making it a selection among those people who happen to be at home when the interviewer calls.

The more often the randomly selected respondents cannot be contacted or refuse to be interviewed, the more the sample departs from its original design. Probability samples, with either face-to-face or telephone interviews, can result in unrepresentative samples if the *nonresponse rate* is high. The nonresponse rate refers to the number of respondents originally selected who, for whatever reason, are not interviewed and thus do not appear in the sample.[1] Should these nonrespondents share some characteristic disproportionately, the resulting sample will underrepresent that type of person. For example, residents of high-crime neighborhoods and the elderly may be reluctant to answer the door for a face-to-face interview; busy people with multiple jobs may not be at home enough to be reached by telephone. When this happens, the sample will have fewer of these people than occur in the population and thus the sample will be biased. All the polling organizations take steps to counter these tendencies by weighting the results to compensate for various demographic biases.[2] This is a difficult problem to solve, however. The likelihood is high that the people who consent to be interviewed are different from, and therefore not representative of, those who refuse. If this is the case, counting those who are interviewed more heavily (which is essentially what weighting the sample does) does not eliminate the bias.

Internet polls and exit polls have their own sampling problems. Self-administered Internet polls are new and still uncommon. Random-digit dialing is used to draw a sample of residential telephones, similar to a telephone poll, and create a "panel"—a large group of individuals who agree to answer a questionnaire and participate in future studies. These individuals are provided with Internet access, if necessary, so the panel is not limited to those who already have such access. Each study draws a sample from the larger panel, and these respondents are informed of the opportunity to go online to answer a questionnaire at a secure Web site. Although the sampling design initially produces a representative set of potential respondents, people who are willing to join the panel and participate in particular studies may be different from the rest of the public.

Internet polls have nothing in common with the self-selected "vote on the Internet" polls favored by some television programs. When people take the initiative to respond, instead of being chosen to respond through a random selection procedure, there can be no claim that it is a representative sample of the public.

Exit polls involve random selection of polling places. Then interviewers go to each of the randomly selected polling places and are instructed to select, say, every tenth voter emerging from the polling place for an interview. At midday the interviewers call in the results of the first set of completed interviews, and at this time the central office may adjust the interval of voters to speed up or slow down the pace of interviewing. A number of biases can be introduced in the sampling process, as busy voters refuse to be interviewed and other voters avoid interviewers on the basis of age or race.

Questionnaire Constructing

In survey questionnaires, several types of questions will ordinarily be used. Public opinion surveys began years ago with forced-choice questions that a respondent was asked to answer by choosing among a set of offered alternatives. For example, forced-choice questions frequently take the form of stating a position on public policy and asking the respondent to "agree" or "disagree" with the statement. The analysis in chapter 6 was based in part on the answers to forced-choice questions on public policy that were used in ANES questionnaires in which respondents were asked to "agree strongly," "agree," "disagree," or "disagree strongly." Some respondents either gave qualified answers that did not fit into these prearranged categories or had no opinions.

A major innovation associated with the Survey Research Center at the University of Michigan is the use of open-ended questioning. Open-ended questions give respondents the opportunity to express their opinions in their own way without being forced to select among categories provided by the questionnaire. Questions such as "Is there anything in particular you like about the Democratic Party?" or "What are the most important problems facing the country today?" permit the respondents to answer in their own terms. Interviewers encourage respondents to answer such questions as fully as they can with neutral "probes" such as "Could you tell me more about that?" or "Anything else?" or similar queries that draw forth more discussion. Open-ended questions are a superior method of eliciting accurate expressions of opinion.

Open-ended questioning has two major disadvantages: (1) it places more of a burden on interviewers to record the responses; and (2) the burden of reducing the many responses to a dimension that can be analyzed is left for the coders. For example, if Americans are asked, "Do you think of yourself as a Democrat, a Republican, or an independent?" almost all the responses will fit usefully into the designated categories:

1. Democrat
2. Independent
3. Republican
4. Other party
5. I'm nothing; apolitical
6. Don't know
7. Refused to say
8. Not ascertained

If a relatively unstructured, open-ended question is used, however—such as "How do you think of yourself politically?"—some people would answer with "Democrat," "Republican," and so forth, but many others might give answers that were substantially different, such as "liberal," "conservative," "radical," "moderate," "pragmatic," or "apathetic"— and these could not easily be compared with the partisan categories. Analysts often intend to force responses into a single dimension, such as partisanship, whether the respondents would have volunteered an answer along that dimension or not. This is essential if researchers are to develop single dimensions for analytic purposes. Modern survey research includes questions and techniques considerably more complex than these examples for establishing dimensions.

Questionnaires differ a great deal in their complexity and sophistication. Face-to-face interviews with well-trained interviewers may have many open-ended questions or questions with branching, conditional on the responses to previous questions. Telephone interviews using computer-assisted telephone interview (CATI) technology and online Internet polls can also be complex, relying on computer branching to guide the respondent through the questionnaire. At the other extreme, exit polls are entirely forced-choice questions that can be completed quickly by the voter without instruction.

Writing good interview questions is an art. The questions should be clear, direct, and able to be understood in the same way by all respondents, regardless of age, education, or regional or subcultural differences. They need to avoid various technical mistakes, like asking two things in one question (a so-called "double-barreled" question). A professionally done poll that seeks accurate results, whether an academic survey, a journalistic poll, or a political poll that wants both the good news and the bad news for its client, will try very hard to write unbiased questions that reflect the actual opinions of the respondents rather than leading them to answer in any particular way. Not all survey operations have this as a goal, however. The following example comes from the 'True Patriot Survey,' conducted in August 2008:

> *Question:* "Now I'm going to read you some proposals that a candidate for president might make because he says they embody America's best, most patriotic ideals. After each one, please tell me whether it is a good way or bad way to express America's patriotism.... Protect the right to keep and bear arms, which our Founders knew would let law-abiding citizens protect themselves against both crime and tyranny...."[3]

Amazingly, 26 percent of the sample didn't take the hint and answered that it was a "bad way."

Interviewing

The selection of the sample depends in part on the interviewer, but even more important is the role of the interviewer in asking questions of the respondent and in recording the answers. Motivated, well-trained interviewers are crucial to the success of survey research. The interviewer has several major responsibilities. First, the interviewer must select the respondent according to sampling instructions. Second, the interviewer must develop rapport with the respondent so that he or she will be willing to go through with the interview, which may last an hour or more. Third, the interviewer must ask the questions in a friendly way and encourage the respondent to answer fully without leading the respondent to distort his or her views. Fourth, the interviewer must record the answers of the respondent fully and accurately. The best survey organizations keep a permanent staff of highly trained interviewers for this purpose.

A technological innovation used in telephone interviewing is the CATI system. The interviewer sits at the telephone, with the questionnaire appearing on a computer screen. As the interviewer moves through the questionnaire, responses are entered directly into the computer and automatically coded. Complicated branching to different questions, conditional on the responses given to preceding questions, is possible.

Telephone interviewing has some real advantages. The travel costs of a field staff are eliminated. Having interviewing conducted from a call-room allows for direct supervision of the interviewing staff, enhancing the uniformity of the administration of the questionnaires. Within-interview "experiments" are possible with the CATI system. Also, changing the content of the questionnaire during the course of the study is easy and inexpensive. The great disadvantage is that face-to-face interviews yield higher-quality data.

In Internet polling, on the one hand, there are no interviewers, which is a great saving in cost. On the other hand, there is no interviewer to help the respondent navigate the questionnaire or to keep the respondent motivated—or to make judgments about the plausibility of the responses.

Exit polls generally use a combination of self-administered questionnaires with interviewers available to read the questionnaires and record responses for those voters who need assistance. Given that exit polls might provide one day of work every couple of years, exit poll interviewers are not seasoned professionals. They also work in scattered locations with no direct supervision. Errors in implementing the sampling technique or in administering the questionnaires would rarely be caught and unlikely to be corrected in the short time span of election day.

Coding

Once the interviewers administer the questionnaires to respondents, the verbal information is reduced to a numerical form, according to a code. Numeric information, unlike verbal information, can be processed and manipulated by high-speed, data-processing equipment.

The coder's task may be simple or complex. For example, to code the respondent's gender requires a simple code: 1 = male, 2 = female. A data field that contains information on the respondent will have a location designated for indicating the respondent's gender. A value of 1 will indicate male, and a value of 2 will indicate female. The list of partisan categories above gives the coding numbers that would stand for various responses. Printed questionnaires for face-to-face interviews are pre-coded for many of the more straightforward questions, and the CATI system allows precoded categories to be assigned automatically as the interviewer records the respondent's answers.

Some coding is complicated, with elaborate arrays of categories. For example, coding the responses to a question such as "Is there anything in particular you like about the Democratic Party?" might include hundreds of categories covering such details as "I like the party's farm policies," "I like the party's tax program," and "I've just always been a Democrat." Some codes require coders to make judgments about the respondents' answers. In political surveys these codes have included judgments on the level of sophistication of the respondents' answers and about the main reason for respondents' vote choices.

After the verbal information has been converted into numbers according to the coding instructions, the data are ready for analysis by computer. At this point, the survey research process ends and the political analysts take over to make what use of the data they can.

Validity of Survey Questions

A frequent set of criticisms directed at public opinion research questions the validity of the responses to survey items. *Validity* simply means the extent to which there is correspondence between the verbal response to a question and the attitude or behavior of the respondent that the question is designed to measure. There is no one answer to doubts about validity, because each item has a validity applicable to it alone. Some items are notoriously invalid; others have nearly perfect validity. Many survey items have not been independently tested for their validity, and for practical purposes, the researcher is forced to say that he or she is interested in analyzing the responses, whatever they mean to the respondent. In other instances the sample result can be compared with the known population value.

The items with the most questionable validity in political studies come from those situations in which respondents have some incentive to misrepresent the facts or when their memories may not be accurate. Questions about voter turnout or level of income are noteworthy in this regard. Validity checks reveal that respondents are about as likely to

Advantages and Disadvantages of Different Types of Surveys

Face-to-face interviews with respondents drawn from a sample of households

Advantages	High-quality data
	Allows for longer, more in-depth interviews
Disadvantages	High cost
	Slow data collection and processing

Telephone interviews of respondents drawn from a sample of residential and cell phone numbers

Advantages	Lower cost
	Fast turnaround especially using a computer-assisted telephone interview system
	Allows direct supervision of interviewing process
Disadvantages	No-phone households are excluded
	Call-screening and resistance to stranger calls further degrades the sample

Self-administered Internet polls

Advantages	Less expensive once the panel is set up
	Subsamples with particular characteristics can be drawn from the panel
Disadvantages	Those who agree to participate may be unrepresentative of the population

Exit polls

Advantages	Provides a large number of journalists with material for reporting and commentary immediately after an election
Disadvantages	Lack of training and supervision of interviewers
	With increase in absentee and mail-in voting, poll needs to be supplemented with telephone survey of voters who do not go to a polling place

underestimate their income as overestimate it, and a noticeable percentage of respondents claim to have voted when they did not.[4]

Recall of past voting behavior falls victim to failing memories and intervening events. Changes in party identification, past votes cast, the party identification of one's parents—all may contain substantial error. For example, during November and December immediately after the 1960 election, respondents were asked how they had voted for president. Most remembered voting for either John F. Kennedy or Richard

TABLE A-1   Recalled Vote for President in 1960, 1962, and 1964

Recalled vote	1960	1962	1964	Actual vote in 1960[a]
John F. Kennedy	49%	56%	64%	49.7%
Richard M. Nixon	51	43	36	49.5
Other	b	b	b	0.7
Total	100%	99%	100%	99.9%
(N)	(1,428)	(940)	(1,124)	

Sources: National Election Studies, available at www.electionstudies.org, and U.S. House of Representatives, Office of the Clerk, clerk.house.gov.

[a] The 1960 popular vote can be tallied in a number of ways, including those that show Nixon with a slight popular vote majority. No matter how the votes are counted, the election was very close.

[b] Less than 0.5 percent.

M. Nixon, and, as shown in Table A-1, they were divided about evenly between the two. (The slight deviation of 1 percent from the actual results is within sampling error by any reasonable standards.) The 1962 and 1964 sample estimates of the 1960 vote reveal increasing departures from the actual outcome. Granting that some change in the population over four years may affect vote-choice percentages, a substantial proportion of the 1964 sample gave responses to the question of 1960 presidential vote choice that misrepresented their vote. The validity of this item always declines over a four-year period, but President Kennedy's assassination in the intervening years created an unusually large distortion in recalled vote.

Validity versus Continuity

One of the important features of the ANES is its continuity over an almost sixty-year time span. Samples of the American population have been asked the same questions during every national election campaign throughout this period, offering an extraordinary opportunity for studying trends in the attitudes of the American electorate. The development of this valuable, continuous series does have one unfortunate aspect, however. Because the value of the series depends on the comparability of the questions, researchers are reluctant to alter questions, even when doubts about their validity arise. Improving the questions undermines comparability. Therefore, a choice between continuity and validity must be made.

The ANES questions concerning religious preference provide a recent example in which validity was chosen over continuity. For years, respondents were simply asked, "What is your religious preference?" Although a small percentage in each survey answered "None," it was clear that a significant number of those answering "Protestant," and fewer numbers citing other religions, had no meaningful religious affiliation. In the 1992 survey, the ANES began asking the question differently. Respondents were first asked, "Do you ever attend religious services, apart from occasional weddings, baptisms, and funerals?" Those who answered "no" were asked an additional question about their religious preference: "Regardless of whether you now attend any religious services, do you ever think of yourself as part of a particular church or denomination?" Those who did not answer "yes" to one of these two screening questions were not asked the traditional question about religious affiliation that then followed. As a result, the percentage of the population categorized as having no religious affiliation increased dramatically. This new question more validly reflects the religious sentiments of the American public, but it is now impossible to compare these later results with those of previous years. We cannot infer a large drop in religious affiliation on the basis of the responses to these new and different questions. In this instance, continuity has been sacrificed in favor of validity.

Despite inevitable concerns about validity, survey research provides the best means of investigating the attitudes and behavior of large populations of individuals such as the American electorate.

Notes

1. See John Brehm, *The Phantom Respondents* (Ann Arbor: University of Michigan Press, 1993).
2. *Public Opinion* 4 (February/March 1981): 20.
3. True Patriot Survey, by Eric Liu and Nick Hanaver, conducted by Greenberg Quinlan Rosner Research, August 12–14, 2008; data available from the Roper Center for Public Opinion Research.
4. Paul Abramson and William Claggett, "Race-Related Differences in Self-Reported and Validated Turnout," *Journal of Politics* 46 (August 1984): 719–738.

Suggested Readings

Asher, Herbert. *Polling and the Public*, 5th ed. Washington, D.C.: CQ Press, 2001.
   A good discussion of how polls are conducted and how they are used.
Groves, Robert M., et al. *Survey Methodology*, Hoboken, N.J.: John Wiley and Sons, 2009. Excellent coverage of the many topics of survey methods.

Kish, Leslie. *Survey Sampling*. New York: Wiley, 1965. By far the most authoritative work on survey sampling.

Mann, Thomas E., and Gary R. Orren, eds. *Media Polls in American Politics*. Washington, D.C.: Brookings Institution Press, 1992. An excellent collection of essays on the use of polls in contemporary media analysis.

Weisberg, Herbert F. *The Total Survey Error Approach*. Chicago: University of Chicago Press, 2005. A comprehensive treatment of survey research methods.

Weisberg, Herbert F., Jon Krosnick, and Bruce D. Bowen. *An Introduction to Survey Research and Data Analysis*. San Francisco: W. H. Freeman, 1989. A good, methodological textbook on survey research and the interpretation of statistical analysis.

Internet Resources

The Web site of the American National Election Studies, www.electionstudies.org, has extensive information on survey methodology.

Some other Web sites with methodological information are the Gallup Poll, www.gallup.com, and the General Social Survey, www.norc.org/GSS+Website.

The Pew Research Center for the People and the Press, www.people-press.org, has done interesting methodological analysis, most recently on sampling cell phone–only households.

Index

ABC News, 36, 156, 189
Abelson, Robert P., 204
Abolition, 41, 76, 221
Abortion, attitude toward, 67, 128,
    137–138, 148–152, 167, 223–224
Abramowitz, Alan, 132
Abramson, Paul R., 102, 108, 109
Absentee ballots, 15, 17, 60. *See also*
    Vote-by-mail
ACORN (Association of Community
    Organizations for Reform Now), 59
Ad watches, 179, 198
Advertising, 14, 142, 179, 191, 194–198, 203
    negative advertising, 14, 197–198
Affirmative action, 143
Afghanistan, 7, 50, 85, 155, 157–158, 182
Age, 40. *See also* Eighteen-year-old vote
    and attitudes, 149
    and partisan change, 100–104
    and partisanship, 78, 119–120
    and turnout, 54–55, 56
Age cohorts, 101–102
Agenda setting, 179, 180
Alaska, 235
Aldrich, John H., 108
Alford, John R., 170
Alger, Dean E., 198–199, 206
Alienation, 53. *See also* Cynicism

Almond, Gabriel, 36
Amendments, constitutional, 20, 40, 43,
    45, 232
American Independent Party, 96
American Medical Association, 142
American National Election Study
    (ANES), 9–10, 20, 25–27, 55, 58, 60,
    74, 78–81, 84, 92, 94, 97 98, 101, 108,
    111, 115, 117–119, 123, 125 –128,
    131, 140, 141–145, 149–155, 158–159,
    161–163, 167, 184, 191, 211–213,
    215–217, 220, 223–225, 229
American Party, 96
Andersen, Kristi, 100, 165, 170
Anderson, John, 91, 96, 97, 106
Approval ratings, presidential, 1, 7, 156,
    180, 186–190, 194, 220
Apter, David, 168
Arizona, 191
Asian Americans, 210
Association of Community Organizations
    for Reform Now (ACORN), 59
Attitude change, 175, 176–179, 203
Attitudes. *See also* Issues; Public opinion
    toward domestic economic policy, 20,
    77, 136–137
    toward health care, 138, 139, 140,
    141–142, 143, 167

toward homeland security, 153–154
toward international affairs, 5,
    154–159, 165
toward racial issues, 50, 55, 142–148
    and social characteristics, 162–163
toward social issues, 148–153
    and vote choice, 227
toward war on terrorism, 153–154,
    155, 157–158, 167
Attitudinal cross-pressure, 131
Attractiveness of presidential
    candidates, 50
Australian ballot, 48. *See also* Secret
    ballot
Avoidance reaction, 130
Ayers, William, 4, 194

Bailouts, 35
Balance of power between parties,
    116, 130
Baldi, Stephane, 37
Ballot. *See* Vote counting
Ballot form, 16–17, 48
Barber, James D., 206
Barr, Robert, 14
Barr, Stephen, 37
Bartels, Larry, 108
Battleground states, 8, 52, 126–127, 231
Bay of Pigs invasion, 156
Beck, Paul A., 106
Berelson, Bernard, 129, 131, 133
Biden, Joe, 192
Blacks, 167, 223, 226, 229. *See also* Race
    attitudes of, 140
    first black American president, 1, 56
    partisanship of, 111, 114, 115–116,
        121–122, 125
    registration and turnout of, 6, 15, 43,
        46, 55–56, 148, 210–212
    suffrage and disfranchisement, 15, 40,
        41–45, 50
    violence against, 42
Blackwell, Kenneth, 16
Bloc voting, 111
Blue states, 10, 126–128
Bobo, Lawrence, 169
Bogue, Allan, 64

Boyd, Richard, 238
Bradley, Thomas, 51
Bradley Effect, 51
Brady, Henry E., 28–29, 37
Brainwashing, 173
Braun, Alan G., 239
Brehm, Jack W., 204
Brody, Richard, 238
Bruner, Jere W., 106
Bryan, William Jennings, 77
Buchanan, Pat, 14, 16, 96
Bureau of Applied Social Research, 129
Burnham, Walter Dean, 45, 47, 49, 64,
    68, 86
Bush, George H. W., 50, 62, 117, 156,
    187–188, 196–197, 200, 217, 220,
    236–237
Bush, George W., 1, 5, 6–8, 17–18, 25–26,
    50, 52, 54, 78, 85, 95, 98, 117,
    122–123, 138–140, 152, 154, 156,
    184–189, 197, 201–202, 217, 220,
    227, 229–231, 237
Bush v. Gore, 7
Busing, attitudes toward, 143, 168
Butler, David, 102
Butterfly ballot, 16

C-SPAN, 178
Cable News Network (CNN), 178, 188, 189
California, 2, 231
Calling the election early, 61
Campaigns, 50–52, 61, 190–199. *See also*
    Mass media; Participation; Turnout
    negative campaigning, 197–198
    participation, 12, 29
    strategy, 3–4, 202–204, 231
Campbell, Angus, 49, 65, 73, 74, 86,
    93–95, 108, 121, 132, 164, 169,
    209, 238
Campbell, David, 29, 37
Campbell, James E., 206
Candidate image, 50, 72, 89–91, 95,
    196–199, 216–219
Cantril, Hadley, 144
Capitalism, attitudes toward, 20
Carmines, Edward G., 116, 132, 138,
    153, 169

Carter, Jimmy, 78, 95, 156, 196, 199, 201, 227, 236

Catholics, 94, 114, 115, 121–122, 124, 127, 129–130, 149–151, 162, 210–212, 218. *See also* Religion

Caucuses, 3, 200

Causality, funnel of, 209–210, 214

CBS News, 5, 26, 153, 154, 158, 185, 189, 190, 193

Center for the Study of the American Electorate, 45, 46, 49, 58, 60

Chads, 16

Challenger space shuttle, 180

Chambers, William N., 86

Cherry, Lynna L., 206

Childhood socialization. *See* Socialization

China, 30

Christian conservatives. *See* Evangelical Protestants, Fundamentalists; Religion

Church attendance, 122–124, 127, 149–151

Citizen roles, 27–29, 32–33, 53, 62

Civic Education Study, 30–32

Civil liberties, 22, 153. *See also* Democratic values

Civil rights. *See* Attitudes, toward racial issues

Civil Rights Commission. *See* U.S. Commission on Civil Rights

Civil War. *See* Realignment

Climate change, 139

Clinton, Bill, 2, 4, 50–51, 62, 78, 84, 117, 122, 138, 141–142, 148, 179, 188, 190, 196, 217, 220, 237

Clinton, Hillary Rodham, 1–5, 141–142, 148, 193, 201–202, 218

Clubb, Jerome M., 49, 65, 68, 71, 72, 86

CNN, 178, 188, 189

Cognitive dissonance, 186

Cohen, Bernard C., 205

Cohort analysis, 101–102

Colorado, 6

Communication, political, 173–204. *See also* Campaigns; Mass media

Compartmentalization, 175, 190

Competitiveness, 12–18, 47, 50–52, 72–73, 75–76, 107, 130–131

Conceptualization, levels of, 164

Congress, 24, 25, 74, 106–107, 234–235. *See also* Congressional elections

Congressional elections, 237. *See also* Congress; Vote choice
of 1994, 9, 83, 93, 162, 236
of 2000, 7
of 2006, 1, 6–7, 93, 234–235
of 2008, 6, 17, 82, 93, 234–235
turnout in, 48–49, 51–52, 93
voting in, 82, 91–95, 97, 233–235

Conservatism, 47, 54, 82–83, 127, 135–137, 147, 160–163, 165–166, 225–226. *See also* Ideology

Constitutional amendments, 20, 40, 43, 45, 232

Constitutional Convention, 231

Contract with America, 236

Convention bounce, 194

Conventions, nominating, 2, 3, 4–5, 194–195, 199

Converse, Philip E., 64, 65, 71, 73, 74, 86, 102, 108, 109, 121, 132, 137, 164, 165, 168, 169, 170, 183, 205, 209, 238

Conversion, partisan, 100

Cook, Timothy F., 198–199, 206

Coombs, Steven L., 205

Corruption, 47–48. *See also* Fraud

Couric, Katie, 5, 192

Crigler, Ann N., 198–199, 206

Crockett, H. J., 36

Cross-pressure hypothesis, 129–131, 175

Cynicism, 34, 53. *See also* Alienation; Trust in government

Dealignment, 75, 83, 85, 91. *See also* Partisanship, change in

Dean, Howard, 8, 199, 200–201

Death penalty, 137

Debates, 5–6, 14, 61, 177, 192

Delaware, 191

Democracy, 30, 231. *See also* Democratic procedures; Democratic values

maintaining, 33–36
political culture as foundation for,
18–33
Democratic Party, 59, 67–68, 70–71, 72,
73, 75–78, 82–85, 136–137, 147, 148.
See also Partisans; Partisanship
image of, 219–221
Democratic procedures, 21–24. *See also*
Democracy; Democratic values;
Rules of the game
Democratic values, 20–21, 52. *See also*
Democracy; Democratic procedures;
Equality; Freedom of speech
Democrats. *See* Partisans; Partisanship
Dennis, Everette E., 205
Dennis, Jack, 37
Deviating electoral change, 73
Directive opinion, 168
Disfranchisement. *See* Blacks,
suffrage and
Disruptive activities, 34, 53
Dissonance, 175. *See also* Cognitive
dissonance
Dissonance reduction, 186, 190
District representation system, 232–233
Divided control of government, 108
Dobson, L. Douglas, 106
Dole, Elizabeth, 235
Dole, Robert, 50, 200
Domestic economic policy. *See* Attitudes,
toward domestic economic policy;
Issues, domestic economic
Downs, Anthony, 182, 205
Dukakis, Michael S., 50, 198, 200, 220

Early voting, 15, 44, 60
Easton, David, 30, 31, 37
Economic crisis (2008), 35, 50, 85, 125,
138, 182
Editorial endorsements, 178–179
Education, 168
and attitudes, 21, 27, 138, 140–141,
149, 162, 165
and partisanship, 114, 116, 124
relation to turnout, 39, 53–54
and socialization, 30–33
Edwards, John, 1–2
Effectiveness of government, 19

Efficacy, political, 27, 62
Eighteen-year-old vote, 40, 41–42, 44–45,
54, 61. *See also* Age
Eisenhower, Dwight D., 50, 73, 89, 216
Elections. *See also* Congressional elections;
Electoral system; Presidential
elections
fair and free, 11, 12–18
meaning of, 235–238
Electoral college, 7, 8, 14, 15, 17–18, 52,
131, 230–233
and campaign strategy, 231
proposals for change, 20, 48, 231–233
Electoral mandate, 74, 236–238
Electoral system, 7, 18
Electronic database of registered voters,
15, 44
Elites. *See* Leadership
Emotional appeals, 53
Enfranchisement. *See* Suffrage
Environment, 139, 140, 167
Epstein, Laurily K., 65
Equal Rights Amendment, 167
Equality, 20–21, 41. *See also* Democratic
values
Era of Good Feelings, 76
Erikson, Robert S., 100, 109
Evangelical Protestants, 114, 116,
122–123, 127, 140, 150–151, 162,
210–212. *See also* Fundamentalists;
Religion
Exit polls, 238
Expected vote, 70–72, 73, 74, 99
External political efficacy, 27

Fair and free elections, 11, 12–18
Fair employment, attitudes toward, 143,
144, 145
Family socialization. *See* Socialization
FEC v. Wisconsin Right to Life, Inc., 206
Federal Election Commission, 60
Federal Elections Assistance
Commission, 16
Federalist Party, 75
Feeling thermometer, 216
Feldman, Jacob J., 206
Felons, 15, 43, 44
Festinger, Leon, 204, 205

Fey, Tina, 5
Financial sector collapse (2008), 35, 50,
    85, 125, 138, 182
Fiorina, Morris P., 132, 219, 238
First Amendment, 13–14, 24, 198
Flag burning, 24
Flanigan, William H., 49, 64, 65, 68, 71,
    72, 86
Florida, 2–4, 6–7, 15, 16, 17, 24, 44, 63,
    78, 233
Florida Supreme Court, 18
Forbes, Steve, 191, 199
Ford, Gerald R., 95, 201
Forecasting models, 190–191
Foreign policy. *See* Attitudes, toward
    international affairs; Issues,
    international affairs
Fox News, 178, 185
Framing, 196
Franchise, 39. *See also* Suffrage
Franken, Al, 85
Fraud, 15–18, 48, 59. *See also*
    Corruption
Freedom, 19, 20, 126
Freedom Forum, 36
Freedom of speech, 13–14, 21–22, 24.
    See also Democratic values
Front-loading (of primaries),
    200, 201
Fundamentalists, 114, 116, 122–124,
    127. *See also* Evangelical Protestants;
    Religion
Funk, Carolyn L., 170
Funnel of causality, 209–210, 214

Gallup Poll, 100, 188, 189, 193
Gans, Curtis, 46, 60
Gasoline prices, 182
Gatekeeping, 178, 180
Gaudet, Hazel, 133
Gay marriage, 8, 128, 148, 152–153, 167
Gay rights, 148, 167
Gays in the military, 67
Gelman, Andrew, 190, 206
Gender, 40
    and attitudes, 149
    and partisanship, 117–119
    and turnout, 40, 42, 55–56, 57

Gender gap, 117–119, 211
General Social Survey, 132, 139. *See also*
    National Opinion Research Center
    (NORC)
Generation effect, 101–102, 104–105
Get Out the Vote (GOTV), 51, 61
Gingrich, Newt, 182
Giuliani, Rudolph, 2–3
Goldwater, Barry, 78, 89–90, 95, 164,
    216, 222, 227
Gore, Al, 6–7, 16, 17, 68, 78, 95, 117,
    217, 230
Government
    divided control of, 108
    effectiveness of, 19
    services and spending, 139–142, 155,
        222–223, 226
    trust in, 25–27, 33, 62, 106
    unified control of, 85
Gramm, Phil, 191
Great Compromise, 231
Great Depression, 35, 77, 100, 102
Green Party, 96
Greenberg, Elizabeth, 37
Gresham's law of information,
    195–196
Group conflict, 146

Habitual nonvoters, 54–56
Hadley, Arthur T., 65
Hagner, Paul R., 170
Hahn, Carole, 37
Hansen, John Mark, 62, 65
Harris Poll, 37
Hart, Gary, 199, 200
Headline service, 178, 179
Health care reform, 84, 85, 138, 139, 140,
    141–142, 143, 167, 237
Help America Vote Act (HAVA), 15, 16,
    17, 44, 59
Hess, Robert D., 30, 31, 37
Hibbing, John R., 25, 37, 170
High-stimulus elections, 48–52, 94
Hispanics, 6, 111, 114–115, 116, 140,
    210–212
Homeland security, 7, 153–154
Honeymoon effect, 186, 190
Horton, Willie, 198

House of Representatives, 6, 82–84, 93, 138, 178, 230–231, 234–237

Hovland, Carl I., 204, 205

Huckabee, Mike, 2, 3

Hurricane Katrina, 4, 85, 182, 187

Hussein, Saddam, 7, 184–186, 189

Ideology, 135–137, 160–166, 209, 210. *See also* Conservatism; Liberalism
    and issues, 167
    and partisanship, 106, 162
    and social characteristics, 162–163
    and vote choice, 212–214, 215, 224–225

Income, 111, 114, 124, 138

Incumbency, 218, 220, 222, 234, 237

Independent candidates. *See* Third-party candidates

Independents, 74, 84, 93–99, 101–104. *See also* Partisanship
    increase in, 78, 105–106
    social characteristics of, 111–131

Indiana, 6, 127

Individualism, 20, 21, 41, 126, 144

Inflation, 50

Information, 12, 14, 16, 47, 52–53, 91–92, 130, 175–183, 195–196

Instant run-off, 232

Integration. *See* Issues, racial

Inter-university Consortium for Political and Social Research (ICPSR), 9, 49, 57, 68, 104, 107, 158

Interest in politics, 52–53, 58–59, 62, 94–95, 97–99, 130, 165, 183

Internal political efficacy, 27

International affairs. *See* Issues, international affairs

Internationalism, 158, 165

Internet, 13, 14, 29, 30, 34, 178, 179, 182, 197

Iowa, 2, 3, 8, 200, 201

Iran, 30, 50, 227, 236

Iraq, war in, 1, 5, 7–8, 50–51, 85, 128, 154– 158, 167, 180, 182, 184–189, 224, 229

Isolationism, 158, 165

Issue advocacy, 14, 198

Issue constraint, 165–166

Issues, 49–50, 72, 136, 174, 210. *See also* Attitudes; Public opinion
    abortion, 137, 138, 148, 149–152, 167
    domestic economic, 5–6, 138–142, 165, 187, 189, 227
    environmental, 139, 140, 167
    government spending, 139–142, 155, 222–223, 226
    health care, 138, 139, 140, 141–142, 143, 167
    international affairs, 5, 154–159, 165, 187, 227
    and partisanship, 127, 159–160
    racial, 50, 55, 142–148
    social, 148–153
    and vote choice, 202–204, 221–226
    welfare, 139, 140, 165

Jackson, Andrew, 76

Jackson, Michael, 179

Jacoby, William G., 86, 164, 170, 228, 238

Jamieson, Kathleen Hall, 198, 205, 206

Jeffersonian Republicans, 76

Jeffords, James M., 7

Jennings, M. Kent, 33, 37, 103, 105, 109

Jews, 121–122

Johnson, Lyndon B., 90, 95, 157, 164, 216, 222

Just, Marion R., 198–199, 206

Katz, Elihu, 204, 206

Kennedy, Edward M., 196

Kennedy, John F., 94, 95, 123–124, 156, 177, 192, 218

Kern, Montague, 198–199, 206

Kerry, John, 8, 95, 184–185, 194, 210, 217

Kessel, John, 238

Key, V. O., 86

Kinder, Donald R., 147, 169

King, Gary, 190, 206

Kopechne, Mary Jo, 196

Korean War, 155

Kousser, J. Morgan, 64

Kraus, Sidney, 206

Kull, Steven, 205

Kuwait, 156

Lane, Robert, 45
Lazarsfeld, Paul F., 129, 131, 133, 204
Leadership, 8, 11–13, 18–19, 22–24,
 35–36, 41, 62, 83, 107–108, 147,
 165–168, 222, 237
Leege, David C., 122, 132
Legal restrictions on suffrage.
 See Suffrage
Legitimacy, 19
Leighton, Melissa Voorhees, 132
Levels of conceptualization, 164
Lewinsky, Monica, 179, 190
Lewis-Beck, Michael S., 86, 164, 170, 206,
 227, 228, 238
Liberalism, 83, 135–137, 139, 147,
 160–163, 165–167, 225–226. *See also*
 Ideology
Lieberman, Joseph, 10
Life-cycle effect, 101–103
Linquiti, Peter, 65
Lipset, Seymour Martin, 86
Literacy tests, 40, 42, 43
Longley, Lawrence D., 239
Lopez, Mark Hugo, 65
Los Angeles Times Mirror, 180
Low-stimulus elections, 48–52

MacKuen, Michael B., 205
Mail-in voting. *See* Vote-by-mail
Maine, 230, 232
Mandate, electoral, 74, 236–237
Manipulation, 47, 53, 196–198, 204
Marcus, George E., 36
Marijuana, legalizing, 167
Markus, Gregory B., 109
Marriage gap, 119–120, 211
Mass media, 14, 52, 106–107, 173,
 176–178, 184–186, 201. *See also*
 Campaigns; Newspapers; Radio;
 Television
 attention to, 106, 179–184
 and attitude changes, 24, 30, 157–158,
 176–179
 and presidential approval ratings,
 186–190
 and turnout, 49–50, 61
Massachusetts Supreme Court, 8, 152
Matthews, Donald R., 43, 64

McCain, John, 2–3, 5–6, 50, 52, 67, 91,
 108, 122, 192–197, 202, 210–213,
 215, 217–218, 222–227, 229
McCain-Feingold Act, 206
McClosky, Herbert, 23, 36
McClure, Robert, 195, 206
McDonald, Michael, 46, 64
McGinniss, Joe, 206
McGovern, George, 90, 195, 216, 227
McPhee, William, 131, 133
McQuire, William J., 204
Michigan, 3, 6
Middle class. *See* Social class
Midwest. *See* Region
Miller, Arthur H., 108, 227, 228, 238
Miller, Warren E., 65, 73, 74, 85, 108,
 121, 132, 164, 169, 209, 220, 222,
 227, 238, 239
Minnesota, 6, 17, 84
Minor parties. *See* Third-party candidates
Missouri, 127
Mobility, 43, 54, 56–57, 62
Mobility, social, 125–126
Mobilization, 51, 62, 63, 100
Mondale, Walter F., 95, 122, 200, 236
Motor voter law, 59, 60
Mountain states. *See* Region
MoveOn.org, 13
MSNBC, 178
MTV Rock the Vote, 62
Mueller, John E., 169

Nader, Ralph, 7, 14, 68, 83, 96, 103
National Election Studies (NES), 57.
 See also American National Election
 Study (ANES)
National Opinion Research Center
 (NORC), 140, 144. *See also* General
 Social Survey
National Republican Party, 82
NBC News, 26, 144, 189
Nebraska, 230, 232
Nelson, Dawn, 37
New Deal. *See* Realignment, New Deal
New England. *See* Region
New Hampshire, 3, 8, 200, 201
New Mexico, 6, 8
New York, 48

New York Times, 10, 26, 185
Newman, Jody, 132
News Interest Index, 182
News stories, 179–183, 195, 197–198
Newspapers, 14, 31, 49, 177–180,
    182–183. *See also* Mass media
Nicaraguan contras, 24
Nie, Norman H., 108, 165, 170, 222, 238
Niemi, Richard G., 37, 109, 164, 228
Nixon, Richard M., 23–25, 73, 89, 95,
    157, 177, 192, 197, 217
Noelle-Neumann, Elisabeth, 177, 204
Nominating conventions, 2, 3, 4–5,
    194–195, 199
Nonpartisans. *See* Independents
Nonvoluntary alienation, 53
Nonvoters, 52–56, 58–59, 61–63, 131.
    See also Turnout
Normal vote, 70–72, 73, 74, 99
Norpoth, Helmut, 85, 164, 170, 228, 238
Norrander, Barbara, 54, 65
North, 42, 43, 56, 76, 78, 82–83, 125, 143.
    See also Region
decline in turnout in, 46–47
North Carolina, 6, 78, 127, 235
Nunn, C. Z., 36

Obama, Barack, 1–8, 13, 15, 27, 35, 44,
    50–52, 54, 56, 59, 61, 67, 78, 84–85,
    91, 95, 98, 103, 108, 117, 122,
    125, 138, 141, 148, 157–158, 190,
    192–197, 200–202, 210–213, 215,
    217–218, 222–227, 229, 237
Occupation, 124, 129. *See also* Social
    characteristics; Social class
Ohio, 8, 15, 16, 44
Oklahoma City bombing, 34
Open-ended questions, 217
Opinion change. *See* Attitude change
Opinion elites, 176
Opinion leaders, 176–177, 203
Opinions. *See also* Attitudes; Public
    opinion
consistency in, 175
functions of, 174–175
Oregon, 60

Page, Benjamin, 238
Pakistan, 85

Palin, Sarah, 4–5, 67, 192, 196, 197, 218
Panel data, 100, 103
Participation, 12–16, 28–29, 41, 47, 52.
    See also Campaigns, participation;
    Turnout
Partisan change. *See* Partisanship
Partisan conversion, 100
Partisan realignment. *See* Realignment
Partisans. *See also* Partisanship
political characteristics of, 98–99
social characteristics of, 111–131
Partisanship, 7–8, 47, 58–59, 67–85, 89–108,
    209. *See also* Independents; Partisans;
    Party identification; Party loyalty
and attention to media, 183
change in, 99–105 (*See also* Dealign-
    ment; Realignment)
concept of, 67, 99
decline in, 89, 93–94
defection from, 71, 89–93
future of, 107–108
and ideology, 106, 162
and issues, 152–153, 154, 157–158,
    159–160
measurement of, 69
and social characteristics, 111–131
strength of, 107–108
types of electoral change, 72–75
and vote choice, 212–214
and voting behavior, 89–95
Party base, 67
Party campaign activities. *See* Campaigns
Party identification, 69–72, 97–98, 111,
    114–115, 227. *See also* Partisanship
measurement of, 69
Party image, 219–221
Party loyalty, 47, 67–69, 75, 89, 107.
    See also Partisanship
Party switching, 6, 7, 83
Party systems, 75–83. *See also* Political
    parties
freezing of, 76
Patriotism, 7, 19–20
Patterson, Thomas F., 183, 195, 201,
    205, 206
Paul, Ron, 3
Perie, Marianne, 37
Period effect, 101–102
Permissive opinions, 168

Perot, Ross, 50, 62, 68, 83, 90–91, 95, 96,
     103, 107, 197
Persian Gulf War, 155, 156, 167,
     179–180, 182, 187
Petrocik, John R., 108, 170, 222, 238
Pew Research Center for the People and
     the Press, 18, 51–52, 56, 92, 94, 132,
     153, 178, 180, 181, 182
Pierce, John C., 169, 170
Piereson, James, 36
Pledged delegates, 4
Polarization of political parties, 6–9, 24,
     83, 91, 107, 132, 148, 158, 223–224
Political advertising. *See* Advertising
Political communication, 173–204.
     See also Campaigns; Mass media
Political connectedness, 62
Political culture, 11–36, 41
Political efficacy, 27, 62
Political elites. *See* Leadership
Political ideology. *See* Ideology
Political interest. *See* Interest in politics
Political leadership. *See* Leadership
Political parties, 12, 48, 105–108, 231.
     See also Democratic Party; Party
     systems; Republican Party
     attitudes toward, 36, 108
     social composition of, 114–116
Political socialization. *See* Socialization
Poll tax, 42–43
Pomper, Gerald M., 132–133, 238
Popkin, Samuel L., 64, 183, 195–196,
     205, 206
Popular vote, 1, 7, 8, 15, 17–18, 68,
     230–233
Populists, 77
Pornography, 148
Position issues, 153, 154
Powell, G. Bingham, Jr., 65
Prayer in public schools, 148
Presidential approval. *See* Approval
     ratings, presidential
Presidential elections. *See also* Vote
     choice
     of 1828, 75
     of 1876, 18
     of 1888, 7, 18
     of 1896 (*See* Realignment, of 1896)
     of 1904, 77

of 1912, 7, 68, 77
of 1916, 77
of 1932, 77 (*See also* Realignment,
     New Deal)
of 1952, 1, 9, 50, 72
of 1956, 50, 72, 121
of 1960, 22, 39, 94, 95, 123–124,
     177, 192
of 1964, 78, 89–90, 91, 95, 164, 165, 222
of 1968, 3, 50, 68, 71, 91, 95–97, 197
of 1972, 50, 72, 89, 90
of 1976, 50, 61, 78, 91, 95, 183
of 1980, 50, 54, 91, 97, 196, 236
of 1984, 1, 4, 50–51, 89, 95, 236
of 1988, 45, 50, 54, 91, 198, 222
of 1992, 50, 62, 68, 71, 78, 90–91, 95,
     103, 198–199, 222, 236–237
of 1996, 50, 51, 60, 61, 62, 71, 78, 91,
     95, 237
of 2000, 6–7, 11–12, 14–18 , 24, 44, 51,
     61, 63, 68, 78, 91, 95, 103, 182,
     201–202, 230–231, 233, 237
of 2004, 6–8, 14–16, 18, 22, 44, 50–52,
     63, 68, 71, 85, 91, 95, 117, 122,
     123, 152, 184–185, 210, 230, 237
of 2008, 1–8, 14–15, 18, 39, 44, 50–52,
     58–60, 63, 67–68, 71, 78, 84–85,
     91, 94–95, 117, 122, 148, 182, 192,
     196–197, 210–213, 215, 217–218,
     222–226
aggregate vote totals, 68
red and blue states, 126–128
time of decision, 191
turnout in, 39, 43, 44–50, 54–56, 59,
     93–95
Presidential primaries, 1, 2–4, 5, 54, 93,
     191, 199–202
Primary elections, 16, 48–49, 61, 93
white primary, 42
Primary groups, 117–120
Princeton Survey Research Associates, 144
Print media, 178–179, 180, 182. *See also*
     Newspapers
Program on International Policy
     Attitudes (PIPA), 185
Propaganda, 173
Property requirements, 40
Proportional representation system, 2,
     3, 233

Protestants, 114, 116, 122, 124, 129–130, 140, 149–151, 162, 210–212. *See also* Evangelical Protestants; Fundamentalists; Religion
Prothro, James W., 43, 64
Provisional ballots, 15, 16, 44, 59
Psychological attachments, 174
Public financing, 6, 14, 201–202
Public opinion, 135–159. *See also* Attitudes; Issues
  measurement of, 137–138
  and political leadership, 166–168
Punch-hole ballots, 16
Putnam, Robert D., 28, 29, 37, 62

Question wording, 149

Race, 40, 42, 135. *See also* Blacks
  and attitudes, 137, 140–141, 142–148
  and partisanship, 82–83, 114, 116
  and realignment, 82–83
  and turnout, 51
Racial conservatism, 144, 146, 147
Racial issues. *See* Issues, racial
Racial resentment. *See* Symbolic racism
Radio, 177–178, 179, 182. *See also* Mass media
Rally-round-the-flag phenomenon, 156, 187
Rapid response team, 194
Rational choice theory, 182–183
Rationalization, 175, 186
Reagan, Ronald, 9, 25, 51, 86, 89, 95, 117, 122, 139, 186, 196, 201, 217, 220, 227, 236, 237
Realignment, 73, 77, 83–85, 99–100, 106. *See also* Partisanship, changes in
  of 1896, 77
  Civil War realignment, 73, 76–77, 114, 136
  dealignment, 75, 83, 85, 91
  New Deal realignment, 73, 77–78, 82, 83, 100, 103, 111, 114, 136–137, 140, 148
  party systems and, 75–83
Recession, 35, 77
Recounts, 6–7, 16, 17, 84, 233. *See also* Florida

Red states, 10, 126–128
Reference group, 121. *See also* Secondary groups
Reform Party, 96
Region, 75–83. *See also* North; South
  differences in partisanship, 76–77, 82, 121
  differences in turnout, 48
Registration, 15, 43–44, 48, 54, 56–60
  same-day registration, 44, 59
Religion, 29, 129–130
  differences in attitudes, 140–141, 149–152
  differences in partisanship, 94, 114, 122–123
RePass, David, 238
Republican Party, 17, 41, 59, 67–68, 70–74, 76–77, 82–85, 136–137, 147–148, 221, 236–237
  image of, 219–221
Republicans. *See* Partisans; Partisanship
Residency requirements, 40, 43, 44
Retrospective voting, 219–220
Rezko, Tony, 194
Rice, Tom W., 206
Right to vote, 12–13, 18, 28, 39. *See also* Suffrage
Right track/wrong track questions, 26–27
Roe v. Wade, 149
Rokkan, Stein, 86
Romney, Mitt, 2–3
Roosevelt, Franklin D., 35, 77
Roosevelt, Theodore, 68, 77
Roper Center for Public Opinion Research, 26, 144, 188, 189, 193
Rosenberg, Milton J., 204
Rosenstone, Steven J., 62, 65
Rove, Karl, 108, 122–123
Rule of law, 18
Rules of the game, 18–19, 22. *See also* Democratic procedures
Run-off elections, 232
Rusk, Jerrold D., 42, 48, 64, 65
Russia, 35

Safe states, 52, 126–127, 231
Same-day registration, 44, 59

San Francisco earthquake, 180
Sanders, Lynn M, 147, 169
Saturday Night Live, 5
Saunders, Kyle, 132
Schattschneider, E. E., 47, 64
Schlozman, Kay L., 28–29, 37
Schmitz, John G., 96
School integration, attitudes toward,
    143–144, 145, 168
School prayer, 148
School vouchers, 167
Sears, David, 169
Secondary groups, 117, 120–124.
    See also Reference group; Voluntary
    associations
Secret ballot, 12–13, 48
    See also Australian ballot
Selective exposure, 175
Selective perception, 175
Seltzer, Richard A., 132
Senate, 6, 7, 18, 83, 84, 178, 230, 231,
    234–235, 237
Senate elections. *See* Congressional
    elections
Sentencing Project, 43
Separation of church and state, 31
September 11, 2001, 7, 22, 25, 26, 153,
    156, 179, 180, 182, 184, 187. *See also*
    Terrorism
Sex education, 148
Shanks, J. Merrill, 220, 222, 227, 238
Short-term forces, 70, 72, 94,
    214–226, 227
Shortridge, Ray M., 65
Sidanius, Jim, 169
Silbey, Joel, 64
Sindlinger and Co., 205
Single-issue voting, 221–222
Skidmore, Dan, 37
Slavery, 41, 76
Sniderman, Paul M., 169
Social capital, 28, 62, 120
Social characteristics, 111–131, 162–163,
    209. *See also* Occupation; Social
    class
    and presidential vote choice, 210–212
Social class, 33, 77, 117, 124–126. *See also*
    Occupation; Social characteristics

Social connectedness, 61–62
Social cross-pressures. *See* Cross-pressure
    hypothesis
Social dominance, 146
Social groups, 116–126, 140, 177,
    211–212. *See also* Primary groups;
    Secondary groups; Social class
Social issues. *See* Issues, social
Social mobility, 125–126
Social Security, 139, 237
Socialization, 29–33, 53, 103, 104–105
South, 40, 41, 42–43, 46, 48, 50, 55–56,
    57, 76–78, 82–83, 114, 125, 127, 143,
    200, 211. *See also* Region
Soviet Union, 30, 154–155
Specter, Arlen, 6, 85, 235
Split ticket, 47, 95, 130
Stevens, Ted, 235
Stimson, James A., 116, 132, 138, 153, 169
Stokes, Donald E., 65, 73, 74, 86, 102,
    108, 121, 132, 164, 169, 209, 227,
    238, 239
Stouffer, Samuel, 36
Strom, Gerald, 65
Stucker, John J., 42, 64
Suffrage. *See also* Franchise
    extensions of, 39–42, 46
    restrictions on, 42–44
Sullivan, John L., 36
Super-delegates, 4
Super Tuesday, 3, 200
Supreme Court, 7, 14, 18, 24, 25, 42, 43,
    149, 182, 198, 206
Swift Boat Veterans for Truth, 194
Symbolic racism, 146, 147
Symbolic speech, 24, 164
System support, 19–20

Tedin, Kent L., 100, 109
Teixeira, Ruy A., 45, 61–62, 64, 65
Television, 13–14, 49, 61, 177–183, 195.
    See also Mass media
Terrorism, 7, 8, 22, 34–85, 128, 153–155,
    157–158, 167, 188–189
Tetlock, Philip E., 169
Theiss-Morse, Elizabeth, 25, 36, 37
Third-party candidates, 14, 50, 62, 68,
    71, 90–91, 95–97, 106, 232

Ticket-splitting, 47, 95, 130
Tocqueville, Alexis de, 28
Tolerance, 21–22, 24
Torney, Judith V., 30–31, 37
Torture, 85
Traditional values. *See* Issues, social
Trial heats, 192–194, 201
Trust in government, 25–27, 33, 62, 106.
    See also Cynicism
Turnout, 6, 16, 39, 44–48, 71, 106, 128.
    See also Campaigns; Nonvoters;
    Participation
    calculation of turnout rate, 44–46
    decline in, 39, 46–48, 50, 54, 59,
        60–64, 93
    high- and low-stimulus elections,
        48–52
    voters and nonvoters, 52–56
Two-step flow of communication,
    176–177

Unified control of government, 85
Union members, 114, 120–121, 122
United Nations, 158
U.S. Census Bureau, 45–46, 55, 68, 73, 74
U.S. Commission on Civil Rights, 15, 44
U.S. Election Project, 43, 45, 46, 49
USA PATRIOT Act, 22, 154
USA Today, 188, 189

Valence issues, 153, 154
Verba, Sidney, 28–29, 36, 37, 108, 170,
    222, 238
Vietnam, 23, 25, 41, 50, 137, 155, 157,
    165, 167
Virginia, 78, 127
Voluntary associations, 28, 120–124.
    See also Secondary groups
Vote-by-mail, 15, 44, 60. *See also* Absentee
    ballots
Vote choice, 190–191, 209–210, 235–238.
    See also Congressional elections;
    Presidential elections
    determinants of, 226–229

in non-presidential elections, 233–235
    and social characteristics, 210–212
Vote counting, 12–13, 16–17
Voter registration. *See* Registration
Voting equipment, 16
Voting Rights Act, 43

Wall Street Journal, 26, 189
Wallace, George C., 68, 82, 91, 96, 97
War on terrorism. *See* Terrorism
Washington, George, 231
Washington Post, 25, 156, 189
Wasted votes, 14, 230
Watergate, 25
Wattenberg, Martin P., 108, 227,
    228, 238
Weapons of mass destruction (WMD), 7,
    184–186
Weisberg, Herbert, 86, 164, 170, 228, 238
Welfare. *See* Issues, welfare
West. *See* Region
West, Darrell M., 199, 206
Whig Party, 75–76, 221
White primary, 42
Williams, J. A., 36
Williamson, Chilton, 64
Wink, Kenneth A., 206
Winner-take-all system, 2, 201, 230, 231
Wolfinger, Raymond, 65
Women, 55–56. *See also* Gender
    first candidate for president, 1
    and primary groups, 117–120
    suffrage, 40, 41–42, 44–45
Wood, Sandra L., 36
Working class. *See* Social class
World Trade Center. *See* Terrorism
World Trade Organization, 34
Wright, Jeremiah, 4, 148, 218
Wyoming, 231

Young people. *See* Age

Zaller, John, 36
Zingale, Nancy H., 65, 71, 72, 86